RANDOM HOUSE

LARGE
PRINT

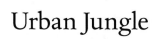

Urban Jungle

Urban Jungle

The History and Future
of Nature in the City

Ben Wilson

RANDOM HOUSE
LARGE PRINT

Front-cover photograph: The Milan Vertical Forest, 2007–2014, Milan, Italy by Boeri Studio. Typology: Architecture, Vertical forest. Design team: Stefano Boeri (founding partner); (executive architects) Davor Popovic, Francesco de Felice; (project architects) Phase 1 — Urban planning and preliminary project: Frederic de Smet (coordination), Daniele Barillari, Julien Boatyard, Matilde Cassani, Andrea Casetto, Francesca Cesa Bianchi, Inge Lengwenus, Corrado Longa, Eleanna Kotsikou, Matteo Marzi, Emanuela Messina, Andrea Sellanes. Phase 2 — Detail project: Gianni Bertoldi (coordination), Alessandro Agosti, Marco Brega, Andrea Casetto, Matteo Colognese, Angela Parrozzani, Stefano Onnis. Consultants: Arup Italia s.r.l. (structural engineering); Deerns Italia S.p.A. (facilities design); Tekne s.p.a. (detailed design); LAND s.r.l. (open space design); Alpina S.p.A. (infrastructure design); MI.PR.AV. s.r.l. (contract administration [DL]); Studio Emanuela Borio and Laura Gatti (landscape design)

Cover photograph by Andrea/EyeEm
Cover design by John Fontana

The Library of Congress has established a Cataloging-in-Publication record for this title.

ISBN: 978-0-593-86373-2

www.penguinrandomhouse.com/large-print-format-books

FIRST LARGE PRINT EDITION

145407060

Contents

List of Illustrations

Old tree in King George V Memorial Park, Hong Kong, south east entry, 2019. (Kenny Ho, CC BY-SA 4.0 <https://creativecommons.org/licenses/by-sa/4.0>, via Wikimedia Commons)

George Cruikshank, 'London going out of Town – or – The March of Bricks and Mortar', 1829. (Author's collection)

The Mughal Emperor Babur receives the envoys Uzbeg and Rauput in the garden at Agra, 18 December 1528. (Bridgeman Images)

A couple examining wildflowers growing on a bombsite in Gresham Street in the City of London in July 1943. (Popperfoto / Getty Images)

Protest against further development of the banks of the Spree River in Kreuzberg. (Björn Kietzmann / ImageBROKER / Alamy Stock Photo)

Prairie Garde, Lincoln, Nebraska, photograph, 2020. (www.monarchgard.com)

9th Street Community Garden Park in the East Village, New York City. (John Bilous / Shutterstock.com)

Introduction

Their thick roots twist around masonry in a mesmerising, tangled mass that is at once beautiful and terrifying. They smash roads and rip through concrete. Mighty banyans are the slayers of cities. Their seeds, carried on the wind or dropped by birds, settle in tiny crevices in the structures built by humans. The roots push outwards and downwards seeking nutrients, enveloping the stone, concrete or asphalt in a mesh until they can exploit a crack in which to find sustenance. Banyans are perfectly suited to the dry, hard, urban environment. There is no barrier they can't overcome. They clamp defenceless walls and buildings with roots coiling like the tentacles of a mythic sea monster, strangling its prey in a crushing embrace of death.

What chance does a city have against such power? The site of Angkor Wat in Cambodia, with its helpless temples in the talons of the banyan, reveals what happens when they run amok.

Yet banyans, for all their city-shredding potential, are a quintessential urban tree across south-east Asia. Guangzhou has an astonishing 276,200. Walk along Forbes Street in Hong Kong and you can see the majestic power of banyan trees as twenty-two grip on to a section of wall, their canopies shading the street below. No one planted them, but they thrive here nonetheless. Like any true urbanite, they can adapt to a hostile environment. Hong Kong's 'Tree Professor' Jim Chi-yung has counted 1,275 epiphytes – tropical trees that can begin life on almost any surface – growing against the odds out of 505 humanmade structures in the city. The most common is **Ficus microcarpa,** the Chinese banyan, and some specimens have grown to twenty metres. 'They do not occupy significant ground space,' he explains, 'and grow spontaneously with little human intervention or care . . . they present a special habitat with a rich complement of flora, adding significantly to the otherwise treeless streetscape.'[1]

Hong Kong is known for its skyscrapers and density; but look at it another way, and it is a city of gravity-defying banyans, nature's skyscrapers, a hanging forest that amalgamates human culture and wild nature. The Forbes Street banyans recall an ancient form of Asian urbanism. Trees such as the banyan found a place in the cityscape, despite their enormous size and destructive powers, because they were sacred. They also offered environmental services, being providers of cooling shade. When Europeans reached the Indian Ocean, the Straits of Malacca and the South China Sea in the wake of Portuguese colonial expansion from the late fifteenth century CE, they encountered cities quite unlike the compact, tree-starved metropolises of Europe. A French Jesuit described the great Sumatran port city of Aceh in the seventeenth century: 'Imagine a forest of coconut trees, bamboos, pineapples and bananas . . . put into this forest an incredible number of houses . . . divide [the] various quarters by meadows and woods; spread throughout this forest as many people as you see in your towns, when they are well populated; [and] you will form a pretty accurate idea of Aceh . . . Everything is neglected and natural, rustic and even a little wild. When one is at anchor one sees not a single vestige or appearance of a city, because the great trees along the shore hide all its houses.'[2]

Neglected, natural, rustic and wild: this is city and nature entwined in ways we have been trained to overlook or disregard. This ruralopolis might have been characteristic of the tropics and Mesoamerica, but in cities in almost all latitudes, the veneer of civilisation is paper-thin. Scratch at the carapace and you discover a world teeming with wildlife.

In writing **Urban Jungle,** I set myself the task of exploring the wild side of cities – the parts of urban life that long fell outside the purview of the historian: the middens and rubbish dumps, the abandoned sites and empty rooftops, the strips of land behind chain-link fences and alongside railway lines. For much of history, wild patches in cities, with their diverse flora and fauna, provided food for the pot, fuel for the fire, ingredients for medicines, and places for play and recreation. The dividing line between city and countryside was blurry. Only comparatively recently did we break from those traditions.

The messy side of cities – the alternate city of pavement gaps, building sites, forgotten swamps and raggedy wastelands – is where nature gets a free reign and flourishes with wild abandon. What surprised me most when researching **Urban Jungle** was not so much the extraordinary abundance of nature in cities (although that is undoubtedly remarkable) as the sheer dynamism of the urban ecosystem. The natural part of cities is as restless, fast-paced and cosmopolitan as the human. Incredible things happen in cities. We all know that. But often they happen in cracks in the concrete or in unassuming suburban back gardens. I chose a historical and global approach because only by looking deep into the past, examining the present and casting an eye to the future can we really begin to understand the bountiful potential of this most fascinating of ecosystems.

Today, we are very interested in nature in the city, and for good reason in an age of climate emergency and collapsing biodiversity. In this book, I go beyond this awakening awareness and examine the long and complicated relationship between city-dwellers and the environment both within and immediately around their metropolises. There is a deep and intrinsic connection between urbanisation and nature; the city **is** an ecosystem. We only have to discover – or rediscover – it. This is, most importantly, a story of the people who craved greenery amid the grey, about how they fought against developers, planners and investors. Above all, I want to warn of what happens when that connection breaks down.

New York contains more species than Yosemite National Park. An abandoned oil refinery in Canvey Island, Essex, has been nicknamed 'England's rainforest', so abundant are its rare plants and insects. Australian cities shelter more endangered species per square kilometre than non-urban areas. Rather than being sterile or deadening, urban areas and their peripheries are stunningly biodiverse, often far more so than nearby countryside. It has taken us a long time to realise this.

'Nowhere has mankind been farther removed from organic nature than under the conditions of life characteristic of great cities.' So wrote the American sociologist Louis Wirth in the 1930s. We perhaps see things differently now, or are beginning to, but Wirth put his finger on a common feeling. City and countryside were assumed to be two irreconcilably divided realms. If you wanted arcadian scenes and wildness, you had to leave the city. In **Little Dorrit** (1857), Charles Dickens conjured up the deadness of the nineteenth-century city: 'Melancholy streets in a penitential garb of soot, steeped the souls of the people who were condemned to look at them out of windows, in dire despondency . . . No pictures, no unfamiliar animals, no rare plants or flowers, no natural or artificial wonders of the ancient world . . . Nothing to see but streets, streets, streets. Nothing to breathe but streets, streets, streets. Nothing to change the brooding mind, or raise it up . . . Miles of close wells and pits of houses, where the inhabitants gasped for air, stretched far away towards every point of the compass. Through the heart of the town a deadly sewer ebbed and flowed, in the place of a fine fresh river.'

That last sentence, for me, eloquently sums up why attitudes to nature in the city had become so pessimistic. Where once rivers, streams and ponds had been life-giving, they had, by the industrialised nineteenth century, become stinking reservoirs of death, polluted with industrial effluence, rotting offal and raw sewage. Likewise, the animal life of the city – the thousands of horses that kept the city moving, the sheep, cows, poultry and pigs slaughtered every day, the packs of dogs that scavenged the rubbish heaps – became a transmitter of lethal zoonotic diseases.

The widespread urban myth of the sewer-dwelling alligator is a revealing one. Wildlife in the city had become a lurking threat, a mutated, warped, **un**natural danger that sustained itself on the foul effluence of humanity. The urban ecosystem was seen as a polluted, poisoned threat to human health. Ecologists followed suit: **real** nature existed elsewhere, far from the smoky, toxic metropolis with its diseased animals, foul rats and sinister invasive vegetation. Until well into the twentieth century, the city was not a fit subject for study by a self-respecting botanist.

The messiness of cities had become a matter of death. The move to tidy them up and make them sanitary entailed an assault on natural processes. Rivers and streams were let underground and integrated into the sewer system. Marshes and wetlands were paved over. A few pages after Dickens's dismal portrayal of the death of nature in the modern city in **Little Dorrit,** we encounter an old house festooned with a 'jumble of roots' and 'overgrown with weeds'. Aha: so there is greenery in the monotone city after all. But, alas, it is the wrong kind.

Industrial cities were once bedecked with vegetation. But by the nineteenth century, tolerance for spontaneous vegetation – much of it once a source of food – had vanished. The extensive weedscapes of European and American cities in particular, which were once allowed to flourish, generated social anxieties. A clue as to why comes from George R. Stewart's classic post-apocalyptic novel **Earth Abides** (1949): 'Grass and weeds were showing green at every little crack in the concrete' soon after a pandemic wipes out most of the human population. Signs of nature reclaiming the anthropic environment have become markers of social breakdown and dereliction. Percy Bysshe Shelley described the Roman Colosseum in the early nineteenth century as almost indistinguishable from a rocky Mediterranean hill overgrown with wild olive, myrtle and figs: 'The copsewood overshadows you as you wander through its labyrinths, and the wild weeds of this climate of flowers bloom under your feet.'

The Colosseum had, for centuries, been a biodiverse haven, with 420 species of plants, many of them exotic, in the middle of the nineteenth century. But they would soon be stripped away as the ancient buildings of Rome were restored to be monuments and tourist attractions. The victory of nature in the urban setting – most conspicuous in Rome – was taken as horrifying evidence of the defeat of civilisation. Later in the nineteenth century, the lost Mayan city of Tikal and the remains of Angkor Wat, both devoured by rainforests, gripped imaginations: here was the eventual fate of all cities set out in vivid detail. The lost cities of the jungle and decaying monuments like the Colosseum served as potent warnings about the dangers of letting nature go feral. Unregulated vegetation, the intertwining of buildings and nature, symbolised neglect and, ultimately, the fall of civilisations.

Shelley imagined a future London as 'shapeless and nameless ruins in the midst of an unpeopled marsh' with only booming bitterns breaking the silence of the 'islets of reeds and osiers'. Shelley's soggy London of the future is also the London of the past – a bog that existed before humans came and drained it. It could be Berlin or Lagos, New York or Shanghai, Paris or Bangkok – indeed any of the hundreds of cities built on top of oozing wetlands. Eventually, one day, the mud will re-assert itself and swallow everything up. The trope is familiar from novels and movies: once disaster strikes, the city gradually slides back to a natural state, overgrown with trees and weeds that shatter masonry and cleave steel-framed skyscrapers, populated by wild animals. The vision reminds us of our insecurity and the awesome and inevitable power of nature.

The flora of cities came under attack – from stern weed ordinances and, later, oceans of chemical weedkiller and battalions of workers armed with strimmers. Urban vegetation – of the kind that is detailed in chapter 3 – came to be ranked along-side pollution as a source of social anxiety. Because they are (like many a city-dweller) unruly, tenacious and resilient, they became loathed as weeds. When these plants lost their utility as foods and medicines, they became unloved, unwanted and, consequently, unsightly. The same could be said for rivers once water came piped in from elsewhere, and for urban forests once wood was replaced with coal and gas as the main sources of fuel. It also happened to the urban farmscape – once so productive and visible in cities – when food was flown in cheaply from distant fields. Little wonder that the imaginary divide between city and countryside became wider and wider. When cities became independent of the ecosystems of their immediate hinterlands, the link between environmental and urban health became harder to discern. Hard engineering and technology took over from natural processes. The balance between nature and the city was lost; we are only now trying to come to terms with that.

That is not to say that nature didn't exist in the city. On the contrary: industrialisation marked the birth of the modern city park. But the park went hand-in-hand with a new conception of nature. I call it urbane nature, as opposed to urban nature. City parks are places where nature is tidied up and simplified; where the spontaneity and messiness of wildlife is kept in check; where the human urge for domination is most apparent. If nature was to exist in the metropolis, it would do so on strictly human terms. The process is typified by the lawn – all those acres of manicured, fertilised, pesticide-soaked and often lifeless grass. Our standards of beauty and acceptability underwent a massive shift – or, at least, the standards of those who had power, who could impose them on poorer citizens and on colonised people. Weeds and spontaneous growth, smelly farms and shaggy meadows, wild animals and untamed rivers, all alike betokened dereliction when they manifested in the urban realm.

But for all the time and money spent on beautifying cities, the unwanted and despised forms of nature survived. The seeds remained, like hidden fugitives; they found habitats in the places we boarded off and ignored. Wild animals quietly infiltrated the labyrinth, building up their numbers and learning ways to live alongside humans. Without much attention being paid, urban ecosystems continued to evolve in startling ways. Only in very recent times have we begun to appreciate the incalculable value of these ecosystems and of wildness in all its messy glory.

In the face of the climate emergency, cities are in a precarious position. For all their marvels of engineering, they are simply not designed to cope with higher temperatures, unpredictable storms and rising sea levels. Engineering is not enough to save city-dwellers; instead, the focus has switched to what is called green infrastructure.

Cities badly need re-naturalised rivers, restored wetlands, rehabilitated tidal marshes and the shady canopies of urban forests to withstand the climate crisis. If you picture the city of the future, think less of smart tech, flying cars and skyscrapers; think more of cascading foliage, farms on flat roofs, rough urban meadows and dense groves of forest. Cities are changing fast, as they always have done. The tendency in the twenty-first century will be for them to go greener, as a form of self-defence if nothing else. The dividing line between city and wildness is going to get blurrier.

Cities have a lot of green areas, but there are plenty more opportunities to extend greenery into every nook and cranny if we want. Urban areas abound with unused and underutilised space. Think of all those barren flat roofs, all that idle space between buildings and along roads, and the immense acreage dedicated to the driving and parking of cars. And then there are suburban back gardens, which can account for around a quarter of a city's area. Forget about parks – nature is capable of insinuating itself almost anywhere in the built environment if we only allow its growth. The space we **could** make for nature is vast. The challenge for the twenty-first century is to make cities that are, for the first time, biophilic, that actively encourage and maximise a functioning ecosystem.

Why should we transform our cities in this way? Urban wildness makes cities more biodiverse and helps mitigate the effects of climate change in ways that will, quite frankly, help us to survive. It makes them places that we want to live in. Encouraging and maximising unrestrained vegetation make cities beautiful; urban environments are, after all, our predominant habitat, and we remain instinctively drawn to nature. Most importantly, studies have shown that easy access to green space significantly improves mental and physical health. It reduces stress to boot and improves cognitive development in children. And it is not just any kind of 'nature'. The psychological and physical benefits of urban greenspaces are strongly correlated with species richness. The kinds of biodiversity found in semi-wild urban areas are much better for us than simplified landscapes such as parks. What benefits the bee and the butterfly, the falcon and the fox, makes us healthier and happier, too. We should make our modern metropolises a bit more like early modern Aceh – neglected, natural, rustic and wild – because biodiversity thrives in tangled messiness, and we thrive with it. It is becoming ever clearer that cities, if they are managed right, can provide havens for plants, animals and insects that are seeing their habitats destroyed by intensive farming and climate change. With up to a fifth of the surface area of a city lying fallow as vacant building sites, a quarter being private gardens, and up to a tenth consisting of grassland alongside roads and on roundabouts, urban areas have a lot of green space that can be managed for biological complexity. When you add in parks, cemeteries, golf courses, rivers, allotments, flat roofs and networks of neglected marginal land, you discover an intricate mosaic of varying habitats. Human activities and natural processes are woven together. What we make of that relationship is up to us.[3]

Throughout our time as an urban species, we have

sought, in different ways, to make cities more live-able by making them more verdant. Oftentimes, people have rejected the traditional city and sought something else, inventing garden cities or sub-urbanising on a titanic scale in search of the sweet spot between city and countryside.

The history I unravel attests to the strength of that urge to live with nature. In many places across the globe today, cities **are** becoming much greener than they ever were. But in most (though not all) cases, this movement is most apparent in wealthy, post-industrial metropolises. For the majority of urbanites – particularly the billion or so people who live in slums, shanty towns and other infor-mal settlements – access to any kind of nature is a rare commodity. It was ever thus. The greenest, most pleasant parts of cities were always reserved for the wealthy. Extending the benefits of urban nature to all parts of the metropolis is a matter of social justice.

My hope is that if we come to see cities as in-triguing, valuable ecosystems in their own right, we might re-examine the position of cities within the planetary ecosystem. For all their latent or hidden biodiversity, and all the changes we are making, cit-ies are still violently destructive forces, responsible for the lion's share of carbon emissions, pollution, resource extraction waste and species extinction. New York, for example, consumes more energy and emits more pollution than all of sub-Saharan

Africa. One of the urgent issues of the present is to create sustainable cities with vastly reduced ecological footprints. A good starting point is surely to understand and appreciate the peculiar ecosystem we have shaped that lies, sometimes unseen, on our doorsteps and beneath our feet.

1.

On the Edge

The edge. The fringe. The urban-wilderness interface. Desakota. Twilight zone. Interzone. Rurban. Peri-urban. Suburbia. Exurbia. Terrain vague. The hinterland. There are many words for the eerie edgelands of the metropolis, the place where city crashes into nature. Victor Hugo called it 'bastard countryside': 'To observe the city edge is to observe an amphibian. End of trees, beginning of roofs, end of grass, beginning of paving stones, end of ploughed field, beginning of shops . . .'

If only it could be so clear cut. Often, the urban edge is a transition zone. The term 'desakota' is made up from the Indonesian words **desa** ('village') and **kota** ('town'). It describes a liminal area where intensive agriculture and village life are jumbled up with industry, suburbs, squatter villages and spiralling road systems. Applied to endless sprawl in the rural-urban regions of developing countries in south-east Asia, the subcontinent and Africa, 'desakota' is expressive of the strange, blurred hybridity of modern urban edgelands the world over, with their uneasy mix of uses – farms and shopping malls, office parks and patches of ancient woodland, golf courses and trailer parks, reservoirs and rubbish dumps, out-of-town offices and derelict wastelands. We all know these edgelands.[1]

This eerie never-zone was the inspiration for Ernest Lawson in New York at the turn of the nineteenth and twentieth centuries. In his paintings of the margins of the metropolis, we can see the sorry state of Manhattan's countryside as apartment blocks encroach like a besieging army. All that is rural and wild will become a level grid of streets once the rock has been dynamited, the land flattened and the trees cut down. In the meantime, this is a place of abandoned fields taken over by weeds. 'Who but Lawson can bring beauty out of a region infested with squalid cabins, desolate trees, dumping grounds, and all the other impossible familiarities of any suburban wilderness?' asked one of his patrons.

Lawson captured the moment just before nature is converted into concrete. The frontline never stays still for long. Writing at about the same time, the naturalist James Reuel Smith said that the terrain beyond New York's 72nd Street had been 'a forest in a primitive state' as recently as the 1880s. All that had gone within two decades, replaced by 'asphalt walks and close-cropped lawns'. You had to venture to Washington Heights, close to what would become 171st Street, to witness the 'almost un-broken woods, up hill and down dale, interspersed with deep ravines, with numerous noisy brooks, rocks, a fallen tree, and all the wilderness of a place far out in the country' by the 1900s. But not for long: all this was daily 'disappearing from sight with such celerity that it is merely a matter of months when there will be none whatever left in view upon Manhattan Island'.[2]

The total reordering of the landscape had begun with European settlement and accelerated in the nine-teenth century as New York's population grew from 33,000 in 1790 to 515,000 by 1850 and 3.48 mil-lion by 1900. As the population grew, the city ex-panded into the wetlands and meadows that made the Hudson Bay estuary one of the most biodiverse areas on the planet. As detailed in Ted Steinberg's chilling, magnificent book, **Gotham Unbound: the ecological history of Greater New York,** hills were flattened, and bogs were filled with the debris and heaps of garbage. Draining, filling and urbanising 'unsightly', 'worthless' wetlands was hailed as a 'pub-lic improvement' by press, politicians, planners and real estate dealers as a way of converting unproductive emptiness into dollars. In the 1930s and 40s, areas of wetland collectively equal to the size of Manhattan disappeared in a fury of development. And that was just the curtain raiser to a more sustained onslaught in the decades that followed.[3]

LaGuardia, JFK and Newark international airports were built upon filled wetlands, as were major shipping terminals. The 32,000 acres of white cedar swamp at the Hackensack Meadows in New Jersey – a wilderness just five miles from the Empire State Building – were greedily eyed up as 'potentially the most valuable unbuilt area of its kind in the whole world'. Rubble from the London Blitz – brought as ballast on returning ships – was tossed into the marshes, along with garbage and chemical waste. By 1976 it had been pared down to 6,600 acres. New York's master planner Robert Moses looked at one of the metropolis's last major intact marshlands in the 1940s – 2,600 acres of wetland at Fresh Kills on Staten Island – and licked his lips at an 'immense acreage of meadow land . . . which is presently valueless'. The first step in its conversion from ecological treasure house to valuable real estate was – as ever – to fill it up with trash. Fresh Kills became the largest garbage dump in the world by 1955. For years on end, it received 29,000 tons of waste generated by the city every day. The flat salt marshes had been transformed, within a few years, into a mountain range of human waste, the peaks of which reached 225 feet. Within sight of the skyscrapers of Manhattan, Fresh Kills became a nightmarish monument to what cities do to the ecosystem. They consume the natural world with a ferocious appetite, and their outputs are pollution and waste, poisoning rivers and wetlands, converting natural habitats into toxic landfill.[4]

Amid this orgy of destruction at Fresh Kills, in 1970, former New York Sanitation Commissioner Samuel J. Kearing looked at the rapidly accelerating destruction of the wetland wilderness and asked which was more important, unthinking urban development 'or the preservation of wild birds and the biological community of which they — and we — are a part'. 'I'd vote in favour of the birds,' he declared. 'I think many more would vote that way, too, if they had been with me when I made my first inspection of the Sanitation Department's landfill at Fresh Kills. It had a certain nightmare quality. I can still recall looking down on the operation from a control tower and thinking that Fresh Kills . . . had for thousands of years been a magnificent, teeming, literally life-enhancing tidal marsh. And in just 25 years it was gone, buried under millions of tons of New York City's refuse.'[5]

His was a lonely voice. 'We have pushed back the sea and filled in the swamp for parks and airports,' the **New York Times** exalted in 1946, celebrating the victory of the metropolis over the constraints imposed on it by nature. The 'path to progress', it said, was the result of the 'wise use of the garbage pail and other refuse' in creating dry land out of bog. Natural limits to growth had been obliterated. The ecology and landscape of the edgelands was a resource to be consumed, transformed and entirely remade, and there was little compromise; by the end of the twentieth century, 90 per cent of the tidal and freshwater wetlands were gone for ever.[6]

The conversion of nature into city, the reclamation of the apparently useless into something profitable and the near-total transformation of the landscape in the greater New York region, was a forerunner for developments across the world in the later twentieth century. Take Singapore, where, as in New York, an unpromising location was re-engineered to exploit its geographical advantages as a trading hub. During its colonial period, Singapore added 740 acres to its landmass by filling mangrove swamps, draining marshes and expanding the shoreline. In the three decades that followed full independence in 1965, the city state reclaimed an additional 34,100 acres from the sea, massively expanding its size in the process and (literally) setting the stage for its economic ascendancy. As a result, more or less the entire coastline of Singapore is artificial, with devastating consequences for the area's profuse biodiversity. A mere 5 per cent of the thirty square miles of mangrove forests that existed in 1819 survive today. Most of the sandy beaches are gone, while 60 per cent of the forty square miles of coral reefs were obliterated.

So it goes with city after city across the world: entire ecosystems are remade to pave the way for economic take-off. The destroyed aquatic edgelands of cities – the unlovely marshes, the thick mangrove forests and unseen coral reefs – represent the confrontation between city and nature and, more importantly, the Anthropocene.

The rapid loss of Lawson's gritty New York edgelands became a feature of cities all over the planet in the later twentieth century and beyond as the rest of the world emulated America's turbo-charged urbanisation. An observer of the modern Bangladeshi 'bastard countryside' wrote, 'There are few horizons which are devoid of settlement, but where they begin and end is often impossible to judge.' Between 1982 and 2012, 43 million acres of farmland, forest and wilderness were suburbanised in the United States, an area the size of Washington State. That's two acres of open land claimed by the suburbs every minute.[7]

Urban edges and dull suburbs are hardly the thing of romance; we hurry past them. But we need to pay attention to this easily avoided, unloved interzone. Edgelands represent the fastest-changing habitat on the planet. They are the site of eco-apocalypse, the graveyard of endangered flora and fauna. The urban-rural fringe is also becoming the predominant habitat of the species **Homo sapiens.**

Every day, an area of land the size of Manhattan Island is urbanised. This is city as mass extinction event. In 2010, 50 per cent of humans were living in cities; by the middle of the century, the figure will be 75 per cent. And we are spreading ourselves out: the proportion of land covered by concrete and asphalt is growing significantly faster than population. By 2030, two-thirds of urban land will have been built since 2000. It is not the scale that should alarm us, so much as the **location** of this land-grab. We have chosen to site our cities on deltas, rainforests, woodlands, grasslands and wetlands – the most important biodiversity hotspots on the planet containing ecosystems that are vital for our survival. The local impact on ecology is grave, but cumulatively, the damage to the global ecosystem is disastrous and irreversible.[8]

Across the planet, some 423 fast-expanding cities are devouring the habitats of over 3,000 already critically endangered animal species. The Amazon, Indonesian and Congo Basin rainforests are being eroded. The bountiful tropical wetlands of the Indo-Burma region, West Africa and China are in steep decline because of urbanisation. Addis Ababa lost 24 per cent of its peri-urban agriculture in a mere five years. The Jakarta metropolitan area has swallowed up 700 square miles of vegetation on its borders in the last three decades; agriculture has been pushed further out from the city by the bow-wave of urbanisation, destroying once remote and untouched forests. The result of devouring surrounding wilderness is a city being wrecked by floods and rising sea levels: Java's very existence is at risk. Both New York and New Orleans have sacrificed the vast expanses of wetlands that once defended them against hurricanes, floods and rises in sea levels. Delhi and Beijing are facing desertification after they destroyed the green mantle of forests that shielded them against dust and sand. There can be few more important places than the overlooked, unlovely, fragmented edges of cities for the future of humanity and the planet. This is the story of global climate change told on millions of local scales.

A city's edgelands are its life support system; a functioning ecosystem of forests, grasslands, wet-lands and tidal marshes are essential buffers against the manifold effects of climate change. Yet this is the terrain most vulnerable to our greed for develop-ment. The dangers are clear and present. Intrusions into hitherto untouched ecosystems mean that more human settlements are thrust into close en-counters with wildlife. Fauna in degraded habi-tats on the urban fringe are more likely to become sources of zoonotic diseases carrying deadly new pathogens; cities packed with humans are their perfect breeding grounds, from which pandemics spread throughout the planetary urban network with astonishing speed. If we care about our future on earth, we should focus on the frontier between cities and nature: it is a battleground.

A warm spring evening brings people swarming out of the claustrophobic, rule-bound city through the gates in its walls and into the wild freedom of the countryside. It is a jostling, colourful mass of people. The townsfolk shed their urban ways, ap-prentices rubbing shoulders with civic dignitaries, men consorting with women, class and gender rules temporarily forgotten in the fresh air and fields.

This is the famous second scene of Goethe's **Faust,** as the people stream out of small, fortified Leipzig for an evening of freedom. The boundary between city and countryside, order and freedom, is stark. But escape from the confines of the city is never far away. In German literature, cities are surrounded by primeval forests and wildernesses, the hiding places of the Brothers Grimm's wolves, fairies, dwarfs and magical animals. Forests were more important than arable fields because they provided one of the city's key needs – fuel. A medieval city such as Nuremberg drew its food from up to one hundred miles away; but it needed its timber (which was costly to transport) close to hand, in the forests that abutted its walls. This is the yin and yang of urban life: the civilisation and security of the city is juxtaposed with the wildness and weirdness of the countryside and woodland. The downsides of the crowded and unsanitary city are balanced by the easy accessibility of forests and fields.[9]

Who ever thought of a park when the real, untamed nature was a stroll away?

If the German urban imagination was fed by the forests that environed cities, the English had another kind of wildness upon which the mind could feast. An unprofitable marsh on the edge of the City of London known as Moorfields, which extended from the Roman wall northwards to Islington and connected with yet more open space at Finsbury Fields, was central to urban life long into the eighteenth century. This undrained fen, thick with sedge, rushes and flag lilies, was the place where the people of the city – particularly young Londoners – went for sports, rowdy games, sex, festivities, protests, fights, archery practice and exercise. The monk William Fitzstephen, author of **A Description of London,** recorded Londoners skating on the frozen bog in the late twelfth century. At about the same time, young men played the first recorded football games there, involving hundreds taking part in tumultuous, disorderly matches.

Up until the nineteenth century, London was surrounded by 45,000 acres of commons and heathlands to its north and west, and an almost identical area to the south. Like forests, grasslands and marshes provided indispensable sources of energy – hay for the tens of thousands of horses that hauled, carted and carried. Much of the countryside surrounding London was given over to grassland. One of the most famous tracts, Hounslow Heath, extended five miles from the west of London to beyond the hamlet of Heathrow and encompassed over 6,000 acres of grass, furze, broom, heather and stands of trees. 'Time was when the heath seemed illimitable, stretching north and south . . . [and] far out towards the horizon.'[10]

The primeval native ecology of London's edgelands was the forest that had grown since the end of the last Ice Age. The heaths – wild as they looked – were the result of deforestation and grazing. But for all that, these huge areas of lightly grazed acidic grassland provided an exceptionally productive habitat for grasses, lichens, mosses, fungi, herbaceous plants, small wildflowers, shrubs, burrowing insects, small mammals and butterflies. Heaths abounded in gorse, used as a cheap or free source of firewood, along with bracken and heather which were used for thatching and animal litter. The southward road out of London 'opened out into one wild heath after another', a 'beautiful chain of commons' easily accessible from the city. The semi-wild environment that enveloped London also provided habitat for 'wild life': highwaymen used the cover of the furze to rob stagecoaches along the lonely roads.[11]

'In the month of May . . . every man, except impediment, would walke into the sweete meadowes and greene woods,' wrote John Stow of Londoners in the sixteenth century, 'there to rejoice their spirities with the beauty and savour of sweete flowers, and with the harmony of birds, praising God in their kind.' The edges of cities throughout Europe represented not just leisure but opportunity. The urban poor relied upon edgeland commons and forests for building materials and firewood, as well as for grazing their animals and foraging – matters of brute survival, not just enjoyment. In the wetland fringes of New York, from the seventeenth century through to as late as the mid twentieth, urban trappers caught muskrats in marshes such as Flushing

Meadows in Queens, Jamaica Bay on Long Island and Fresh Kills on Staten Island, selling the furs to augment their paltry incomes. The marshes yielded game and fish for the pot, berries, mushrooms and firewood. On the wild frontier of Berlin in the late nineteenth century, many of the poor who lived peripherally in self-built shanty towns were able to survive because their lives were balanced between urban and rural. The wastelands on the edge, created by the growth of the city, became **de facto** commons for gleaning and guerrilla gardening.[12]

What made London 'glorious' according to the essayist Leigh Hunt were its 'green pastures' close to hand: '**There** we have fields; there one can walk on real positive turf . . . and have hedges, stiles, field-paths, sheep and oxen, and other pastoral amenities.' At weekends until the early nineteenth century, Londoners – just like Leipzigers and New Yorkers – strolled out of the metropolis to tea gardens, taverns and theatres in the rural fringe. The boundary between city and countryside was porous. Thomas De Quincey captured the nearness of nature and its role as an antidote to urban claustrophobia when he wrote of the joy of walking along Oxford Street by night and glancing along a side street 'which pierces northwards through the heart of Marylebone to the fields and the woods'.[13]

Writing in the 1820s, the satirist, journalist and lifelong Londoner William Hone could remember that 'In my boyhood, I had only to obtain parental permission, and stroll in fields now no more, – to scenes now deformed, or that I have been wholly robbed of, by "the spirit of improvement". Five and thirty years have altered everything.' Hone's close friend George Cruikshank depicted the scene in a cartoon entitled 'The March of Bricks and Mortar' in 1829, a nightmarish scene of serried ranks of terraced houses and factories, led by a robotic infantry battalion of picks, shovels and hods, belching smoke and bombarding London's arcadian fringe with cannonades of bricks. Trees cower in terror; cows and sheep run from the invaders. This is city as destructive force, expansion as naked violence and runaway suburbanisation as ecocide.[14]

The image may seem hackneyed now. But it had a visceral impact when it was published. For it was here, on the cherished northern outskirts of London, that the swift, unstoppable juggernaut of suburbanisation first got going on the omnivorous scale we now know all too well. 'The rage for building', wrote a contemporary critic, 'fills every pleasant outlet with bricks, mortar, rubbish and eternal scaffold-poles, which, whether you walk east, west, north, or south, seems to be running after you.'[15]

Known as 'wastes' and 'wildernesses', these unproductive peri-urban common lands were regarded by agricultural improvers as 'disgraceful . . . and insulting to the inhabitants of the metropolis'. Walking out of London to the suburban village of Kew in 1819, Sir Richard Phillips railed at the immense tracts of unused land, looking forward to the 'fullest triumph . . . of the fortunate combinations of human art over the inaptitude and primitive barbarity of nature'. More bombastically, during the Napoleonic Wars, the president of the Board of Agriculture, Sir John Sinclair, declared war on the 'wastes': 'Let us not be satisfied with the liberation of Egypt, or the subjugation of Malta, but let us subdue Finchley Common; let us conquer Hounslow Heath; let us compel Epping Forest to submit to the yoke of improvement.'[16]

By the time Finchley Common was enclosed for sale in 1816, encroachments had already reduced its size from over 1,240 acres to 900; thereafter, almost all of the green space was surrendered to suburban development. Lewisham lost 850 acres of commons in 1810 and Sydenham Common – the 500 acres of which had reminded Washington Irving of the wilds of America – went entirely. The 60,000 acres of commons and heaths that existed in the eighteenth century dwindled to 13,000 by the 1890s; today, only 3,889 acres of this precious ecosystem remains. The once-mighty Hounslow Heath has been reduced from 6,000 acres to 200 by suburbanisation and, later, airport development.[17]

It marked a cardinal moment in urban history. London had always been growing, of course. But never at this velocity and never into the beloved pockets of countryside around Islington and Hampstead where Londoners flocked at weekends to escape the smoke, stench and congestion of the city. The age of mass-produced housing had arrived. That timeless experience of leaving the bricks and mortar and stepping into semi-wild edgelands was going. It meant the alienation of city-dwellers from nature. In a famous musical song, a working-class Londoner stretches his imagination to believe he is living in a rural bliss. He has filled his miserable inner-city backyard with vegetables grown in pots and he boasts he could enjoy the sweeping vistas to far-off Chingford, Hendon and Wembley 'if it wasn't for the 'ouses in between'. People were sealed in the city, distanced from nature by seemingly endless terraces.

Or, at least, the poor were. George Cruikshank may have been horrified by the march of the city; but he was deeply implicated in it. He had moved to a new suburban development in Pentonville in 1823, built for middle-class families to enjoy a semi-rural lifestyle close to the city. Overlooking fields and streams, it was little wonder that Cruikshank wanted to stop other families swarming his arcadia, where they would block his views and chew up his fields. London had expanded just far enough for him.[18]

Cruikshank, then, was one of the pioneers of modern suburbia, a NIMBY before it became fashionable. Cheap finance became available in the 1820s, opening the way for rapid development of the 'burbs. Omnibuses, followed by trams and trains, made commuting possible for the first time. Then, the industrial revolution made cities cramped and polluted, plagued by cholera and crime. People were leaving the land and coming to town; by 1851, Britain had a majority urban population. During the second half of the century, London's outer ring of suburbs grew by 50 per cent each decade; these places experienced the fastest population growth anywhere in England. In this time of monstrous growth and rapid, discombobulating change, confidence in cities collapsed. If you had the cash, you decamped to the rural edgelands. Then, you decamped again if, like George Cruikshank, you feared that others were coming to spoil the party. Districts that possessed a rural charm rapidly became densified, as wastes, fields, market gardens and private gardens experienced in-fill. Pleasantness was often a fleeting quality, spurring further leapfrogging to new edgelands. The ''ouses in between' kept mushrooming.[19]

Edgelands possess magic. They are the sweet spot. No wonder people have been attracted to live there since the earliest cities and **en masse** from the early nineteenth century. But they are in constant flux as cities sprawl outwards. Suburbia had its champion in the remarkable Scottish polymath and landscape gardener John Claudius Loudon, whose influence deeply affected the ecology of modern cities. Worried at the velocity of change in London, he made an extraordinarily visionary proposal in 1829, the same year as Cruikshank's cartoon. What had motivated both of them was the impending sale of rugged Hampstead Heath, the city's most popular and cherished wild heathland, to developers. According to Loudon, the government should buy existing rural and common land on the margins of the capital – a circle at a distance of a mile from St Paul's Cathedral. This would produce a mile of countryside, which would then give way to a mile of urban development, and then another mile of countryside, and so on. If this was done, wrote Loudon, 'there could never be an inhabitant who would be farther than half a mile from an open airy situation, in which he was free to walk or ride'. The rural zones would be planted with trees and shrubs in a semi-wild landscape of rivers and lakes with 'rocks, quarries, stones, wild places in imitation of heaths and caverns, grottoes, dells, dingles, ravines, hills, valleys, and other natural-looking scenes'. Whatever it was to be, this was not a call to preserve farmland or create parks: it was a plea for wildness to be integrated into the expanding urban matrix.[20]

'I am now twenty-three years of age,' Loudon had written back in 1806, 'and perhaps a third of my life has passed away, and yet what have I done to benefit my fellow men?' Those anguished words, confided to his journal in the year that he was left crippled by an attack of rheumatic fever, tell us a lot about him. Dedicated to public service, he combined his profession as a landscape architect, inventor and botanical writer with radical political activism. Making modern cities more habitable, particularly for the poor, was central to his reformist vision. He advocated access to green space of all kinds – including squares, public parks and cemeteries – as an antidote to the confinement and disease of the industrial metropolis. Contact with nature, he believed, should be the hallmark of modern cities, and, just as importantly, cities should be landscaped like a garden.

Loudon wrote his pamphlet soon after he returned from a tour of France and Germany. In Leipzig and several other German and Austrian cities, obsolete city walls were pulled down throughout the late eighteenth and the nineteenth centuries and replaced with public promenades lined with linden trees that encircled historic city centres. These parklands – the most famous example is the Ringstraße in Vienna – preserved the distinctiveness of the urban core even after de-fortification. Loudon's green belt proposal almost certainly influenced the design of Adelaide in south Australia. Laid out by William Light from 1837, Adelaide consisted of two built clusters either side of the River Torrens surrounded by 2,332 acres of parkland – an unbroken figure-of-eight green belt.

Long before John Loudon, there had been attempts to halt the growth of London. Both Elizabeth I and Oliver Cromwell had banned high-density building on the fringe of the metropolis.

John Evelyn demanded a green girdle of gardens and orchards which would make London 'one of the sweetest and most delicious Habitations in the world'. Loudon went beyond these simple, restrictive ideas. For a start, he accepted and embraced the inevitability and desirability of urban expansion. An urbanist at heart, he loved the energy of cities. But he knew that frenetic urban life had to be counterbalanced by retreat into nature. His was a call to preserve the huge heaths that teemed with life before the builder and speculator got to them. The city should grow round these areas of outstanding wildness, not crash into them.

The ideal of **rus in urbe** – the countryside in the city – has been with us since the first cities. The sizeable urban parks that appeared in the nineteenth century only partially satisfied that urge to live alongside nature as well as the sources of wealth and power. In an age of accelerated urban growth, the connection between city life and the countryside was disappearing for ever. How could that link be preserved? There was no shortage of visionaries.

Sixty-nine years after the publication of Loudon's essay, in 1898, Sir Ebenezer Howard came up with the concept of the 'Garden City', a compact settlement surrounded by a buffer of countryside. In marked contrast to Loudon, Howard was anti-urban. His ideal settlement was an oversized village, a rural-urban hybrid in which every dwelling would be surrounded by a garden. Between 1895 and 1910, Arturo Soria y Mata came up with his highly influential **Ciudad Lineal** – 'lineal city' – plan. He wanted Madrid to expand into its surrounding countryside along thin transport corridors with a single row of houses on either side. Everyone would have a close, intimate relationship with nature because the edge would always be easily accessible from your back door. Soria's ambition, like Howard's, was nothing less than to 'ruralise the city and urbanise the countryside'. [21]

Ebenezer Howard called his Garden City concept the beginning of a new civilisation. In the same utopian vein, the American architect Frank Lloyd Wright envisaged 'Broadacre City' in 1932, a new metropolis which he said would exist everywhere and nowhere at the same time. It would be a decentralised city, spread through the countryside. Broadacre City, like Garden City, would be the anti-city, a complete reordering of the metropolis as it had existed for millennia. 'Modern transportation may scatter the city,' he declared with relish, 'open breathing spaces in it, green it and beautify it, making it fit for a superior order of human beings.'[22]

Radical ideas came out of Berlin, the fastest-growing city in Europe at the end of the nineteenth century. Max Hilzheimer, the city's commissioner for the care of natural monuments, argued for the right of Berliners imprisoned in the 'desert of stone' to experience the 'secret beauty' in 'the surroundings of our city Berlin' – the untouched forests, bogs, sand dunes, lakes and creeks that characterised the post-glacial Brandenburg region. It was there, in Berlin's edgelands, said Hilzheimer, that city folk could discover 'the image of the free nature, where one can indulge at will, and in which trees and bushes grow without having been directed and put in place by human hand, where sources, creeks and rivers search their way according to their own laws'. Wild fringe ecologies were so valuable precisely because they existed so close to artificial cities and their nature-starved masses. There was no need to travel to distant wildernesses if there was one on your doorstep.[23]

A strategy for preserving fringe ecologies even while Berlin grew culminated in a bold 'Comprehensive Green Space Plan' in 1929 which demanded twenty-six green wedges radiating out continuously from the city centre to large nature reserves on the wild edgelands. This plan, farsighted as it was in reinventing the modern city, fell victim first to the financial constraints of the Great Depression and, finally, to the Nazis. Following the destruction inflicted on cities during the Second World War, the British town planner Patrick Abercrombie revived the plan, demanding that the density of pre-Blitz London be replaced with these lavish green wedges. He imagined every Londoner walking 'from garden to park, from park to parkway, from parkway to green wedge and from green wedge to Green Belt', a route from inner city to peripheral countryside clear of buildings and traffic.[24]

Green wedges, garden cities, lineal cities, Broadacre City – all these proposals to, as Lloyd Wright put it, destroy 'the artificial divisions set up between urban and rural life', met failure. They came at a time when walking out of the city into a natural landscape had become almost impossible, particularly for the poor: it would take a bus or train journey to see a rural vista. Only in the post-war period did London impose a Green Belt on its fringes, by which time most of its adjacent countryside, including its rough heaths, had been eaten up by suburbia. London's Green Belt was widely copied around the world as a means of preventing sprawl and protecting countryside from development. Restrictive in intent, it did little to re-imagine the urban edgelands as places for biodiversity or to radically impact ecology within cities.

Modern green belts are a long way from the proposal made by John Claudius Loudon back in 1829 for landscaping the city with a mixture of alternating wild and artificial zones. But although Loudon (and his successors) did not succeed in changing the city on the macro scale, they did on the micro. As cities expanded, their edgelands were converted from one ecosystem to another. If the traditional European and American city was compact and dense, the city emerging in the nineteenth century was ringed and interlaced with greenery. It may not have been the publicly owned, remnant wild space made up of green wedges that campaigners wanted, but it was nonetheless brimming with vegetation.

Today, almost a quarter of London's surface area is made up of suburban gardens encircling the dense, built-over core; in Brisbane, it is closer to a third; in continental Europe, where cities are denser, it is about a fifth. Residential backyards in the United States, the majority planted in suburbia since 1945, cover an area collectively the size of the state of Georgia. In León, Nicaragua, 86 per cent of all green space consists of private patios. The predominant ecosystem type in cities is not, as one might think, parks, recreation grounds and cemeteries, but private gardens. Few did more to nurture into life the domestic back garden, and hence the ecologies of modern cities, than John Claudius Loudon.[25]

Go to numbers 3–5 Porchester Terrace and you find yourself in one of the ritziest districts of London, the home turf of Middle Eastern royals, enigmatic oligarchs and well-upholstered ambassadors. But the house you find there has an odd historic pedigree: it is the great-great-grandfather of the suburban semi, the house that spawned millions of imitators and helped inculcate an aspirational lifestyle.

Built in 1825 by Loudon, the property showcased a new way of living in the city. With its glass-domed conservatory and veranda, it epitomised middle-class domesticity. Affordability was masked by an illusion of grandeur because, as Loudon wrote, the aim was to give two small houses the appearance of being one large, fairly grand building, bequeathing to both the outward vestige of 'dignity and consequence'.

Loudon loved the suburbs; he celebrated the new way of living as it was emerging in the 1820s. Suburbs, as he saw them, blended the best of city and countryside while avoiding their pitfalls. They also created a new type of nature. Loudon stood at the forefront of popularising gardening as a leisure pursuit. He wrote for as large an audience as possible, aiming to diffuse, for the first time, knowledge about horticulture and gardening to men and women of all sections of society. The author of **An Encyclopaedia of Gardening** (1822), he was also the founder and editor of the **Gardener's Magazine,** the first periodical dedicated to horticulture, and the **Magazine of Natural History.** Much of his prodigious output was written in collaboration with his wife Jane, an author and illustrator of books and articles on gardening. The Loudons became the most widely read garden writers of the early nineteenth century; their influence extended down the generations.[26]

In 1838, John published **The Suburban Gardener, and Villa Companion,** a how-to guide to creating the perfect garden in a brand new house on the expanding urban fringe. In fact, the book was not merely a DIY gardening book but a massive manual on becoming suburban. Loudon and his wife could help you choose the right kind of plants; but they could also advise you on how to make your house, inside and out, a place of beauty and respectability, how to decorate your bookshelves and lay out your furniture. The Loudon couple were Victorian lifestyle gurus.

Numbers 3–5 Porchester Terrace might not have been the very first semi-detached villa ever built, but it became the template for the suburban way of life, a living showcase for the aspirational middle classes of early Victorian Britain. Most important was the Loudons' garden. The pillars of their veranda were twined with China roses, wisteria, jasmines and japonicas. All around the veranda were planters filled with flowering seasonal plants. The garden itself, smaller than the area of two tennis courts, was crammed with 2,000 species of exotic plants, 'specimens of almost all the kinds of trees and shrubs that could, in 1823 and 1824, be procured in the London nurseries', as well as numerous varieties of apples, pears, plums, cherries, peaches, nectarines, apricots, figs and vines. The aim was to create a miniature and manageable version of the landed estate within the metropolis, a new way of living for professional and commercial families.[27]

Loudon presented gardening as a lifestyle choice for the new breed of suburbanites: it was about exercise, intellectual curiosity and conspicuous consumption. It allowed men and women to reconnect with their rustic instincts in a setting that was neither countryside nor city but poised between the

two. Gardening, in Loudon's view, was about gain-
ing mastery over a piece of land and bending it
to your will. The bestselling garden writer in the
world, Loudon helped create the Victorian garden
not only in Britain but in Australia, New Zealand,
America and Europe. His design, which was known
as 'gardenesque' – with neat lawn, groupings of ornamental shrubs, flowerbeds and carefully placed
trees – has conquered the globe, as has the rustic style of low-density 'garden suburbs' planned
around private gardens, avenues and open spaces.

Loudon's garden design, as it took shape in
Porchester Terrace, emphasised display and orna-
mentation; it sought out an eclectic assortment of
trees and shrubs from all over the world that would
have been considered bizarre and incongruous by
earlier generations. In his columns in **Gardener's
Magazine,** Loudon enthusiastically promoted newly
imported plants as they came on sale. As one observer
of the growth of middle-class London suburbia put
it: 'In the place of [ancient manor houses] we behold
the modern villa, with its spruce though pigmy appurtenances of pleasure-ground, garden and green
house, where the exotic productions of southern
climes have supplanted the gigantic patrimonial timber.' Under Loudon's influence, this novel ecosystem,
as we would call it today, was, with its cultured mix
of alien and native plants, making suburbia a surprising cornucopia of botanical cosmopolitanism.[28]

The plant palette in British cities represented the

spoils of empire and London's position at the centre of a worldwide network of trade routes. In turn, suburbanisation was a form of internal colonisation as cities consumed villages and farms and transformed their ecologies with bricks and bougainvillea. Suburbia itself was shaped by empire: much of the investment capital that fuelled the building boom came from profits brought from India and elsewhere in the empire.

The garden character of modern suburbia was, in fact, not so much an English invention as an import from abroad. Rather than live cheek-by-jowl with locals in the established Indian centres of commerce, trade and religion, British officials, merchants and military officers took to segregating themselves in 'garden houses' on the outskirts of cities such as Madras and Calcutta from the eighteenth century. South Asian cities were a lot greener and more expansive than European ones. Madras, it was said, 'seems to be less a city than a vast garden where houses happen'; the buildings of Bangalore were 'completely hidden' in a forest of trees. Emma Roberts described Madras in 1836: 'The roads planted on either side with trees, the villas . . . nestling in gardens, where the richest flush of flowers is tempered by the grateful shade of umbrageous groves, leave nothing to be wished for that can delight the eye or enchant the imagination.' Unlike in Europe, Englishmen 'live entirely in their garden-houses, as they properly call them; for these are all surrounded by gardens so closely planted, that the neighbouring house is rarely visible'.[29]

Parts of London began to take on this Asian aspect as colonial adventurers retired to semi-detached villas in new suburbs such as St John's Wood, Kensington and Bayswater, which was known as 'Asia Minor' because of its pronounced Anglo-Indian character. Many of the new semis reflected the architectural styles of the garden quarters of Calcutta and Madras, with verandas, balconies, pergolas, loggias, gazeboes, bay windows and, critically, ornamental gardens. John Loudon's famous semi-detached villa was itself in Bayswater.

An extensive industry of nurseries and seed catalogues emerged to meet the demand for colourful, exotic plants and trees. London's floral inventory was augmented through businesses such as James Colvill's Exotic Nursery based near Sloane Square, which offered, among other things, Mexican dahlias; rhododendrons from the Himalayas; yuccas, Californian poppies and mountain laurel from the United States; magnolias, peonies and roses from China; and, one of its bestsellers, Japanese spotted laurel. George Cruikshank may have depicted the countryside being bombarded with bricks, but he could equally have drawn cannonades of alien seeds spraying down on the urban edge. The suburban environment was beginning to gain an abundance of species that exceeded the countryside thanks to the fashions for exotic plants promoted by people like John and Jane Loudon.

The taste for exotics extended to the working poor who lived in cramped houses devoid of gardens in the inner city or rapidly urbanising suburbs such as Bethnal Green. The journalist and social campaigner Henry Mayhew, in his 1851 portrait of working-class Londoners, **London Labour and the London Poor,** made much of the love of bright, exotic flowers in the East End. When the gardens of working people were filled in by housing, the trade in seeds had fallen away. But it was replaced by a profitable business in the mid-nineteenth century. Towards the end of May, the stalls and barrows of flower-sellers were 'exceedingly beautiful, the barrow often resembling a moving garden'. They were selling potted roots: geraniums, mignonette, dahlias, fuchsias and polyanthuses that could be grown in window boxes or flowerpots. The founding of the Tower Hamlets Chrysanthemum Society in 1859 attested the tremendous popularity of that plant among working people. The first annual Window Garden Show for working-class entrants was held in 1860; four years later, Charles Dickens was among thousands who admired the overflowing roses, fuchsias, geraniums, balsam, convolvulus, mignonette and dahlias. Much later, in 1939, **Picture Post** commented, 'Every Londoner longs for a garden. Few can afford a big one. But thousands grow glorious flowers in backyards, and window-boxes, even on roof-tops.'[30]

The demand for a greener city, the desire for a private garden in which to cultivate chrysanthemums, dahlias and vegetables, motivated Ebenezer Howard to design his Garden City as a way of distributing land to the landless and satisfying the instinctive human desire to grow and cultivate. If Howard did not achieve a revolution in urbanisation, his ideas fundamentally reshaped existing cities around the globe. The garden suburb became the prevailing model of the twentieth century for expansive city growth, consisting of low-density family homes shrouded in greenery. After the First World War, around 4 million new homes were built in Britain. London doubled in size while its population grew by just 10 per cent: this was a policy of dispersal just as it was a sudden and violent revolution in the landscape of London's environs. London County Council built eight huge 'cottage estates' on the agricultural outer rim of the capital for working-class people, most notably the Becontree Estate which was, with 25,769 predominately semi-detached houses for 116,000 people, the largest housing development in the world.

The experience of leaving the cramped slums of the inner city for the garden suburb was recorded in a 1991 book called **Just Like the Country: memories of London families who settled the new cottage estates, 1919-1939.** May Millbank remembered moving as a child from a tenement in Somers Town, Kings Cross, to the Watling cottage estate in Burnt Oak. 'We looked out of the window and my brother who was two years younger than me said, "What's that over there?" He couldn't make out what the green was or what the flowers in the garden were and I was glad he asked because I wasn't sure if the flowers were also called grass.'[31]

Watling Estate is a quintessential interwar garden suburb, a reaction against the harsh nineteenth-century slum and a representation of the desire to return to England's lost (or, rather, imagined) past of villages and rural simplicity. Many street trees were ancient survivors from the hedgerows that had only recently divided fields or lined country lanes. The estate was landscaped with generous green verges, street corners and traffic roundabouts, along with parks and recreation grounds, to give it a village-y, open feel. And then there were the houses (or 'cottages'), set back from the street with private gardens behind privet hedges.

'My parents set about developing a garden,' remembered Joyce Milan of the time her family moved to Page Estate in Eltham, 'something they had never known but had longed for. Mum was mainly in charge of the operations and it was remarkable what she achieved over the years . . . Every inch of the garden was used, growing flowers of every kind . . . Beyond the gate, we grew vegetables of all kinds, potatoes, carrots, cabbage and

Brussels sprouts. Even celery and cucumbers were given a try. Mum planted a small apple tree which produced delicious fruit.' Joyce Milan's mum was not alone: the 1930s were a heyday of gardening, as semi-detached neighbourhoods became the predominant habitation for the working as well as the middle classes. Many took to gardening because of the sheer exhilaration of owning a patch of green after a lifetime in the inner city. In 1938, a whopping 65,000 people entered the competition run by the London Gardens Society for that year's best-kept garden. Even if you didn't want to win a prize there was every incentive to get out with a hoe and trowel: a neat, well-cultivated garden was a condition of tenancy in cottage estates.[32]

For a long time, urbanisation was regarded as a destructive force as far as nature was concerned. **Real** nature – untouched, native, uncultivated – existed elsewhere, in the countryside, in reserves, mountains and forests. Domestic gardens were dismissed by a leading ecologist in 1966 as 'biological deserts'. In reality, the suburban ecosystem had hardly been studied.[33]

It took the zoologist Dr Jennifer Owen to change that. Owen graduated from Oxford University in 1958, gained her PhD from the University of Michigan and took up academic posts in Uganda and Sierra Leone. In the latter country, she made the observation that there was more wildlife in her garden than in the nearby forest. In 1971, back in Britain at the University of Leicester, she began a thirty-year study of her suburban garden of just 741 square metres. During that period, she recorded 2,673 species, made up of 474 plants, 1,997 insects, 138 other invertebrates and sixty-four vertebrates. Because she was unable to study tiny flies and soil creatures, Owen estimated that the true number of insect species was 8,450. Similarly, she calculated the plant diversity of suburbia to be 3,563 species per hectare (an African rainforest has up to 135 plant species per hectare). Owen's garden was not managed as a purposefully biodiverse habitat; it was an ordinary back garden. Yet around 9 per cent of all the species in Britain were found there.[34]

Further scientific studies of gardens in other cities have backed up Jennifer Owen's findings: urban gardens support a greater number of species than an equivalent-sized semi-wild rural habitat. They are the opposite of 'biological deserts': that designation more readily applies to countless acres of monoculture agriculture in the countryside. Suburbia blooms in comparison.[35]

This bounteousness is partly due to the fact that people stuff their gardens with a range of plants not seen in the natural world. It is an extremely complex environment, the long-term global legacy of gardeners such as Loudon. Gravel paths mimic coastline habitats; compost heaps are like detritus layers in woodlands; shrubs and hedges resemble

deciduous forest habitats; lawns stand in for grazed
pastures, sheltering as many as 159 small plant species. There can be a mosaic of different habitats
crammed within a modest garden, some wet, some
dry, some shaded. In London, there are 2.5 million mature trees in private gardens, making up a
considerable proportion of the urban forest. No
garden has an identical inventory of plants, so a
corridor of suburban yards yields an even greater
diversity of food resources for foraging species.
Intriguingly, biodiversity is directly correlated to
human population size: a small town will have an
average of 530–560 plant species; a city with up to
400,000 people will have around 1,000; but once
a city passes the million-person mark the number
rockets above 1,300.[36]

City gardens, therefore, make up a collective
urban habitat consisting of thousands of unique
microhabitats. It is an ever-changing ecosystem:
there are 1,625 native plant species in the British
Isles but 55,000 taxa available for sale to domestic
gardeners (many of them are almost indistinguishable; the list includes 6,413 varieties of daffodil),
and fashions continually change. Of the plants in a
typical garden, 30 per cent are native and 70 per
cent are alien. Owen counted 214 non-British
species in her garden from all over Europe, the
Americas, Africa and Asia, providing an abundance
of food for herbivores. The flora of the world had
travelled to Leicester and made it home.[37]

The emergence of the suburban jungle escaped
the attention of ecologists until relatively recently.
As we will see throughout this book, the green
fringes of cities the world over have, as their ecosystems have matured, become an alluring habitat
for an impressive and increasing array of animals,
birds and insects, many of them endangered by intensive farming and climate change. But none of
this was clear during the onslaught of bulldozers
and builders. Ecologists saw only destruction.

Los Angeles, the global emblem of nature-
devouring suburbanisation, was a particularly potent
example. Promoted as a refreshing corrective to industrial urbanisation, L.A. in its early years offered the
perfect combination of city and nature. According
to the congregationalist minister and L.A. booster,
a 'pauper lives like a king' in sun-kissed southern
California, blessed with a garden in which to grow
vegetables and keep chickens, as well as easy access to
beaches, mountains, forests and countryside.

It proved too attractive. Looking out of the plane
window while flying from L.A. to San Bernardino
in 1958 was 'an unnerving lesson in man's infinite
capacity to mess up his environment' for an appalled William H. Whyte: 'the traveler can see a legion of bulldozers gnawing into the last remaining
tract of green between the two cities, and from San
Bernadino another legion of bulldozers gnawing
westward'. L.A. turned from dream green city to ecological nightmare, driven – ironically perhaps – by

the deep-seated desire of millions of people to live amid nature. The prevailing vegetation types of the region – chaparral and coastal sage scrub dominated by drought-deciduous shrubs – were almost entirely eliminated. The destruction of more or less the entire ecology of Greater Los Angeles, bar a few scattered remnant patches, was a shocking revelation of the power of twentieth-century urbanisation.[38]

Photographs of the post-war subdivisions that eradicated the peri-urban landscape show rows of identical, mass-produced bungalows occupying moonscapes denuded of trees and plants. It looks like the very definition of ecocide, but this was a landscape also poised on the brink of renewal. Within years, such landscapes would develop a canopy and a covering of exotic plants.

The humanmade biome of Los Angeles is now more forested, more colourful, more shaded and greener than the ecosystem it replaced. Part of the reason is that it is now a wetter place, with vast amounts of water piped hundreds of miles first from the Owens River and then the Colorado River. Water sprinklers became commercially available after the Second World War, and this heavily irrigated landscape now supports a mighty assemblage of flora collected from every continent on the planet, which thrives in southern California's balmy Mediterranean climate. Areas of coastal sage scrub do not contain many trees or grasses. By the 1960s, L.A. possessed an area of lawn the size of four Manhattan islands, ninety-five square miles. A survey published in 2019 found 564 species of trees in residential yards compared to four in natural areas. There was a sevenfold increase in plant species per square metre in cultivated areas compared to surviving patches of native habitat.[39]

Anything could grow in Angeleno soil, it was said, if it was watered well enough. L.A.'s new inhabitants took up the challenge: by the 1960s, L.A. led the country in sales of ornamental stock. Settlers from the east coast and the Midwest brought their preferences for the English aesthetic which went back to the time of John Loudon – an orderly gardenesque landscape of lawn, eclectic exotic ornamentals and stately, shady trees. They had little appreciation for the native plants of coastal sage scrubland, which is brown for much of the year. In one of the nation's first mass-produced blue-collar suburbs, Lakewood, there was a fad for jacarandas from the Amazon, pepper trees from Peru and rubber trees from India. Orange and avocado trees took hold in suburban yards. The insatiable desire for a verdant lawn was made possible in the 1960s by hybrid crosses of African Bermuda grass with other African variants that retained their greenness all year round. We are talking about an almost complete species turnover during the course of a century, an urban biome created by generations of residents that is totally different from the native ecosystem.[40]

We tend to think of the city's assault on nature

as being one of asphalt and concrete, bricks and mortar. But urbanisation reshapes the edgelands of cities in a more fundamental way: due to the immense acreage of gardens, it replaces native species with alien ones. In temperate countries in Europe, this might not be so much of a problem. For one thing, most of the plants require tender human care and would not live long on their own, so only a few become invasive. For another, garden fashions introduce a lot of resource-rich plants from diverse origins that provide food for insects, upon which all life ultimately depends, including our own.

In Mediterranean-climate and tropical cities, however, alien plants can impact on the regional ecosystem when they escape and become invasive. **Lantana camara** (from the verbena family), introduced to Indian gardens from South and Central America, has had a devastating effect on biodiversity, particularly in forest understories. The pretty Amazonian water hyacinth has wreaked untold carnage on riverine and wetland ecosystems the world over. In New Zealand, the colonial desire to Englishify the cityscape with plants familiar to settlers has been fatal to local ecosystems. In Christchurch, out of 317 vascular plant species found in the city, only forty-eight are natives. Many of the surviving native herbaceous plants are considered weeds. Since the arrival of British colonists, over 20,000 alien species have been introduced, many of which out-compete the indigenous flora. In fast-growing cities in Central and South America, Africa and Asia – many of them located in biodiverse hotspots – escapee plants find the climate and soil entirely to their tastes. A study of Ensenada, Mexico, found that 61 per cent of plant species growing wild in the city outside parks and gardens were non-native; a similar investigation in Concepción, Chile, discovered 113 alien plants in streets and waste grounds and hardly any natives at all. As the next chapter details, huge proportions of cities all over the globe are carpeted in manicured lawns. Outside Europe, many of the grass seeds are imported from abroad and, because they are non-native, require oceans of water, pesticide and fertiliser to keep out indigenous flora and preserve the vaunted greenness. Swathes of lawn adorning suburban areas bear no resemblance to the ecosystems they conquer and are often lifeless as a result. Turfgrasses are some of the most destructive invasive species assailing the planet.[41]

In the temperate regions of the northern hemisphere, the story is less dramatic, but it is a cause for concern all the same. Pelham Bay Park, the largest natural area in New York City, lost an average of 2.8 native plant species and gained 4.9 alien species every year over five decades. In the late nineteenth and early twentieth centuries, surveys of Central Park found 356 plant species, 74 per cent of which were natives and 26 per cent non-native. In 2007, there were 362 species, of which 40 per cent were native and 60 per cent non-native. The pattern is strikingly common the world over: urbanisation **increases** the total number of species present while at the same time inflicting local extinctions. We talk about global cities as monotonous, with similar skyscrapers, cuisines, brands and cafés. But globalisation exerts its force in other ways, largely unseen and rarely discussed. The globalisation of urban nature is known as 'biotic homogenisation'.[42]

Over the last century, we have transformed the edgelands of cities from their wild, semi-wild or agricultural state to something else – an expansive realm of suburbia, a good proportion of which is a complicated tessellation of very different kinds of open spaces. Generations of ecologists saw this is a bad thing: the modification of the landscape and the replacement of native plants with aliens made it a degraded, profoundly unnatural, messed up place. True nature existed in 'pristine' or untouched areas, while suburbia represented all that was bad about the interactions between humans and natural processes.

But there is another way of looking at it. The suburbanisation of the edgelands on a global scale has created 'novel ecosystems', hybrid habitats where the artificial mixes with the natural. Urbanisation is a shocking, destructive event for native wildlife. Yet new ways of life are created in the process. Like it or not, this kind of habitat is a reality, and it is irreversible. Better to embrace it than wish it away. Right in front of our noses is a lavish, vital ecosystem that needs to be valued if it is to thrive. The challenge now is to optimise these vast, often disregarded edgelands ringing our urban centres. Because, like other habitats on our planets, it is endangered.

Imagine the outcry if the London authorities sold off Hyde Park, Regent's Park, Victoria Park, Hampstead Heath and Epping Forest to developers. It would be an unmitigated tragedy, an ecological crisis for the metropolis, entailing the sacrifice of 3,000 hectares of recreational space and wildlife habitat. Yet that was the amount of green space lost in London between 1998 and 2006 as gardens were paved over, turned into decking or built upon. And these gardens can be just as ecologically valuable as parks, if not more so.[43]

Although a quarter of London's surface is designated as garden space, just 58 per cent of it is vegetated. The remaining 42 per cent of potential greenery (10 per cent of London) is simply part of the grey jungle. A massive 12.4 square miles of the metropolis is made up of paved-over front gardens devoted to car parking. In California, meanwhile, 33,881 'accessory dwelling unit' (ADU) permits were issued between 2018 and 2020 after changes in the law allowed separate buildings to be built in suburban backyards in an effort to ease the state's housing crisis. In Germany, by contrast, paving over your garden entails higher water bills as compensation for your part in reducing greenspace. In 2021, there was a campaign in the Netherlands named 'Breaking the Tiles', in which cities competed to rip up paved areas in front of homes, apartments and offices and replace them with plants and bushes. Rotterdam went head-to-head with Amsterdam in a battle to remove the most tiles. In the end, the score was Rotterdam 47,942, Amsterdam 46,484.[44]

The global trend is going the other way, however, with fewer gardens and more asphalt. As gardens begin to disappear or change use, so large amounts of the urban habitat shrink. Furthermore, there are gardens and there are gardens: some contribute far more to the health of the city than others.

Brad and Amy Henderson, a young couple in their 30s, were cited by the city of Lawndale, Los Angeles, for creating a nuisance in 2003. Their crime? – contributing to urban 'blight' and creating 'slum' conditions by allowing 'excessive overgrown vegetation in [their] frontyard'. According to Preston Lerner of the **Los Angeles Times,** Brad and Amy had rejected the neat suburban garden ideal of trimmed lawn, tidy shrubs and regimented flowerbeds in favour of a 'chaotic, writhing, tangled hodgepodge of purple sage, dun buckwheat, coyote bush, needlegrass and dozens of other drought-tolerant native plants, all growing in nature's version of a rugby scrum'.[45]

Brad and Amy were rebels against the ecologically

destructive cult of the suburban lawn that had given their city, Lawndale, its bucolic name. Lawns cover 40 million acres in the United States. For city enforcement officials, their yard was a public nuisance; for them, it was a native wildlife garden, 'an island in the middle of a totally urbanized environment' in the words of Brad, which did not require destructive inputs of water and pesticides.[46]

In the end, the Hendersons gained the support of their community and won, agreeing to trim their wild plants when they encroached on the sidewalk. It was a victory for urban gardens that are grown for ecological, as opposed to ornamental, purposes. Gardens that are a little wild, a bit **messy** – with tall herbaceous plants, infrequently mown lawns and spontaneous growth – fall foul of long-established ideals of suburban beauty and local weed ordinances, but they overflow with resources for wildlife, including vital pollinators and invertebrates.

Cities and suburbs need more people like the Hendersons. That is why it is so important to understand and broadcast the potential biodiverse power of gardens, which are, after all, the keystone of the urban ecosystem. They have the capacity to be a boon for nature if we tend them accordingly; they are not merely ornamental or recreational but key microhabitats that can be **more** biodiverse than the countryside or a city park. The greening of the urban environment can only happen one garden, one flowerpot, at a time. It can only happen when gardeners fully appreciate the vital contribution their plots could make to biodiversity.

The term 'ecotone' is used by biologists to describe the transition zone between two distinct biomes, where ecologies collide and intermingle. It could be the place where a forest meets grassland, or where a river encounters a marsh. The word comes from the Greek **oikos** (home) and **tonus** (tension). It is a dynamic environment which is constantly being remade: it is a zone of struggle and co-dependency. Ecotones are places of exceptional biodiversity, species richness and adaptation as a result.

We should start seeing urban edgelands as ecotones – as the half-wild interface between human and natural habitats where biodiversity can flourish. In 1978, W. G. 'Bunny' Teagle published a short but highly influential pamphlet, 'The Endless Village', the result of his pioneering 1,300-mile journey by bus and foot through the post-industrial edgelands of the Birmingham and Black Country conurbation in the West Midlands of England. This scarred terrain had been the founding forge of the industrial revolution that engulfed the world, a human-altered landscape of quarries, mines, slag heaps, factories, furnaces, railway lines, canals, power stations, housing estates and motorways – a 'jumbled mosaic', as Teagle called it, capturing the intertwining of human activities and nature. This derelict, abused terrain, Teagle discovered to his surprise, was profuse with life. Neglect had allowed nature to flourish; it had found a niche in these abandoned edgelands, in the scrub, heath, bogs, marshes and woods that had been left to regenerate. This is the new wild. Or perhaps it is the **old** wild, a throwback to the scrubby, rugged edgelandia that once girdled cities and provided a retreat for urban dwellers.

Teagle's findings were specific to the Black Country; but almost every city has a comparable belt of left-over land. It is a wildscape, an ecotone where the artificial and the natural become deeply imbricated. Just over twenty years after Bunny Teagle's ground-breaking survey of the Black Country edgelands, another discovery was made in the UK, this time in the industrial landscape of Essex. An abandoned oil terminal covering 240 acres, wedged between refineries, new housing, roundabouts and a super-store on Canvey Island, had been fenced off and left for thirty years. This is classic feral edgeland: it had been used for bonfires, trail biking and illegal rub-bish dumping. Yet despite its roughness, it contains magic. 'Canvey's Rainforest', as it is nicknamed, has more species, including a number of rare and en-dangered species, per square metre than a nature reserve. 'Nowhere else in the UK has such a rich-ness of nature,' Matt Shardlow of the conservation trust Buglife told the **Guardian.** 'It's ridiculously high quality. I cannot think of any site of this size which has such diversity.'[47]

For much of the last century, biodiversity conservation strategies focused on pristine natural environments, overlooking urban habitats and scruffy fringes. At the same time, green belts were preserved for agriculture and to limit sprawl; their value for biodiversity and wildlife was disregarded. But the time has come for the urban-rural ecotone to become a priority for nature conservation, because it can be an incredibly productive habitat.

Green belts are a misstep. What the planet needs are wild belts or ecological buffer zones on the edges of cities – wildlife reserves that conserve native ecologies while also serving as defensive walls against severe flooding, poisoned air, water shortages and desertification. These semi-wild mantles are not merely nice add-ons but economic and existential necessities. As we shall see, New York has reason to rue the near-total loss of its tidal wetlands, and Delhi its encircling forests. We could forget how a city relates to its hinterland once we dispensed of the need for its food, fuel, building materials and water – instead procuring those energy inputs from ever greater distances – but climate change is forcing us to re-examine the city's place within its immediate environment.

Writing in 1894, the historian Thomas Janvier bitterly fulminated that the opportunity 'to create a beautiful city' in New York was simply 'wasted and thrown away'. If the street plan had formed around the natural topography of Manhattan rather than a grid, New York would have looked very different, with roads curving with the contours of the land around hills, tracts of woodland and 'reservations [preserved] for beauty's sake alone'. As it was, the city planners decreed 'that the forests should be cut away, the hills levelled, the hollows filled in, the streams buried' to make way for the rigid, undeviating rectangular street plan.[48]

The alternative New York imagined by Janvier, which grew around its natural topography rather than smothering it, while preserving sizeable tracts of wildness, would nowadays be called 'landscape urbanism', a way of designing cities to exist in some sort of harmony with their natural surroundings. It is a concept of urban planning that extends back in time to Loudon, who looked upon cities as having the potential to be gardens writ large. Bio-sensitive urban growth is centred on what is called the 'patch-corridor' model. Cities can, will and should grow, according to this model, but they can minimise their environmental impact if they concentrate new developments in dense, moderately sized hubs set amid substantial patches of remnant native vegetation, particularly areas of rainforest, woodland, wetland, grassland, savannahs and rivers. These patches have to be linked by green corridors because that ensures the survival of indigenous species and allows room for animals to range without being fragmented, trapped and isolated by urbanisation. This brings us back to the wild spaces envisaged by Loudon almost two centuries ago, to the demands for green belts and wedges that followed as cities everywhere began to grow at hyperspeed. Only today, the need for such interventions is determined by pressing environmental priorities and developments in ecological science. To put it another way, we have moved from focusing on aesthetics to self-preservation.[49]

We now know that the shadowlands of cities can be exceptionally good for nature, even if they don't look like conventional wildernesses. It is where wildlife adapts to living in close proximity to humans, an urgent need in the Anthropocene when our greed and waste touch every ecosystem. Urban edgelands can become the wildlife reserves of the future, refuges for numerous species from the intensities of the city on one side and industrialised agriculture on the other, if we preserve them. In the past, the forests ringing German cities, the wetlands surrounding New York and the heaths encircling London were rugged, semi-wild places of escape for the inhabitants of the urban jungle. Imagine if that were the case today – if we could walk, cycle or take a train out of the city not into fields but straight into wildscapes and nature reserves. As we shall see throughout the rest of this book, edgelands will become vital to shield cities from the dire effects of climate change. But they are places of pleasure and escape as well. Fresh Kills on Staten Island was for the second half of the twentieth century a by-word for the malign effects of a city on its local eco-system. But even this site of rampant destruction is becoming the home of a new urban wild.

2.

Parks & Rec

Deep underground, microbes turn half a century's worth of city waste into methane. The gases and leachate are extracted through an extensive network of subterranean pipes and then used to power 22,000 nearby homes. While 150 million tons of garbage gradually decomposes unseen below the surface, above ground, the former dump reverts to meadows, woodland and saltwater marshes, providing a haven for wildlife and a massive park for the people of New York.

This is Fresh Kills in the 2020s. In 2001, the infamous landfill received its last, and saddest, consignments – the charred debris of the World Trade Center. Since then, it has been transformed into a 2,315-acre public park. Three times bigger than Central Park, it is the largest new green public space created within New York City for over a century, a mixture of wildlife habitats, bike trails, sports fields, art exhibits and playgrounds. This is poisoned land: fifty years' worth of landfill has killed for ever one of the city's most productive wetland ecosystems. Restoration is impossible. Instead, a brand new ecosystem is emerging on top of the toxic garbage.

It is doing so thanks to human engineering. The waste is separated from the environment by impermeable plastic covers, geotextiles and a thin layer of soil; the toxic liquids and gases are pumped away. The garbage slopes have undergone a process known as strip cropping; fast-growing plants on the mounds were ploughed repeatedly back into the soil to add organic matter. When the soil became fertile, the next step was the planting of 'workhorse' species: tough native meadow grass and wildflowers such as Indiangrass, little bluestem, gamagrass, aster and goldenrod.

The tough grassland provides a habitat for initial colonisers – the plants, microorganisms, insects, small mammals and birds that come first. This is the world's largest experiment in reclaiming contaminated land and returning it to nature. Already, the grassy matrix has created the conditions for life: numerous plant and tree species have appeared in the last decade, along with muskrats, painted turtles, bald eagles, ospreys, herons and the endangered grasshopper sparrow. What happens next is largely outside human control. Over the next decades, the vast extent of Freshkills Park (as it was renamed) will be reclaimed by whatever species are attracted to the foundations of grasses. Nature will do the bulk of the work, not human beings. Biodiversity

will steadily build as winds and birds bring seeds to
the site. This process of spontaneous successional
growth is how nature rebounds from natural disasters such as forest fires, earthquakes, volcanic activity and climate upheaval. Only, in this case, the
disaster was humanmade.[1]

One scholar has dubbed typical urban parks as
'Potemkin gardens', named after the fake 'Potemkin
villages' supposedly created to impress the Empress
Catherine II with an illusion of prosperity when
she visited Crimea in 1787. Just like the villages,
urban parks present a façade of nature, which, in
reality, provide limited ecological value. Most parks
were designed to look picturesque and provide recreation. They were not intended to enhance urban
ecologies. Freshkills is not, however, a typical park.[2]

It is called 'lifescape', as opposed to 'landscape' – that
is to say, a terrain continually shaped by unpredictable natural processes rather than a masterplan. It is
an act of atonement and redemption after years of
destruction. It is also a response to the need to carve
public parks out of the existing dense cityscape by
reclaiming vacant land. In cities around the world,
parks are being created out of landfills, disused factory sites, airports, military bases, water treatment
facilities, quarries and prisons. Vegetation and pioneer forest are engulfing the decomposing remains
of the Thyssen-Meiderich blast furnaces at the
heavily-polluted Landschaftspark Duisburg-Nord,

providing diverse habitats for endangered species. Rainham Marshes in east London had long been used as an army shooting range and a dumping-place for estuarine silt; it lies between extensive warehouses, breakers' yards, landfills and industrial estates. The A13 motorway and the Channel Tunnel rail link scythe through it. Yet since 2000, it has been rehabilitated as a wetland nature reserve, a 'wildscape for a world city' nestled within intensive urbanisation.

Such urban rewilding projects, with Freshkills as the leading exemplar, offer a new concept of public parks in the twenty-first century, focused primarily on biodiversity and the rehabilitation of native ecologies after decades or centuries of abuse. Above all, they broadcast the reassuring message that, however hard we try to spoil nature, wildlife possesses the power to recover. They are new, to be sure, in their environmental concerns. But they connect back to millennia-long attempts to create natural idylls in cities. The notion of what is considered idyllic always changes. Today it revolves around ideas of wildness and the restoration of native ecologies as acts of redemption in an age of climate change. For most of our urban history, however, greenery in cities was intended to demonstrate the absolute mastery of humans over the wildness, danger and instability of the natural world. The ambition in sculpting green spaces in grey cities – from ancient Babylon to Central Park in New York – was not to import nature into the metropolis; it was to create **better** nature.

The large artificial green mountain made up of ascending tiered gardens overflowing with trees, shrubs and vines that existed in ancient Babylon was the product of some of the most advanced engineering on the planet. Evidence for the existence of the Hanging Gardens of Babylon is sketchy. It has been argued by the historian Stephanie Dalley that such gardens existed in Nineveh. Certainly, the Assyrian king Sennacherib (704–681 BCE) created extraordinarily lavish gardens in Nineveh fed by waters carried over fifty miles through automatic sluice gates, aqueducts and water screws, which made possible the irrigation of vegetation high up on raised terraces above the cityscape. Olives, figs, date palms, oaks, cedars, vines and junipers draped over Sennacherib's brick mountain in defiance of, and in striking juxtaposition to, the arid natural environment and the density of mudbrick buildings. The effect of such gardens, in Nineveh and Babylon, would have been stunning, a manifestation of human domination over the world and of the king's power over everything.

The emperor Nero made clear the extent of his manic, untrammelled power when he brought the countryside into the very heart of Rome. The fire that destroyed the imperial capital in CE 64 cleared the space, previously occupied by the poor, for

Nero's Domus Aurea, a palatial estate of 200 acres in what would later become the site of the Colosseum. Enclosed by the gentle slopes of the Palatine, Oppian and Caelian Hills, the landscaping of the Domus Aurea gave the illusion of uncultivated wildness rather than formal gardening. With groves, pastures, vineyards and a large artificial lake, it was the most audacious attempt at **rus in urbe** seen thus far in history. As it was said of Nero, 'the real luxury was not in gold and jewels, which were common by this time, but in having country meadows and parks in the middle of the town, where one found, in complete seclusion, first shady thicket, then open lawns, vineyards, pasture lands, or hunting grounds'.

The whole project was 'ruinously prodigal', according to Suetonius, an extreme example of hubris and megalomania in attempting to convert a portion of the imperial megacity into an idealised arcadian dreamscape. In doing so, Nero was attempting to live up to, and exceed, the Roman veneration of, and nostalgia for, a lost world where humans and nature were in harmony. This pining for the pastoral, expressed in art and poetry, came at a time of intense urbanisation, when Rome was marching towards becoming a city of a million souls. Rome itself was endowed with the first public parks – ornamental gardens in theatre, temple and bath complexes bequeathed to the people by powerful politicians such as Pompey, Caesar and Agrippa in the century before Nero built his pleasure grounds. Under the emperor Augustus, the Campus Martius, the Field of Mars, was transformed into something like a public park, an open area with temples, tombs and mausoleums. When he was bequeathed an enormous house, Augustus had it pulled down and turned into the beautiful Portico of Livia, with a public garden that included a vine growing over the walkways, capable, according to Pliny the Elder, of producing twelve amphorae of wine a year. Green space in the city was an expression of ostentation and power, a gift from the benevolent super-rich to the nature-starved masses. Above all it showed the supremacy of humans over the life-giving element of water: only the fabulously wealthy could manipulate the environment in this way, overcoming the aridity of the cityscape to provide year-round greenery through elaborate and expensive technologies.[3]

Urban greenery has been cultivated since the very earliest cities. Just as Nero's outrageous urban estate attempted to recreate lost arcadian virtues, royal Aztec gardens were designed to establish links to both mythology and the numinous. In the centre of Tenochtitlan, for example, there was a garden that recreated the rugged desert terrain of northern Mexico, where plants such as cactus, agave and yucca grew on humanmade cliffs.

The desert garden took the Aztecs back to the depths of time, to the harsh ancestral landscape from which they had migrated centuries before the creation of Tenochtitlan; it was the starting point for ceremonies that recalled their mythic past, their long journey from the arid wilderness to the metropolis that stood at the centre of the world. Elsewhere, botanic gardens and zoos contained collections of plants and animals that had been transplanted from great distances, forming a vivid, symbolic recreation of Tenochtitlan's extensive imperial reach. As with later European colonial botanic gardens, they were trophies of conquest. For the Aztecs, urban gardens existed as sacred spaces that obliterated time and space by providing sensory connections with distant topographies.[4]

Nero's attempt to create a natural-looking arcadia aside, most projects to green cities involved forcing nature into geometric patterns. If nature in the wild was rough and shaggy, in the city, it became ordered, neat and harmonious. There is no better example of this need to regulate nature than the Uzbek ruler and founder of the Mughal Empire, Babur. Under his rule in the early sixteenth century CE, cities stretching from Kabul to Agra were remodelled as stunning garden cities.

As with the Aztecs, urban gardens provided a link back to the ruler's dynastic origins. Babur's courtly life took place in outdoor garden settings in the midst of cities. Pavilions and tents recalled his ancestors' nomadic lifestyles on the steppes, the great Mongol conqueror Genghis Khan and the Turkic empire builder Timur (Tamerlane). Creating gardens in Afghan and Indian cities linked Babur most closely with Timur, who had made gardens the pre-eminent symbol of central Asian civilisation after his wars of conquest in the fourteenth century. Timur's gardens adopted the ancient Persian **chahar bagh** style that went back all the way to the time of Cyrus the Great in the sixth century BCE, a rectangular, walled garden divided into quarters by straight canals. The quartered garden represented the division of the universe into four – the four seasons and the four elements, earth, wind, water and fire. Its symmetry mirrored the underlying harmony of the cosmos. The English word 'paradise' comes from the Latin **paradisus,** borrowed from the Greek **paradeisos** which in turn comes from the Old Persian **pairidaēza,** which means walled garden. Heaven was a cultivated, idyllic garden.

The ancient, beautiful, geometric form of garden, with its lawns, flowing streams, octagonal pools and shady fruit trees, was taken by Muslims as a terrestrial representation of the paradise described in the Qur'an. The four watercourses that defined the **chahar bagh** were the four rivers of honey, milk, wine and water found in heaven. Gardens in Iran and central Asia were constructed on terraces that allowed water to flow in managed cascades and waterfalls. Nature was made orderly and geometrical in an effort to fuse its principles with humanity's and thereby fashion something divine. Timur's magnificently crafted gardens in Samarkand underlined his status as ruler of the world and legitimised his conquests.

In his autobiography, Babur never mentioned constructing mosques or madrassas in the wake of conquest. Instead, he was preoccupied with the many gardens he built. Clearly, then, garden design embodied and reflected his statecraft. More than that: gardens were at the centre of his world view. To say he was obsessed with them would be to put it mildly. As a boy he visited the gardens of his ancestors in Samarkand. It left an impression that would last a lifetime: 'For beauty, and air and view, few [gardens] will equal Darwesh Muhammad Tarkans's **chaharbagh** . . . it is arranged symmetrically, terrace above terrace, and is planted with beautiful narwan and cypresses and white poplar'.

Driven out of his ancestral lands in the Fergana Valley, Babur spent much of his early life on the run, estranged from those wonderful gardens. An itinerant prince looking to make his fortune, he finally captured Kabul in 1504. He set about making gardens in the time-honoured manner of his ancestors. He transformed Kabul into a verdant city with a series of **chahar bagh** gardens. These gardens, alive with orange and pomegranate trees, flowers, streams and pools, became his private paradise and put him on par with his ancestor Timur. The gardens were the very first things created after the conquest of Hindustan because they broadcast what Mughal rule meant: their evergreen lushness represented the infinite bounty of the godlike emperor; their symmetry betokened orderly government.

They were **better** than nature. If paradise was a geometrical walled garden full of the good and beautiful things, the world was chaotic and sinful, full of rank weeds, irregular landscapes and wild beasts. In cultivating perfect gardens, Babur was bringing order to chaos, purging unsightly and irregular nature. Once, Babur came upon a stream in a garden which was 'zig-zag and irregular; I made it straight and orderly; so the place became very beautiful'. Creating an earthly paradise in this way was an expression not so much of piety as of kingship: only the emperor had the power to surround himself in life with the beauties promised in the afterlife; only he could straighten rivers and command the elements. The walled city garden became a microcosm of a perfected world, shorn of its tangles and tares. Cities gave garden creators the perfect tabula rasa; all that was beautiful and agreeable could be incorporated; all that was ugly, messy or dangerous could be banished.

Gardens served another purpose. For one thing they were an indelible stamp of conquest and subjugation: what could demonstrate more power than rearranging entire landscapes? Gardens also made cities more hospitable. The Mughal elite did not much like the dust and heat of Agra and wanted to leave with their loot. By fashioning it into a city of gardens reminiscent of Kabul, Babur aimed to make Agra more familiar to his central Asian command- ers in both its appearance and its microclimate. His gardens produced melons and grapes – fruits he introduced to India from home. The topography of Hindustan, according to Babur, was 'disorderly' and its cities 'unpleasant'. It was also lacking in running water, so 'it kept coming to my mind that waters should be made to flow by means of wheels erected wherever I might settle down, also that grounds should be laid out in an orderly and sym- metrical way'. The garden thus became a showcase of advanced technologies that aimed to recreate the streams of the Fergana Valley.

The passion for gardens evinced by Babur, his suc- cessors, the nobility and wealthy merchants trans- formed cities. The gardens themselves weren't parks as we would know them. They were the settings for court and administrative life, for business and plea- sure among the elite. On select occasions they were open to the public, and some became parks as the Mughal Empire waned. But they did fundamen- tally affect urban spaces in India as cities developed around these generous wellsprings of greenery and coolness. Trees, flowers, herbs and fruits were gath- ered from around India and central Asia, creating new biodiversity in the cityscape. Mughal gardens were suffused with dense foliage, thick with flowers and fruit trees, many of which had never existed in the region. A visitor described Ahmadabad: 'from [the gate of Shahi Bagh] to Hajipur the road on both sides is shaded by tall, green, trees, beyond which lie the beautiful gardens of the Nazims and nobles. The whole scene appeared as a dream in emerald.'[5]

A 'city of gardens' they called Ahmadabad, so profuse was the greenery. The same name was given to Lahore, where Emperor Shah Jahan created one of the greatest of all Mughal gardens. Constructed between 1641 and 1643, the Shalimar Gardens mark the zenith of Mughal garden design; they were called 'an example of the highest paradise'. The upper terrace of the Shalimar Gardens was reserved for the harem; the middle, with its elaborate waterworks, for the emperor; and the lower for noblemen and sometimes the public.

The completion of Shah Jahan's paradise changed the face of Lahore, with nobles competing to create paradise gardens of their own. In Lahore, landscaping was used consciously to fuse city and countryside, the human and the natural, into a unified whole. This aspiration for harmony between the artificial and the natural impelled the chain of garden cities that stretched from Persia to the Bay of Bengal, similar in many ways to the expansive city states of Mesoamerica before the Spanish conquest. As late as 1885, long after the fall of the Mughals, the Marchioness of Dufferin, the wife of the British Viceroy of India, raved about the verdancy of Lahore. Even in the midst of the city, she could not see much evidence of a town because it was lost in 'luxuriant foliage and flowers' and 'enveloped in trees'; everywhere she drove Lady Dufferin saw thick hedges of roses. Whenever an inhabitant of Lahore left his dwelling and narrow street, she rhapsodised, 'he finds himself amongst plantains, and roses, and palms, and mangoes, and peepul-trees, and lovely flowering pomegranates'.[6]

Babur's gardens in Mughal India tell us a lot about nature in cities. We have always wanted to create landscapes of order. The same could be said about the temple gardens of Japanese and Chinese cities or the formal gardens of Renaissance Italy, places that sought to create models of a regulated, improved world and a terrestrial paradise. We have sought to tame the wildness of nature. Cities allow us to do this. They are relatively segregated from the natural world and become controlled environments in which we can experiment. Just as the city itself evinced humanity's achievement in constructing a productive anthropic environment, the garden in the city signified humankind's domination over nature. Public parks, when they came into the urban realm, would emerge out of these political, imperial, aesthetic and moral impulses.

Visitors to New York's Central Park might think it is a remnant of Manhattan's primeval landscape preserved amid the remorseless human cityscape, a chunk of left-over nature existing within the iron logic of the grid. But it is a reflection of the human-made environment around it, as engineered and artificial as Shah Jahan's Shalimar Gardens or, indeed, present-day Freshkills Park. Before 1857, it was a swampy, rocky piece of land covered with low scrub. The site had been used extensively over the years, variously for military encampments, quarries, rubbish dumps, piggeries, farms and bone-boiling factories. In the 1850s, it was home to a large squatter camp. This was not virgin terrain. 'It would have been difficult to find another body of land of six hundred acres upon the island which possessed less of . . . the most desirable characteristics of a park, or upon which more time, labor, and expense would be required to establish them.'[7]

Those were the words of Central Park's co-creator, Frederick Law Olmsted. Time, labour and expense were the key ingredients in bending nature to New York's will. Olmsted and his business partner Calvert Vaux won the competition to design the park in 1858. Over the course of the next few years, more gunpowder was used to clear the site than was discharged at the Battle of Gettysburg. Around 140,000 cubic metres of soil and rocks were removed and replaced with more suitable topsoil imported from New Jersey and Long Island. Hills and slopes were reshaped; humanmade cliffs were installed. Brooks disappeared underground into an enormous latticework of pipes, which redirected water from the meadow marshes to ponds and cascades where it looked most scenic. Hundreds of thousands of plants and shrubs were imported from nurseries in England, Scotland and France. Olmsted and Vaux reordered the entire area; during construction, for the native flora and fauna, it was no less destructive than if the site had been built upon.

Olmsted's parks were designed as poems in green – pastoral landscapes characterised by curvilinear paths that took strollers through a choreographed sequence of sensory experiences and alternating scenery. He wanted his parks to possess a 'pleasing uncertainty and delicate mysterious tone'. Visitors to Central Park were to be enfolded in a gentle rolling landscape that offered a series of vistas. Olmsted gave his parks the illusion of 'rural spaciousness' by camouflaging the adjacent city with greenery. The hand of the creator should be obscured by the organic feel of the park, with no hard boundaries and trees, shrubs, lawns, ravines and ponds blending with one another. When he was designing South Park in Chicago, Olmsted was asked where the flowerbeds would go. Anywhere outside the park, he witheringly replied. The total effect of a pastoral landscape was balm for the soul; it did not need fussy details or distracting flowers. According to Olmsted, 'townspeople appear to find, in broad spaces of greensward, over which they are allowed unrestricted movement, the most exhilarating contrast to the walled-in floors or pavements to which they are ordinarily confined by their business'. If the word 'paradise' originally meant a garden, Central Park was intended to be paradise for a secular, urbanised age.[8]

The word we use for urban recreational greenspace, 'park', comes from the Germanic **parrock,** meaning paddock. It passed into Latin as **parcus,** Middle French as **parc** and English as 'park' to refer primarily to a large piece of enclosed woodland and pasture used to rear animals for the hunt. This etymology provides a clue as to why Central Park – and many parks the world over – look as they do. Olmsted's conception of what urban nature should be had specific origins in medieval Europe.

Hunting parks, because they are grazed, have a certain look – a landscape comprising stands of trees set in broad swathes of turf, bordered by scenic woodland. This vista became the kind of perfected landscape favoured by the English aristocracy for their country estates in the late seventeenth and early eighteenth centuries – a perfected arcadian fantasy of gently undulating hills, expansive green pastures interspersed with woodland, and attractive water features. Traces of actual working farms were erased for this artful rural ensemble designed to manifest a painting by Claude Poussin or Salvator Rosa. It was 'Nature still, but Nature methodiz'd': an improved landscape that exemplified the kind of progress and productivity that was revolutionising English agriculture in the eighteenth century.

Just like Babur's gardens, these parks were crafted

as deliberate political statements. Out went the once-fashionable, fussy, geometric designs that imitated Italian and French gardens, which had in turn derived from Akkadian, Roman and Islamic traditions. In came a landscape that appeared to be a spontaneous creation of nature. English parks were shaggier and more naturalistic than formal gardens, a conscious symbol of the supposed organic nature of England's constitution and the triumph of liberty over the tyrannical absolutist monarchies of continental Europe.[9]

The English aristocracy brought their tastes to town. One of London's gifts to global urbanisation is the residential garden square, the distinctive feature first of elite estates on the western edge of London and then of suburbia. The layout of these squares followed the trajectory of changes on rural estates. Squares that had been planted in the seventeenth century with tightly cropped hedges, deciduous shrubs and pruned trees that bordered gravel walkways gave way to large, stately trees such as the London plane and the sycamore; lawn took over from gravel and paving stones. This greening of Europe's largest and fastest-growing metropolis in the eighteenth century was an elite project. As in Lahore, greenery and gardens were features of the affluent districts. And it was political: by replicating the country estate in urban housing estates, the message was that landed power, not commercial wealth, dictated the destinies of the capital. **Rus in urbe** had a double meaning.

The landscaping of London in a wider sense followed this landed aristocratic taste. One of the world's first large urban parks, Hyde Park, had been a deer park owned by Henry VIII from 1536 until the public was given limited access 101 years later. In the 1720s, it was extensively re-landscaped along the lines of a country estate, with the large Serpentine – one of the first artificial lakes to be made to appear natural – as its focal point. Greenwich Park, previously a formal baroque garden, was remodelled on naturalistic lines. These were royal parks, and they were the recreational sites of the nobility and gentry; it is little wonder that the aristocratic informal style became the dominant park design in the eighteenth century, when urban green spaces – often former game reserves – were becoming emmeshed into the urban fabric. It became an exportable commodity. The Englischer Garten in Munich (1789), the Hagaparken in Stockholm (1780–97), the Bois de Boulogne and Bois de Vincennes in Paris (both 1850s) and the Tiergarten in Berlin (1833–40), not to mention Central Park, are all early examples of the international appeal of the English landscape garden in cities.

This park type would come to dominate the cityscape. It was further refined by that doyen of garden design and urban planning, John Claudius Loudon.

His gardenesque style took the essential elements of the informal picturesque parkscape and added exotic annual and perennial flowering plants amassed in curved and circular beds. Regent's Park, laid out by John Nash, was a radical departure in urban development. Here, parkland was carved out of farmland, not former hunting ground, and integrated into the cityscape as part of an aristocratic housing estate. Regent's Park showcased the gardenesque style, with stately ornamental trees and the exuberantly informal flowerbeds that seemed to mimic nature. Yet Loudon was clear that urban parks should never be mistaken for **real** nature: 'Any creation, to be recognised as a work of art, must be such as can never be mistaken for a work of nature.'[10]

Loudon campaigned, successfully, for the walls that bordered Hyde Park to be replaced with railings so that green and grey space could be integrated. In 1840, he was commissioned by the textile mill owner and philanthropist Joseph Strutt to create a recreation ground to 'offer the inhabitants of the town [Derby] the opportunity of enjoying, with their families, exercise and recreation in the fresh air, in public walks and grounds devoted to that purpose'.[11]

A passionate advocate of providing working-class people with nature in the city, Loudon was given his chance in Derby. It came during a time of mounting pressure to green the city on the grounds of public health. Parks were, according to a mayor of New

York, 'essential aids to the public health . . . the **great breathing places** of the toiling masses' during a time of urban upheaval and deadly urban pandemics such as cholera. They dispelled miasmas and poisonous smoke; they were the lungs of the city.[12]

Loudon's Derby Arboretum was the first publicly owned recreation park in England. Loudon planted 800 species of tree – many of them foreign imports – set apart from one another on artificial mounds that recreated the elements of the country estate; the city beyond the park was screened out by grassy banks. Visitors strolled along 6,000 feet of serpentine paths that twisted through the undulating landscape. Derby Arboretum was Loudon's swansong. He died not long after its completion, in 1843 at the age of sixty. But his influence lived on in this dawning age of public parks.

Loudon's devoted assistant, John Robertson, drew up the plans for Birkenhead Park in Merseyside, the first green public space built at public expense in the world and one of the most influential parks in history. Its overall designer, Joseph Paxton, drained the marshy land to create lakes, using the excavated stone and earth to manufacture terraces, hills and rocky outcrops. Nicknamed 'the People's Garden', Birkenhead Park represented the triumph of the aristocratic picturesque and the gardenesque in the civic sphere, and it became the template for urban parks the world over. Most immediately, it was the inspiration for Central Park. When Olmsted visited

Birkenhead in 1850, he wrote: 'I cannot undertake to describe the effect of so much taste and skill as had evidently been employed; I will only tell you, that we passed by winding paths over acres and acres, with a constant varying surface, where on all sides were growing every variety of shrubs and flowers, with more than natural grace, all set in borders of greenest, closest turf, and all kept with consummate neatness.'[13]

The pastoral landscape of English parks and gardens appealed immediately to Olmsted. He believed that parks were needed for public health. But they went further than that; they had a psychological effect. 'A park is a work of art,' he said, 'designed to produce certain effects upon the minds of men.' At the core of Olmsted's thinking was a passion for social justice and democracy. His landscape design made that conviction manifest in the urban realm. The atmosphere he created in Central Park, he believed, had a 'harmonizing and refining influence upon the most unfortunate and most lawless classes of the city – an influence favourable to courtesy, self-control, and temperance'.[14]

If parks were to put a stop to drunkenness and bad behaviour, they had to be designed purposefully to elevate the mind. For Olmsted, it was the 'beautiful sylvian scenes' of the English pastoral landscape that had this harmonising effect on the mind. Weeds and undergrowth – the products of spontaneous vegetation – were places for subversive pleasures. Overgrown Moorfields on the edge of the City of London had long been a preserve for illicit sexual encounters, predominantly homosexual. Parks denuded of undergrowth were, in contrast, places of control in a botanical and human sense. In working-class Bethnal Green in east London, Victoria Park was built as a near-replica of upper-class Regent's Park.

In contrast to scruffy commons and wastelands, the carefully crafted, landscaped park, with its labour-intensive flowerbeds, meandering paths, stately trees and broad vistas embodied a well-ordered, disciplined society. A park should broadcast the fact, as Loudon decreed, that it **was** a work of human art, not a product of nature; the flowers and shrubs should be exhibits to be studied as if it was an outdoor museum. Artifice was to be celebrated as an example of 'improvement'; nurture took precedence over nature. In the mid-nineteenth century, bright sub-tropical bedding plants became popular in parks and then elaborate 'carpet bedding', in which corralled ranks of annual flowers made geometric patterns or replicated coats of arms, flags or butterflies. Addicted to novelty, parks introduced rock gardens, Japanese gardens, rose gardens, botanic gardens and so on. In part, garish sub-tropical plants were introduced because industrial pollution shrouded trees and shrubs in black soot. Colourful flowers stood out. They were also renewed annually before they were poisoned to death by the urban air. Whatever the motivation, the ornate floral displays in public parks were clearly costly and labour intensive, self-consciously demonstrating their manipulation by human hands.

If nature was not enough to make people better on its own, Victorian parks enforced standards of decorum with fences, by-laws and policemen. The rough, unkempt urban commons that had always existed as the unregulated recreation spots of the poor – and which were profuse in unmanaged nature – were (with a few exceptions) enclosed and converted into intensively tended versions of a new kind of tidier, urbane, bourgeois nature. Victoria Park was laid out over Bonner's Fields, formerly a wild sort of wasteland where the working classes indulged in rough sports and political meetings. According to a correspondent for **The Times,** the newly imagined outdoor public space, with its rose bushes and flowerbeds, had improved behaviour: 'Many a man whom I was accustomed to see passing the Sunday in utter idleness, smoking at his door in his shirt sleeves, unwashed and unshaven, now dresses himself as neatly and cleanly as he is able, and with his wife or children is seen walking in the park on the Sunday evening.' When Battersea Fields was landscaped into Battersea Park at enormous cost, the middle-class press celebrated the newfound 'respectability' of the area in terms of both its aesthetics and the behaviour of its visitors. Parks kept out undesirables both human and natural. Urban green areas called for the inclusion of 'suitable' flowers, shrubs, trees and grasses and the methodical elimination of what were seen as weeds.[15]

Outdoor public spaces are strikingly similar if you are in Shanghai or Singapore, London, Dubai or New York. They are the distant relatives of the medieval deer enclosure as translated and handed down by people such as Loudon and Olmsted. Such parks swiftly moved away from their reformist intentions of creating an ordered society through the medium of nature, becoming places in which to play, sunbathe, picnic, walk dogs and exercise; football and cricket pitches, baseball diamonds, tennis courts, swimming pools and playgrounds were added; in recent years, they have become venues for fun runs, marathons and enormous concerts and festivals. Yet the essentials of the nineteenth-century landscaping style remain; the moral and aesthetic motivations of their distant originators can still be traced today, even amid the flying frisbees and passing joggers.

This landscaping ideal remains popular because the informal, wide-open terrain supports a variety of recreational functions better than a formal garden or a forest. Their lines of sight make them feel safe. Above all, the English pastoral aesthetic is redolent of an imagined, pre-industrial nature. Early-twentieth-century modernists – exemplified by Le Corbusier – adopted the free-flowing English picturesque with alacrity as they envisaged the socially democratic city of the future. They wanted residential tower blocks set amid acres of lawn, motivated by the conviction (according to an expert in landscape architecture), 'that people inherently like the picturesque and given the choice would decide to live in a setting not dissimilar to eighteenth century parkland'. Or, to put it another way, people wanted a **simplified** form of nature, a kind of manufactured urban savannah consisting of uncluttered views and a few favoured species maintained at the expense of unwelcome invaders.[16]

It is possible we are hardwired to choose these kinds of landscapes. When early hominins left the woodlands and jungles favoured by their ape ancestors, the open landscape of the savannah suited their upright postures. Long lines of sight provided warnings of predators, while clumps of trees offered protection. If this thesis – known as the Savannah Hypothesis – is correct, it goes a long way to explaining the global popularity of the English landscape garden in park design, with the medley of grassland, woods and water features that accords with our instinctive evolutionary preferences.

A major reason for the ubiquity of this type of park was the vast geographical extent of the British Empire. Brits abroad craved the familiar. And, as we saw with the Mughals, redesigning the landscape is a reflex action of imperialism. In Australia and the treaty ports of China, Singapore, South Africa, New Zealand, Canada, Hong Kong and elsewhere, the

English landscaped park predominated. In Shanghai, the first public parks, Huangpu and Lu Xun, were designed in the English picturesque style.[17]

In the City of Gardens in Lahore, the British attempted to restore the fabulous Shalimar Gardens only to make them more British than Mughal: mango trees and cypresses gave way to flowerbeds. The British built their own park, Lawrence Gardens (now the Bagh-e-Jinnah), in Lahore which had all the characteristics of an English landscaped garden. Some 80,000 trees and 600 plant species – including Maltese orange trees, Italian pomelos, European apple and pear trees, east Asian chrysanthemum and English pansies – were planted alongside expanses of lawn. 'It is easy enough to picture the change,' wrote Constance Villiers-Stuart in 1913, reflecting on the restoration of the great Mughal gardens under British tastes, 'the public parks with their bare acres of unhappy-looking grass, their ugly bandstands, hideous iron railings, and forlorn European statues; their wide objectless roads, scattered flower-beds, and solitary trees, and, worst of all in a hot country, their lack of fountains and running water.'[18]

The British gift to the world was the lawn. Throughout India, Villiers-Stuart commented, the 'fixed belief in the universal virtue of mown grass' on the part of British landscapers had vanquished the traditional flower, fruit and water garden of India. Everywhere they went, the British wanted a

verdant lawn; when she, the wife of a British official, heard a mower being fired up, she 'could almost
fancy we were in England'. In colonial Australia,
New Zealand and India, establishing acres of lawn
symbolised the victory of civilisation – which, like
a lawn, was regulated and neat – over the wildness of the bush. The British cleared 1,300 acres
of tiger-infested jungle in Calcutta to create the
Maidan, which, according to Governor General
Lord Curzon, furnished the metropolis with 'one of
the finest city parks to be seen in any capital in the
world. Situated on the outskirts of the town, and
yet in close proximity to its most crowded quarters,
this great expanse. . . . [presents] a stretch of green
sward . . . interspersed with avenues and clumps of
trees . . . lending itself both to landscape gardening
and to architectural effect.'[19]

The lawn broke out of the English country estate
and conquered the world. In most cities around the
world, regardless of climate, history or local ecologies, 50–70 per cent of public green space is mown
grass. And that is only parks; add in domestic lawns,
corporate headquarters, golf courses, university
campuses, roadsides, sports fields and cemeteries,
and the total area of grass cover is immense – it covers 11 per cent of the total area of Australian cities;
in the United States, it occupies almost a quarter
of cities and a total area of 63,000 square miles.
Close-cropped lawns are particularly appealing in
setting off and enhancing the grandeur of public

architecture. As such, the urban environment is suffused with the green stuff. It forms, therefore, the dominant biotope of urban ecologies. To many city-dwellers, the carpeted acres of greenery represent nature at it is most tangible and satisfying; take a closer look, however, and the lawn is a conspicuous example of how humans have re-engineered ecologies around the world.[20]

Just as the British and Americans exported their love of the lawn, so did they bring their grass seeds. English ryegrass, Kentucky bluegrass, common bent and red fescue dominate the global parkscape. Where these grass types are native – mainly in northern, temperate climates – they can support a teeming ecosystem. A survey of London's Hyde Park in the 1980s discovered that where there had once been medieval fields, twenty-one different species of wild grass, harbouring twenty-nine further species of tiny wildflowers and herbaceous plants, had survived in the sward despite the park's many varieties of use over the centuries and the millions of trampling feet. The biodiversity of grasslands in parks is vital, because they are the habitats of the microbes, funguses, earthworms, insects, butterflies, moths and bees that determine the ultimate health of the wider urban ecosystem.[21]

In the southern hemisphere, in striking contrast, the rage for lawns both for recreation and for quickly greening the urban environment has often resulted in an imported monoculture, a 'green desert' that is bereft of life and unsustainable. It is an invisible disaster, or at least one that is camouflaged by apparent lushness. Scenic turfgrasses native to Europe and North America have been planted on soils and in climates to which they are not suited. Since the 1970s, China has experienced a lawn makeover, with tens of thousands of hectares converted to sward every year. As in other countries with hot climates, turf has to be nurtured into life, with imported soil, extensive watering, the frequent application of fertiliser and pesticides, and weekly mowing. China is following the United States in its obsession with lawns and the environmental catastrophe that comes with them. Every year, Americans collectively deploy 45,000 tons of fertiliser and 39,000 tons of pesticide, at a cost of $40 billion, to keep lawns green and bug- and weed-free. In Florida, half of all public water is lavished on the lawn; in Western states, it can be 70 per cent. In places where heatwaves burn the greensward to a frazzled brown field, synthetic lawns are often simply installed instead. In some parks, the grass is dyed to give it a lusty appearance. Green lawn is as artificial as grey buildings.[22]

The idealised park aesthetic that dominates the urban world comes with huge ecological consequences: maintaining an alien billiard-table lawn means waging never-ending war on native vegetation that would reclaim the precious turf if it could. Species abundance has declined where non-native grasses predominate. In southern Australia, only

11 per cent of native species can be found within lawns. Tall fescue, Kentucky bluegrass and Bermuda grass occupy 90 per cent of managed lawns, crowding out local flora that is not adapted to coexist with European meadow grass: a green desert indeed.[23]

The great Indian urban ecologist, Harini Nagendra, argues that Bangalore was suffused with an exceptionally wide-ranging palette of species introduced in the eighteenth and nineteenth centuries that provided shade, food and medicines. Lal Bagh, created from 1760 by the Sultan of Mysore Hyder Ali and then his son Tipu Sultan, was influenced by northern Indian Mughal gardens. The park contained an incredible diversity of plants and trees imported by the rulers of Mysore from all over the world. The British added to the eclecticism so that by 1891 this urban botanic garden contained 3,222 species.

Today, the list of species in Lal Bagh has declined to 1,854. The slump in biodiversity in the park is indicative of a wider trend in Bangalore. Under British administrators and their Indian successors, Bangalore's public parks replaced dense groves of native fruit trees with exotic imports and introduced 'landscaped lawns that required intensive inputs of pesticides and fertilizers'. In the words of academic Sheetal Patil: 'The chemicals silence crickets, ants, birds, butterflies and bees.' The craze for lawns adorning the perimeters of office hubs, hospitals, schools, campuses, new upmarket housing estates and public parks has a grievous impact not just on the city but on the regional ecosystem. An academic report found that the lucrative market for Mexican turfgrass had transformed the countryside. In just three villages, 350 acres of land had been totally cleared of vegetation and levelled, doused in chemicals and lavished with water in order to produce weed-free lawn to sell to developers. As one farmer told the researchers: 'We have already damaged our land. If we continue this, in the next 10 years these farmlands will become deserts.'[24]

The messiness of fruit trees and groves that characterised the Indian cityscape, and which made urban areas so biodiverse, has given way to the neatness and regularity of turfgrass and a few favoured non-fruiting trees and shrubs. 'A city that once used a wide palette of species', wrote Nagendra, 'has drastically simplified and reduced the diversity of vegetation. This mirrors a parallel simplification of human interactions with biodiversity.' According to her, the people of Bangalore used urban vegetation for food and medicines and valued it for spiritual reasons until recent times; they gleaned resources from all over the city, including public parks and the Lal Bagh botanic garden. Now, such practices are banned. Parks and public green spaces have become heavily controlled and ornamental, landscaped, maintained and used exclusively for recreation and exercise rather than as multidimensional ecological tools. 'It is the beginning of a slippery slope', she writes, 'that makes a park interchangeable with other public utilities such as metro stations or government offices.'[25]

That, in a nutshell, is the history of municipal parks: nature as an exhibit, a backdrop and a token, rather than as something vital, useful and alive.

None of this is surprising, given the long history of **rus in urbe** and the deeply implanted desire to make cities greener. The ecological consequences of creating idealised landscapes in which nature is controlled and simplified have been little understood; indeed, they have been camouflaged behind deceptive green lawns and seductive bright flowers. This is what is meant by 'Potemkin gardens' – parks that hide their sterility behind an illusion of bounty. Yet as the development of Freshkills Park so vividly demonstrates, our attitudes to urban green spaces are changing. Across the globe, many are being transformed to release their latent potential for biodiversity. This too has a long history, one that runs counter to the dominant narrative of landscaping. It is also dictated, as ever, by politics.

In east London, you can step out of the urban maelstrom and into a glorious fragment of lost medieval fringe landscape. In September 2020, longhorn cattle were turned out to graze Wanstead Flats, a park of 334 acres, for the first time in over a century as a means of restoring its biodiversity. London's edgelands were made by rough grazing. For centuries, people used common land such as Wanstead Flats.

Their animals munched through the commons, keeping encroachments of scrub at bay and removing nitrogen from the soil, creating heathland and acidic grassland, with their characteristic palette of gorse and broom, wildflowers and herbage, insects and birds. Remarkably biodiverse, Wanstead Flats is a Site of Special Scientific Interest within the metropolis, with 780 species of plants – including rare and endangered native flowers – 150 of birds, 28 of butterflies and 225 of moths. Its biodiversity and ecological value far outstrip a conventional park.

This fringeland ecology would not exist today had it not been for the working class of London. On 8 July 1871, 30,000 Londoners assembled for a 'monster meeting' at West Ham Hall to protest against the owner of Wanstead Flats, Lord Cowley, who had fenced off portions of the common in order to build upon it. A few years before there had been 9,000 acres open to the public; but that had been whittled down by enclosures to 3,000. After Cowley's latest round of enclosures, Wanstead Flats would be reduced to just 600 acres. The people were angry. Anticipating trouble, the Essex Volunteers conducted a review on the Flats, watched by a large detachment of mounted and unmounted police.

Meanwhile, at West Ham Hall, the crowd grew restive as the meeting was addressed by various local worthies and MPs. 'To the Flats!', people started shouting. 'They're our own,' others chimed in. 'Why should we be prevented meeting there? Wot is there to be afraid.' Men in the crowd took matters into their own hands and dragged the waggons upon which the organisers were seated all the way to the Flats 'at a steady trot'. The furious crowd, waggons and all, descended upon the common, far out-numbering the troops and police. All seemed peace-ful, and eventually the volunteers marched off and the police withdrew. Then, as night began to fall, the mood changed. A group of men began pull-ing at the fence. Within a minute there were fifty people destroying the fences, then a hundred, then hundreds as people rushed from the side roads and pubs to join in. The sound of destruction sounded like volleys fired by ranks of infantry. In five min-utes, the fences were battered to matchwood.

The mounted police charged at the protestors, leaping over the broken fences. One man was ar-rested. 'They mustn't have him,' cried the protes-tors. They advanced on the police, who formed a line and charged at the mob. During the ensuing melee the prisoner, and a boy, were hurried off to the police station in handcuffs.[26]

The Flats were in the 1870s among the last rem-nants of the semi-wild commons and heaths that surrounded London. Most were falling victim to the city's fast growth. Wanstead was particularly cher-ished because it lay within the congested, highly ur-banised East End. One journalist described entering the common in the 1870s: 'The air was peopled with a thousand strange and wondrous insects, and inter-mingled with the grass we trod upon, were wild flow-ers, full of beauty and simple grace . . . the harebell bloomed in close companionship with the daisy and the buttercup.' A City of London dignitary talked in 1869 about 'the very great desire existing in the minds of the working and trading classes to get out of the Metropolis, not into a park, not into Victoria Park, but to get out into some open spaces where some traces of nature remained undisturbed, and where they might enjoy the delights which nature affords'.[27]

The working-class rioters at Wanstead won. In 1875, the Flats were purchased by the City of London, ensuring that it would remain public land. It became part of the much larger Epping Forest. Today, you can walk twenty miles from Manor Park to Epping underground stations through a remnant corridor of medieval landscape while barely touching so much as road. London's working class did not stop with Wanstead Flats; in 1875, 50,000 working people gathered on Hackney Downs, another large area of common land im-perilled by development, to witness and celebrate fences being torn down and burnt. And again, the following year (1876) thousands marched on Plumstead Common to prevent, by force, its enclo-sure and to fill in, with their own hands, gravel pits that marred the open space.

These working Londoners were joining a centuries-long tradition of asserting rights to urban commons. In the mid-nineteenth century, they were aided by middle-class activists. One reason for this was that, as London's suburbs sprawled, well-off householders wanted to preserve open spaces such as Hampstead Heath and Wimbledon Common in order to keep property prices high and retain the semi-rural character of their neighbourhoods. The fight to save Hampstead and Wimbledon in the 1860s led to the foundation of the Commons Preservation Society (CPS) in 1865 and the formation of a parliamentary select committee to examine the state of open space.

The desire to protect edgelands was not just about property prices; it was motivated and justified by appeals to the common good, particularly the health and welfare of the poor in the age of aggressive industrial urbanisation. More fundamentally, the members and supporters of the CPS wanted to reconceive the very idea of the city. The Liberal MP Frederick Doulton told parliament that London used to be 'belted' with 'natural parks', by which he meant the endangered heaths and commons. Doulton did not want these edgelands being 'transformed into neatly trimmed and laid out gardens and parks'. His object was to have them preserved in all their wild and uncultivated condition, and 'it would be a pleasant sight to see the boisterous enjoyment of the working people in places where there did not exist those restrictions which were natural and proper enough in well laid-out gardens.'[28]

Here, then, was a plea for wildness, for the spontaneity of unregulated nature even in the midst of a city. It was an overt criticism of parks, which confined and constricted natural processes and human enjoyment alike. Such attitudes reflected nostalgia for the deep rural past and an awakening appreciation for the beauties of untamed nature that derived from Romanticism. Above all, it evinced widespread rejection of the industrialised city of the nineteenth century and the artificiality of the landscaped and policed municipal parks that were festooned with exotic flowerbeds and mown lawns. The CPS wanted rough patches with 'green turf and gold gorse, their May blossoms and wild rose-bush'. As such, it marked a radical shift in attitudes towards nature from a few decades before, when the 'wastes' were condemned as an affront that could only be improved by modernisation. The concern was not so much with ecology as with the benefits of uncultivated land to hard-pressed city-dwellers. The first major victory came when Hampstead Heath was purchased by the Metropolitan Board of Works in 1871. The board was required by law not only to preserve 'the natural aspect and state of the Heath' but to restore it to its 'beautiful and wild condition' of bygone days.

Over the following years, 3,889 acres of commons were saved and preserved, as far as possible

not as manicured parks but in their rough condition. This marked a different kind of **rus in urbe,**
not the urbane garden but a throwback to ancient
land use made up of native flora. These kinds of
patches are, according to a government commission in the 1950s, 'disproportionally rich in examples of plant and animal communities which have
largely been eliminated from surrounding localities'
including parks.[29]

These were not 'wild' areas. They were survivors
from London's medieval fringe landscape, managed
natural resources that had experienced many different uses over the years. Traditions of gleaning and
common grazing (rather than intensive agriculture
or heavy grazing) kept scrub at bay and permitted the emergence of heathlands and acidic grasslands, with their unique abundance of tall grasses,
flowering plants (many of them rare and endangered), lichens, mosses and fungi. In addition to
urban commons, London's former hunting parks
such as Richmond, Bushy and Greenwich have
been deer-grazed for half a millennium, which has
made them wildlife-rich grasslands. The fifty-plus
species of grasses, rushes and sedges in Richmond
Park provide an excellent habitat for a multitude of
invertebrates, small mammals – such as mice, voles
and shrews – and the predator species that feed on
them, such as kestrels, foxes, badgers, stoats and
tawny owls.[30]

For the Danish architect Steen Eiler Rasmussen,

writing in the 1920s, London was distinguished from other major metropolises because its inhabitants had a more intense, more **primitive** relationship with nature. "If you tell a Londoner what a fine **park** Hampstead Heath is" Rasmussen wrote, "he will look at you astonished and ask; "Do you consider Hampstead Heath a **park**?" . . . To him it is a piece of uncultivated land which – for some unexplained reason – still lies there untouched in spite of the development of the town.' The heath did not feel like an art gallery, as municipal parks often do; Londoners 'walk with delight in the high grass when they escape from the streets. They do not only see, they feel the forms of the land when they wearily plod up the hill.' For Rasmussen, such remnant commons were so important because, with their unregulated roughness and the intimate relationships they enabled between people and wildlife, they had been preserved for the right kind of nature – human nature.[31]

The preservation of heaths and commons in London came at a time when the emphasis around the globe was on simplifying and domesticating nature in parks, rather than consciously preserving wildlife. There were exceptions. One afternoon in February 1896, the zoologist William Temple Hornaday went on a ramble at the edge of New York. He discovered what he described as 'an unbroken wilderness, to the eye almost as wild and unkempt as the heart of the Adirondacks . . . It seemed incredible that such **virgin forest** . . . had been spared in the City of New York in 1896!' Hornaday attempted to preserve the area 'in as natural a condition as possible' as he created the Bronx Zoo on it. Similarly, Inwood Hill, Pelham Bay and Van Cortlandt parks were established in the late nineteenth and early twentieth centuries with substantial amounts of native forests, meadows and salt marshes left intact.[32]

The commons of London and the nature reserves of New York were early forerunners of modern attitudes to urban nature. They are the great-grandfathers of places such as Freshkills Park, where biodiversity is not forced into a straitjacket. Attitudes have slowly changed as people see the dormant potential of urban parks to support natural processes. The urban ecologist Maria Ignatieva has described this as an evolution in our understanding of city park landscaping from 'picturesque' to 'gardenesque' to 'biodiversinesque'. The final stage means moving on from parks simply being places for recreation and scenery to managing them to enhance their ecological potential. Freshkills is another iteration of the idyllic landscapes we have been striving to create in our cities since Babylon. Today, in an era of humanmade environmental degradation, we see beauty in wildness and spontaneity that would have been inconceivable to our recent forebears. We are beginning, tentatively, to appreciate messiness as a source of life.[33]

Let's start at the fundamental battleground for

urban biodiversity, the lawn. Rising temperatures and the need for water conservation will make manicured grassy expanses unsustainable in the future. Native plant species, which are tolerant of local conditions, make for better ground cover in these conditions. In the Midwest of the United States, public parks are turning to prairie plants that are adapted to long dry spells. Some of Beijing's park managers have begun replacing imported turf grass with native groundcover species and wild herbs. In Europe, there has been a tendency since the 1980s to restrict mowing frequency and promote wildflower meadows in parks as a means of maximising biodiversity. This is a form of rewilding the lawn, promoting a mix of grasses with native herbaceous wildflowers that supports pollinators and requires fewer interventions in the form of weed-control, watering and mowing. The end result looks less like the vaunted baize of Wimbledon's tennis courts and more like an ancient, scrubby heath.

Overcoming our addiction to the green stuff is going to be hard. We spend billions perfecting well-groomed lawns. Shaking off that deeply implanted aesthetic preference is vital and will become inevitable in hotter, drier conditions. We have to develop a tolerance for parks that look scruffier: ground-covering vegetation and grass-free areas contain all those weeds that generations have invested so much in eliminating. But we should learn to love that roughness because messiness supports life. We should also learn that the greensward in parks is not just for sitting and playing on; beneath our feet and picnic blankets is a complex ecosystem, vital for a city's health.

The solution cannot be simply to lock the park gates, pack up the mower and the weedkiller, and let nature do the work. In order to support biodiversity, urban parks have to be managed as intensively as Emperor Babur's gardens of paradise. A good example are the London commons. Over the centuries, their biodiversity was maximised by human activity, by grazing, foraging and gleaning. When they became places of public recreation, however, the cows stopped munching. By the end of the twentieth century, woodland had encroached on the commons, engrossing up to 47 per cent of their area, while a further 42 per cent had become mown amenity grass. Both processes reduced the total area of tall grass and wildflower meadows. The reintroduction of cattle into Wanstead Flats is an attempt to revive the kind of ancient management techniques that made it so biodiverse in the first place and an acknowledgement that nature cannot flourish in a city without human involvement. Even the 'wildness' of Hampstead Heath was a human creation.

Neglect, even if it is benign in intention, can lead to not only ecological problems but social nightmare.

In Philadelphia, an urban park called Cobbs Creek became entangled with out-of-control, non-native vegetation, including smothering, coiling, climbing kudzu vines, and Norway maple. To the casual observer it might look like nature exuberantly reclaiming urban land. But the ceding of control to spontaneous growth has led to what has been called an 'ecology of fear', overwhelmingly a gender-specific threat. The neighbourhood of Cobbs Creek is majority African American; the area is plagued by homicide (mainly of women) and rape. The dense, invasive vegetation creates a menacing environment that not only fosters the conditions for violent crime but symbolises the breakdown of order and the neglect of the community more widely.

'Uncontrolled ecologies are interpreted locally as racist ecologies' in Philadelphia as a result, according to the academic Alec Brownlow. Understandably, locals prefer the kind of regulated, simplified parkscapes of the past because 'wildness' is associated with social breakdown and abandoned communities. What is good for biodiversity is not always good for humans in urban environments. Making parks more ecologically productive is therefore a contentious political issue because the untamed is linked to neglect in all its manifestations.[34]

In Zurich, lack of care for the Platzspitz park from the 1940s onwards turned it into a wild sort of place, dense with undergrowth. In formal parks,

the sex lives of plants are under strict control. In unregulated parks, the reproductive urges of flora and
fauna run riot. The unkept state of the Platzspitz
(like Hampstead Heath, Wimbledon Common
and the Ramble in Central Park) made it a popular place for gay cruising. According to the artist
Tom Burr, 'large beech trees towered over everything, and beech saplings had seeded beneath their
canopies and throughout the wooded edges of the
area, creating dense thickets . . . that lent a form
of cover to those who wandered along the pathways, and virtual camouflage to any who strayed off
the designated paths and into the planted regions.'
Weeds added an erotic charge to urban landscapes,
attractive to some but regarded with fear by others.
It also became notorious as 'Needle Park', a magnet
for heroin users. In the 1980s the Platzspitz lost
its concealing undergrowth as the city authorities
regained control over the park, policing spontaneous vegetation in order to create an area of safety.
Letting nature take over is appealing to many because it builds biological complexity. But a park is
a public space. It needs careful, expensive steward-
ship to balance the competing needs of society and
ecology, wildness and safety.[35]

For many people, parks are the only place that
provide publicly accessible nature in their city.
Planners such as Frederick Law Olmsted fenced off
their parks: on one side was nature, on the other

the sterile human city. That perception of division has existed for millennia. But parks represent a fraction of the natural world that exists within the city; they are not isolated patches of biodiversity in the concrete jungle but parts of a lush tapestry of nature within urban areas. Wildness and parks are not fully compatible. Spontaneous, exuberant nature exists outside human control; it does not fit readily into our politicised and changeable concepts of idyllic landscapes. It is in the edges of railways and roads, abandoned lots, canal banks, mortared walls, disused space and cracks in the concrete. That is where wonder is to be found.

3

The Crack in the Concrete

Returning from the horrors of war to his bombed-out hometown of Münster in 1945, a German botanist described his transformed city: 'A dense grove of pussy willows was growing on the rubble left over from a famous restaurant . . . and, in front of it, on the street that leads upwards towards the Horsteberg, pussy willow and mountain maples had taken hold on the slope of the mighty rubble heap. On its peak strawberries were ripening.' The sight of the ruined cathedral was offset by drifts of pretty, yellow mulleins; the main streets of the city were overtaken by copses of willows, birches and elder.[1]

The miraculous and rapid appearance of vegetation drew a 'green veil' over the rubble screes and ruined buildings in cities throughout Europe and parts of Asia. Pulverised and abandoned cityscapes became verdant as never before. The botanist Cornel Schmidt wrote that 'nature, instead of waiting for permission, has pushed itself forwards into the city and has thereby achieved what several city councils have failed to achieve: rubble heaps have disappeared, at least to the eye'. The atomic bomb that detonated over Hiroshima was supposed to wipe out all trace of plant life for seventy-five years. Yet very quickly there was 'a blanket of fresh, vivid, lush, optimistic green' mantling the wreckage. A local eyewitness stated, 'Everywhere were bluets and Spanish bayonets, goosefoot, morning glories and day lilies, the hairy-fruited bean, purslane and clotbur and sesame and panic grass and feverfew.' Even in the centre of the blast, sickle senna pushed up through bricks and cracks in the asphalt. Within months, a patch of oleanders flowered on the irradiated land. Ancient camphor trees, resembling burnt sticks of charcoal, began to sprout buds in defiance of their apparent death.[2]

The renewal of nature amid carnage was balm to the soul. But it was more than a symbol. The widespread destruction of cities gave botanists a rare chance to investigate how nature operated within the urban environment, particularly the kind of spontaneous vegetation that was always suppressed in parks and other formal parts of the city in favour of eye-catching ornamentals. Ultimately, war damage led to the emergence of urban ecology and fundamentally changed how we understand our cities.

When London burnt to the ground in 1666, the ashy ruins were swiftly blanketed with the spicy herb **Sisymbrium irio;** it grew in such profusion that it was named 'London rocket'. Yet during the Blitz of 1940-1, not a single specimen was found.

Its place had been taken by dense pink swathes of rosebay willowherb, or 'bombweed' as it was nicknamed due to its unmissable prevalence in central London. As recently as 1869, rosebay had been considered a rare species outside the Scottish Highlands. Other common bombsite colonisers were the yellow-flowering Oxford ragwort, which had only been introduced from Sicily in 1794, Canadian fleabane, with its profusion of white florets, which had been imported to Europe as stuffing for a dead parrot in the 1680s, and the prolific Peruvian herb **Galinsoga parviflora,** an escapee from Kew Gardens in the nineteenth century.[3]

So the apparent beauties or miracles of nature that war-worn people looked at with hope were not the reassertion of London's lost nature but an entirely new phenomenon. They told a story not only about the city's complicated history but about the way humans had indelibly altered the ecology of their cities. In 1942, the botanist Job Edward Lousley toured the hard-hit districts of the City of London to investigate the processes by which vegetation had colonised parts of the metropolis that had been entirely built over and were, before the Blitz, 'sterile'. Lousley picked through the scree. He peered through the charred door of St Mary's Church, Kennington, which had only been partially damaged and saw the 'most luxuriant vegetation growing in the pavement of the aisles, in which

Epilobium angustifolium [rosebay] was the dominant species'. He looked into an abandoned shop where towards the back 'behind the ruined counter, several plants of **Tussilago farfara** [coltsfoot] and **Senecio vulgaris** [common groundsel] were growing under dimmer, drier conditions than one would have supposed possible'. In all he counted twenty-seven species in the summer after the Blitz. In May 1945, days after Germany surrendered, the director of Kew Gardens, Edward Salisbury, gave a lecture on the botanical diversity of London's bomb craters. The list of plant species had leapt to 157 over the previous three years. An ecosystem was forming.[4]

And it was an amazingly productive one. Disturbance favours biodiversity. In the years after a natural or humanmade disaster, the number of species increases rapidly as plants and insects compete to colonise the barren earth and rubble. Over the years and decades that follow, ecological succession takes place. Biodiversity then decreases as the area comes to be dominated by a few tall, woody species that crowd out the smaller plants. That is why bombsites and building sites are so incredibly profuse with wildlife – and why the shifting urban landscape, cratered with temporary disturbed wastelands and brownfields, is unusually biodiverse.

Many of the seeds reached the bombsites through wind transmission or by bird droppings, but the emerging ecosystems in the ruins of Europe were also the direct result of human activity. Chickweed, shepherd's purse, fat-hen and broadleaf plantain hitched their rides on things that arrived to clear the debris, in the treads of boot-soles and truck tyres or the turn-ups of trousers. Horses brought in to help with the work contributed to the plant palate with their manure, which included wheat, oats, ryegrass and common clovers. Soldiers and refugees carried seeds that had adhered to their clothing and luggage during long journeys. The horses of the second Ukrainian army, which arrived in Berlin in May 1945, were responsible for distributing seeds of **Salsola collina,** a saltwort of the amaranth family native to southern Russia and central Asia, which were transported in the hay stored in their carts. The plant, a notorious tumbleweed, sprouted around Bahnhof Zoo, a railway station later to be the most important in West Berlin.[5]

Rosebay willowherb is also called 'fireweed' because it loves burned-over land; it surges in the wake of forest fires. James Salisbury believed that fires caused by locomotives and cigarettes tossed out of car windows had created a singed pathway for rosebay, which had upped sticks from the Scottish Highlands and followed railway lines and roads into central London in the early twentieth century. Rosebay, instantly recognisable from its dense stands of spiking bright pink flowers, was therefore a symbol of disaster as much as hope.

Similarly, buddleia was introduced to Europe from China in the 1890s as a garden shrub and had been noted in the wild as recently as 1922. An opportunist primed to exploit inhospitable places where it can gain a slight advantage, the tree loved the dryness of the railway environment, growing between tracks and along cuttings, latching on to crumbling masonry and racing along the national network. It was ready to burst onto the bombsites, therefore, in the 1940s. Ever since, it has been the distinctive lilac emblem of urban dereliction – or of unexpected urban ecological wealth, depending on how you see things.

The pioneer species that colonised bombsites are known as 'ruderal', which derives from the Latin word **rudus,** meaning 'rubble'. They were the plants that exploited disturbed land and ruins. The destruction wrought by aerial bombardment had thrown large amounts of carbon and nitrogen into the soil; lime mortar used in construction had likewise introduced calcium. The coarse, dry, calcareous rubble heaps and dusty wastelands were perfect for pioneer colonisers such as rosebay, groundsel and Oxford ragwort, which had evolved on the ashy slopes of Mount Etna. In Berlin, the black locust tree – imported from North America as an ornamental in the seventeenth century – treated the city's downfall as boomtime and it spread with wild abandon, draping its hanging clusters of fragrant white flowers about the ruined metropolis. So too did Jerusalem oak goosefoot (**Dysphania botrys**), which found the rubble, combined with Berlin's heat island-effect, akin to the sandy and stony soils of the Mediterranean. The annual herb is found north of the Alps only in Berlin, where anthropogenic changes to the landscape provide it with an ideal habitat. James Salisbury gave his seminal lecture on London's wartime ecology in front of an audience of female volunteer ambulance drivers. This was appropriate. The vegetation, like the audience, was made up of the first responders to disasters who go in where others fear to tread.[6]

Birds such as wheatears loved post-Blitz London because it recreated the rock-strewn landscapes of their breeding grounds. The cliff-dwelling black redstart migrated to London for the first time from the Mediterranean, attracted by the unique flora and teeming insect life of the bombsites, as well as all the debris in which to nest. In Berlin, the magnificent Tiergarten had been destroyed by bombs and fighting; its trees had been cut down for firewood in the desperate months of 1945. This lunar wasteland became the home of steppe birds, which had never been seen in Berlin before. According to a German botanist, the ocean of rubble strewn across Europe had unintentionally created 'a tremendous natural experiment, which with respect to its size, must be compared to the colonization of new habitats created by volcanic activity'.[7]

Bombs carved out space for nature in cities that

had rarely existed before and certainly not on that kind of scale. Eliot Hodgkin painted the eerie beauty of destruction, paying particular attention to the effects of the weedy growth. The wildness of bombed-out London was conveyed in Rose Macaulay's novel **The World My Wilderness** (1950), the dustjacket illustration of which depicted the area around St Paul's Cathedral as a meadow of wildflowers. The unexpected biodiversity in the heart of modern cities opened people's eyes to the weird and wonderful nature that existed unseen in the urban sphere. Perhaps the inner city was not so sterile after all. In 1945, R. S. R. Fitter's groundbreaking book **London's Natural History** appeared.

What made it so radical was the way Fitter wove human and natural history together. Fitter started his career as an analyst of civilian attitudes to the war for the research organisation Mass Observation; then, he worked for RAF Coastal Command's operation research section, based in London. His service in the capital allowed him to explore the war-damaged city. When the publishers Collins approached him to write the natural history of the Thames Valley for the 'New Naturalist' series, Fitter proposed instead a natural history of London. A lifelong Londoner and explorer of its hidden places, he felt he knew it better than anywhere else. His editors were astonished; no one had ever made a city the subject of ecological investigation before. But

Fitter was a radical thinker and an acute observer of processes and activity invisible to others, including academic ecologists; he got his way.

He was a gifted naturalist and erudite writer, and his work was not of biological taxonomies; it was an analysis of how human and non-human history intertwined. He showed the ways in which animals and plants adapted to the humanmade environment, the effect of air pollution or foreign trade in subjecting the flora and fauna to repeated disturbances. Above all, he revealed how the urban environment created a new kind of hybrid ecology: the natural part of the city was as dynamic, subject to violent change, and as cosmopolitan as the human part. He moved away from the 'official' sites of nature in the city – parks, cemeteries, gardens and commons – and found delight in sewerage systems, reservoirs, disused sandpits, garbage dumps, peeling walls and bomb craters, the 'unofficial', the overlooked. Crucially, the human animal was as much part of this ecosystem as the other animals and the plants.

Fitter's book was a product of war. Because the Second World War had made urban nature so startlingly vivid, it gave his subject a thermal up-current and a plethora of vivid visual references in the real world. Fitter's book was the first systematic study of the natural history of a city, a field of research hitherto eschewed by naturalists. He went through the novel habitats that had been created over the centuries, dividing the metropolis into different eco-systems. With the keen eye of a passionate amateur, he devoted chapters to suburbanisation, digging for building materials, the influence of the water supply, the effects of refuse disposal and pollution; he took account of the way sport, food, gardening, traffic and trade changed the urban ecosystem. Fitter showed, for instance, that the electricity and gasworks needed to fuel industry inadvertently created secret oases of nature in cities. He wrote about the accidental 'gas-works sanctuary' in Bromley-by-Bow 'in the heart of the industrial East End', alive with hedgehogs, rabbits, kestrels, skylarks, butterflies and stag bee-tles in the disused waste ground between infrastruc-ture. The habitat consisted of a jumbled assemblage not found anywhere else, a collection of fruit trees and sycamores, ruderal plants and relics of the semi-maritime Thames-side flora. Few people had ever acknowledged, let alone appreciated, this unique, semi-wild gasworks ecosystem woven through the heavily built, industrialised landscape.

Interest in urban nature was piqued elsewhere. In 1954, Paul Jovet wrote about spontaneous vegeta-tion in Paris. John Kieran's classic **Natural History of New York City** came out in 1959. Kieran, like Fitter, offered a hopeful and very modern view of the twentieth-century city. He pointed out that the widespread 'incursion of humanity and its steel, concrete and asphalt appurtenances' had failed to eradicate New York's indigenous wildlife. Even if the quantity of nature had declined, he declared, remnant patches of meadow and forest had allowed most of the native animal and plant life to remain. 'Let the population of the area increase and multiply as it may, let men build and pave to their heart's content, there will always be many kinds and untold numbers of wild things in the great city.'[8]

Such words sound complacent today – build and destroy as much as you like – but nature's a tough cookie. Books such as Kieran's marked a change in public attitudes towards urban nature in the second half of the twentieth century. At the very least, citizens now had a number of books at their disposal pointing them in the direction of wildlife of all kinds. It came as something as a shock for people to discover that nature existed **at all** in the human city. But the most significant and lasting change in attitudes came from one particular city: West Berlin.

A walled city. A city cut off from its countryside. A city smashed by war. A city crisscrossed with empty streets awaiting the end of the Cold War. The legacy of war and the reality of geopolitics made West Berlin resemble an island and therefore the perfect laboratory to pioneer a brand new field of science – urban ecology.

In most war-scarred cities, rubble was cleared

within a few years and buildings reappeared. Berlin was different. Many large sites were left abandoned for decades, including right in the centre of town. Rubble could not be disposed of outside the city limits, and as a result, large rock peaks – most famously the Teufelsberg ('Devil's Mountain') which rises eighty metres above the Teltow plateau and contains 12 million cubic metres of debris – appeared throughout Berlin's public green areas. Most significant of all was the fact that Berliners had restricted access to countryside. As a result of this claustrophobia, nature became prized by botanists and ordinary Berliners wherever it could be found to a degree unsurpassed anywhere else.

Abandoned places and debris-strewn wastelands – known as **brachen,** or fallow fields – became places of play for children and of illicit activities for adults. They also became the haunts for two young students in post-war Berlin. Hildemar Scholz and Herbert Sukopp scoured the ruined cityscape, detailing the rare and unexpected flora they discovered. Academic botanists such as Scholz and Sukopp were joined by amateur enthusiasts co-ordinated by the long-established Botanischer Verein der Provinz Brandenburg. Here was a unique chance to study what happened in cities when nature was left to itself. In Berlin, you could see how natural succession occurred over long periods of time – how the hardy colonisers paved the way for shrubs and trees. As Scholz recognised very early on, their work went far beyond merely observing natural processes. The war had been such a shocking event to the ecology of Berlin that it rendered previous botanical work on the city all but redundant. The rubble-pickers and wasteland botanists were observing the birth of a new urban ecosystem.[9]

No one in the 1950s knew exactly what form this new environment would take. But one thing was for sure: Berlin was a humanmade place, and the kind of urban nature that was emerging would be radically different from the pre-urban ecosystem. Rather than rewilding, this was 'neo-wilding'. In 1957, Scholz and Sukopp published a list of the wild plant species that had been found in Berlin, the results of years of cataloguing by professionals and amateurs; the inventory was updated in subsequent years as field surveys continued to make new discoveries and the biotypes matured. As time wore on and repeated studies were made of **brachen,** it became clear to researchers such as Sukopp that the plants best adapted to the hostile artificial urban environment and climate were hardy non-native species. The disaster-loving plants seen during the war were not just by-products of human conflict; they had become tough denizens of the inner city, capable of surviving the repeated shocks meted out in the urban environment. Sukopp and others saw that urban ecosystems were unpredictable because they were subject to frequent invasions by alien species. Moments of disturbance – war being the obvious example – clearly favoured invasive species over native ones, and the city was a site character-ised by disturbances of all kinds, from wars to reces-sions to booms to technological changes.[10]

What extensive and intensive research into urban **brachen** revealed was that marginal places in the city had an amazing amount of biodiversity. They nurtured rare plants whose original biotopes had disappeared, and they were taking on a character of their own which no one could have predicted. The black locust tree, box elder, cherry laurel, laburnum and the tree of heaven had all been present in Berlin for at least a century, yet despite being highly fer-tile, only in the later twentieth century did they dis-charge their seeds over the city. What had changed for them was the microclimate: by the 1960s, the centre of Berlin was on average 2°C warmer than the surrounding region (on warm days the differ-ence could be 12°) and there were fewer than sixty-four frost days per year compared to more than 102 in the surrounding area. This pronounced disparity between rural and urban temperatures, caused by surfaces that absorb solar radiation, buildings that block wind and greater concentrations of pollution, is known as the heat island effect. Berlin's **brachen** were revealing their secrets.[11]

Only by studying such places year after year could scientists understand the elaborate interplay between the metropolitan environment and the de-velopment of ecosystems. Sukopp pointed out that an inner-city wasteland in central Berlin, where natural succession was allowed to occur over many years, contained 140 seed plants and 200 species of insect. In contrast, the 'carefully maintained lawns and bushes of the nearby Tiergarten park have at most a quarter as many insect species in the same area'.[12]

Just as importantly, Sukopp and other researchers made the insight that there was no single urban ecosystem. Sites across Berlin had different ecologies depending on their history, microclimate, proximity to the edge of the city and dominant species. Berlin, in all its complexity, was 'a living space, that resembles a mosaic, composed of many different small locations'. Here was a powerful acknowledgement that city and nature were not binary opposites. Every city developed its own unique form of 'nature' in niche spots, where spontaneous vegetation was allowed free rein. The process of urbanisation in Berlin, it was discovered, had **increased** the amount of spontaneously occurring species in the city from 822 in the eighteenth century to 1,392 by the end of the twentieth, despite the extinction of 202 species. Unlike parks, these unofficial manifestations of nature wove crucial green networks throughout the urban frame.[13]

In his study of London, Fitter had celebrated such unlikely spots. Herbert Sukopp made that enthusiasm a science. By the 1970s – that pivotal decade for nature in the city – he was using the term 'urban ecology' to describe his studies of Berlin. In 1973 the Berlin Technische Universität founded an Institute of Ecology, with Sukopp appointed director of its Ecosystem Research and Vegetation Sciences department. From this position, Professor Sukopp now not only studied the city but began to shape it as well. All those untidy, messy wastelands added up to a lot of biodiversity. They were also unique ecosystems which had barely been studied before. They were thus as much in need of conservation as an ancient forest or a rural lake. Indeed, they were extremely vulnerable because they were at once ugly and prime real estate.[14]

Preserving demolition sites for the sake of nature had never been on any one's agenda before. But Sukopp and his colleagues were able to bring, for the first time, decades of sustained scientific findings and reams of data to the table. Their involvement helped shape the Berlin Nature Protection Law of 1979, which established a species protection programme for the urban area of West Berlin. Under a working group led by Sukopp, experts compiled a red list of endangered species and, most radically of all, produced a colour-coded biotope map of West Berlin that revealed the complex mosaic of its different ecosystems.

The stage was set for a battle to protect Berlin's unofficial greenspaces. Sukopp said that he did not want to turn the city 'into a paradise of nature'.

What he wanted to show was that 'city and nature are not opposites. A large number of plants and animals are able to live in direct proximity to the urban dweller.' Nature conservation in the city meant preserving these organisms not only for research purposes, but for the benefit of Berliners who were deprived of contact with nature. Most importantly, inner-city wastelands were more biodiverse and interesting than formal parks and gardens. They were essential for the health of the city's ecosystem services. **Brachen** needed to be the nature reserves of the future.[15]

As Sukopp saw it in 1979, evolution was occurring on these endangered urban and industrial wastelands as species adapted to urban conditions. In such disturbed and humanmade environments, species – many of them recently introduced – were hybridising with each other, creating new gene types. 'These evolutionary processes are going on continuously,' Sukopp wrote. 'The prevailing plants of the future will certainly be those which adjust themselves best to man-made sites.'[16]

Here we see the beginning of a change in sensibilities. Those old eyesores – derelict sites with their tangles of weeds – were becoming places of awe and wonder. Their plants were hardened inner-city types, able to tough out everything the city had to throw at them. The urban weedscape was about to become political in post-industrial cities awakening to the realities of climate change. In doing so, it has cut across some of our deepest prejudices.

'The spectacle of the world, how it is fallen!' lamented the scholar Poggio Bracciolini in 1430. 'How changed! How defaced! The path of victory is obliterated by vines.' Once the icon of urban magnificence and engineering brilliance, the Roman Colosseum was, by the Middle Ages, festooned with weeds.

In 1643, the botanist Domenico Panaroli wrote **Plantarum Amphytheatralium Catalogus** in which he inventoried 337 plants growing in the six-acre site. Plants were so productive in the Colosseum that peasants paid a fee to collect hay and wild herbs. The ruins had a unique microclimate, with conditions dry and warm on the south side and cool and damp on the north, which created different habitats and plant communities. Where spectators had once cheered on gladiatorial contests, the lower galleries now swarmed with pink dianthus; wood anemone preferred the higher tiers. In 1855, the British doctor Richard Deakin recorded an explosion of 420 species of vegetation in the Colosseum. Many of these were exotic plants from the eastern Mediterranean, Africa and further afield, leading Deakin to speculate that the seeds had arrived on the fur of the wild animals brought to be slaughtered 2,000 years before.

Weeds meant decline. They were at once the symptom and the cause of civilisational collapse. After all, what had civilisation been about if not the re-placement of chaos with human order? Urban life represented war against the destructive power of nature; the city was refuge from the caprice of the merciless wild. Weeds were reminders that nature was always lurking, ready to swallow up the greatest creations of humanity. In Giovanni Battista Piranesi's depictions of eighteenth-century Rome, it is the contrast between the ancient grandeur of the build-ings and the rampant invasion of foliage – such as **Arctium lappa** (greater burdock) and **Phragmites australis** (common reed) – that is often so striking. The neglected state of the Colosseum taught that everyone should be on their guard against weeds.

Biologically speaking, there are no such things as weeds. Reaching an objective definition is im-possible, and the Western canon has complacently defined the weed on moral terms. The Bible's men-tion of the word 'wilderness' is invariably negative; 'weeds' are pests with which we have to do battle. In the Old Testament, Edenic beauty is replaced with land that needed to be worked and perfected after the Fall; fruits and flowers existed with thorns and briars; only by labour could the good and bad be separated. In Shakespeare's **Henry V,** political dis-order is equated with wilderness and weeds: once bountiful meadows have been overtaken with 'dar-nel, hemlock, and rank fumitory . . . hateful docks, rough thistles, kecksies [cow parsley], burrs, losing both beauty and utility'. In **Hamlet,** the prince sees the sorry state of Denmark after his father's death as 'an unweeded garden, / That grows to seed; things rank and gross in nature / Possess it merely'.[17]

Accounts of cities rarely strayed into the ruderal vegetation; paintings emphasised the geometry of the humanmade. Yet for all the silence, it is clear that cities have always been full of unsanctioned, spontaneous greenery. The archaeological record speaks where written history is mute. Weeds, such records tell us, were useful and abundant in medieval cities. Faecal evidence found in excavated latrines are rich in wild seeds that supplemented the urban diet in medieval Europe: sloe, bullace, opium poppy, cherry, blackberry, raspberry, wild strawberry, dog rose-hips and hazelnuts. Seeds were constantly being brought into the city. They escaped from the sedges and rushes used for thatching and flooring and germinated in the city, as did grass seeds imported in hay, and stitchworts and chickweed introduced by horses. The edges of breweries were particularly thick with exotic imports, with 692 grain and hay plants around German breweries, for example, and 814 citrus weed species. Exotic seeds spewed out of packing cases in docks made the areas adjacent to warehouses profuse with alien flowering plants. As Swiss botanists noted in 1905, wild flora in cities 'essentially runs parallel to the size and intensity of trade and industry; it is the direct standard of the technical culture'. The quays of premodern Paris – like many other commercial waterside spots – had more wildflowers and herbage than anywhere else in the city.[18]

What later ages would call weeds were, in the Middle Ages, common resources. Griselda in Chaucer's 'Clerke's Tale', 'whan she homward cam, she wolde brynge / Wortes or othere herbes tymes oft, / The whiche she shredde and seeth for hir lyvynge'. The herbalist and Londoner William Gerard, writing in 1597, said that people were wont to 'feast themselves even with varieties of those things the vulgar call weeds'. Nettles were used in soups, young sow thistles and wild clary in salads. The ubiquitous dunghills and middens on the streets sprouted fat-hen, eaten as an iron- and protein-rich cooked vegetable. Medieval brewers flavoured ale with **gruit,** a mixture of herbs that grew in wastelands and alongside buildings: bog myrtle, mugwort, yarrow, ground ivy, meadowsweet and broom. Poor women harvested and sold penny-royal, used for abortions and to soothe toothache, haemorrhoids and itches, as well as henbane, a seda-tive, and coltsfoot, which was used to make cough syrup. Purslane, one of the most distinctive pavement weeds all over the planet, contains extraordinarily high concentrations of omega-3 oils and was a key part of the medieval diet. During the Second World War, the Directorate of Medical Supplies put out a call for wild herbs growing in London that were once commonly foraged but had, in recent years, been im-ported. Plants needed for drugs included foxglove,

male fern, stinging nettle, dandelion, burdock, coltsfoot and henbane. The wartime request brought back
a lost world of urban foraging.[19]

As in Sukopp's Berlin of the twentieth century, the
plants that thrived best in the medieval city were those
pre-adapted to disturbed sites and wastelands: nettles, goosefoot, thistle and dandelion. And, as in the
modern metropolis, the continual activity and movement of goods made the weedscape highly dynamic,
with new species arriving continually and displacing
older residents. In 1823, the Danish botanist Joakim
Schouw forged a new characterisation, **'Plantae
urbanae',** to describe the kinds of vegetation – many
of them exotic ruderal species – that favoured life in
the city over the countryside.[20]

Gerard wrote that, 'narrowly observed', there was
'a great deal of prettiness' in the wildflowers of the
city. He observed that the brick and stone walls of
Elizabethan London were luxuriously curtained
with wall rocket, rue-leaved saxifrage and pellitory-
of-the-wall. By the mid-eighteenth century, London
walls were sprouting a new green garb – ivy-leaved
toadflax, a native of the Mediterranean which had
arrived in Oxford as part of the packing materials for marble statues taken from Italian mansions
and escaped, gone on the lam, and fetched up in
the capital.

'All the dusty, noisome and malodorous pests of all
the world seem here to revel in one grand congenial
democratic orgy,' sniffed the English science writer

Grant Allen of the United States in 1886. Allen saw the weedscape of American cities as a mirror of American cosmopolitanism, marred with the botanical dregs of Europe, Asia, Africa, the Americas and Australia. Invasive, uncultivated species arrived with the first European settlers, introduced deliberately as herbage or accidentally through trade, and spread throughout the continent, edging out the natives.[21]

Others, however, appreciated the rackety beauty that characterised American cities in the nineteenth century. The Bostonian botanist William Rich found an 'almost inexhaustible supply' of wild plants of diverse origins in the 'vacant lots and dumping grounds' of his home city. In his remarkable and far-sighted book **Nature in a City Yard** (1897), Charles Montgomery Skinner revelled in the profusion of wildlife in his Brooklyn plot. It came from all over the world and thrived: aster, chamomile, daisies, dandelions, thyme, goldenrod, oxalis, smartweed, sorrel, thistle, wild parsnip, chickweed and purslane were among a smorgasbord of delights. Skinner harvested 'plebian' wild mustard from mean-looking side streets and planted it in his yard.[22]

The fast but uneven growth of American cities fostered the wildflower bonanza. Towns in the US had a hell of a lot of gaps between buildings in the age of helter-skelter urbanisation. Prairie plants such as sunflowers and black-eyed susans were well adapted to vacant lots, roadsides and other disturbed places.

Acres of waving sunflowers, which thrived on in-hospitable concrete, rubble, cinders and asphalt, made it the characteristic flower of urban America. Out of the copious manure piles of the Chicago stockyards sprouted catmint, clovers, teasel and nightshades. 'Weeds' covered close to 40 per cent of Chicago's land area in the early twentieth century. Cocklebur, dog fennel, green foxtail and sunflowers and sow thistle took up spaces in alleys and at the sides of railroads, industrial sites and other urban edgelands; the poor harvested prickly lettuce. Pre-urban prairie plants such as ironweed, rosinweed and golden ragwort clung on. Washington D.C. was strewn with unofficial vegetation, some of it growing close to the grand federal buildings and even the White House. In 1902, a botanist discovered 'a veritable tropical jungle' in the unused lots of Philadelphia made up of cannabis, the weed of weeds.[23]

For many people, the city represented humankind's estrangement from nature. Nature was flourishing in the city with incredible profuseness; but it was seen as the wrong **kind.** Hated, unacknowledged, overlooked, this greenery was regarded as akin to pollution.

In a study of the pavement vegetation of Paris in 1881, Joseph Vallot wrote that the metropolis had changed radically since 1800: 'we wouldn't find a corner that is not paved, asphalted or macadamized.

An army of workers, equipped with hose pipes and mechanical sweepers, carry out daily cleaning of the streets, and if some small plant is at risk of pushing between the paving stones, attendants – panicking about the cleanliness of the street – rush to rip it out with special tools.' Old cobbled and unpaved streets were interlaced with urban plants; modern ones gave them very little room. Vallot lamented the way that nineteenth-century Paris expurgated the wild vegetation that had once characterised the cityscape. Plants that had been ubiquitous in previous centuries still appeared, most notably between the grills protecting street trees, but they were becoming rarer as Paris's streets became harder and more impermeable.[24]

After the unification of Italy and the transfer of the capital to Rome, the famous wildness of the Colosseum was deemed undignified, and it was stripped of its foliage. During the nineteenth century, attitudes to vagabond foliage hardened as surely as the streets and pavements. Reformers wanted to make cities healthier, cleaner, tidier. The ecology of cities fell under the reformer's stern gaze. Parks and gardens represented the acceptable face of nature; spontaneous vegetation was anarchic, unsafe and unbecoming the modern metropolis.

Smith Patterson Galt was having none of it. He told the court that his weeds were essential both to the 'economy of nature' and the 'preservation of man upon earth'. In July 1900, Galt, a prominent attorney in St Louis, Missouri, had been issued with a 'weed statement' by a city sanitary officer, ordering him to cut down his sunflowers and what he called his 'uncultivated vegetation' and which the courts defined as 'weeds'. Galt fought the order all the way to Missouri's supreme court, strenuously arguing that it violated his rights under the fifth and fourteenth amendments to the constitution.

The city of St Louis did not like wild growth. The **Post-Dispatch** newspaper castigated weeds as 'the tramps and outcasts of the vegetable kingdom'. Like hobos, they hitched rides on trains and congregated menacingly on wastelands. 'Weeds mean neglect', it thundered. 'Give us a trim and up-to-date city.' Galt's stand coincided with a time when uncultivated urban vegetation was coming under attack in American cities. He fell foul of a city ordinance of 1896 that ordered property owners to destroy unrestrained vegetation growth of over one foot. In the supreme court, Galt defended his sunflowers against the grave charge that they were weeds. But according to prosecutors, sunflowers were the quintessential plant of dereliction and neglect. They were weeds simply because they filled the ugly, unused parts of the city and could never escape that stigma. The judge agreed; Galt lost his appeal.[25]

Spontaneous plants were hated because they were immigrants and opportunists that exploited gaps and crevices like a gang of hobos or outlaws. Their preference for waste ground made them even more repellent in an age obsessed with public order, sanitary reform and beautification. Weeds were, in this view, nature's muggers, ganging up on pretty, delicate foliage; they were decidedly not the manifestations of greenery that anyone, except for oddballs like Galt, wanted.

The precedent of **St Louis v. Galt** was used throughout the twentieth century – and still is today – to enforce weed ordinances, even if the term 'weed' remains undefined. Anything that was not deliberately planted for ornamental or culinary purpose, and which was not kept in order, could fall foul of the ordinances. Tidy up or get a hefty fine, people were told. Sunflowers, burdocks, thistles and the like did not represent 'nature' for the beautifiers; they were hostile invaders and public nuisances associated with stench, disease, crime, poverty and uncleanliness. 'The foreign plant immigrant,' sniffed a horrified botanist in 1902, '. . . is apt to be less fastidious, and will often live and spread even amid ashes and rubbish.' Plants that were attracted to nasty spots must be nasty themselves. The association of undesirable plants with lowlife humans made it absolutely clear that these two interwoven forces were fatally undermining the fabric of urban society. Both were environmental problems; both had to be weeded out.[26]

The advent of weedkillers turned the battle into

chemical warfare. The public part of the city had to be maintained as a weed-free environment. In suburbia, vacant lots sprouting with the cornucopia of unregulated nature represented a Pandora's box of dangers to tidy gardens and lawns. The wildness that had always characterised cities was now associated with destitution, dirt and social breakdown. The twentieth century saw an unprecedented public and private assault on urban vegetation in a bid to create sanitised cities.

Not all buildings are like the Colosseum, able to withstand centuries of green growth. Many urban plants do need to be removed because, left unchecked, they will destroy structures. What was different in the twentieth century was the squeamishness about weeds. They had to be obliterated for moral and aesthetic as well as practical reasons. But such plants are the ultimate survivors. They fought back harder than their human neighbours.

Again, the bombs exploded, and the greenery returned. Only this time the bombs – made from glass Christmas baubles – contained wildflower seeds and a little soil. Hurled into fenced-off, empty lots in New York City by roving bands of Green Guerrillas in the 1970s and 80s, the 'greenades' transformed eyesores into urban micro-meadows brimming with the fernlike Queen Anne's lace, with its frothy white umbel, as well as vivid blue chicory, aster, yellow evening primroses, black-eyed Susans, spiking butter-and-eggs, bright orange jewelweed, goldenrod, moth mullein, trailing cinquefoil and violet feral petunias. The Green Guerrillas scattered sunflower seeds onto the central meridians of New York's streets. 'They have not prepared, improved or fertilized the soil, nor have they watered,' wrote the **New York Times** in June 1985, 'yet the wildflowers that were put to bed in these unpromising, even antagonistic circumstances in mid-April are up with a flourish and about to bloom.'[27]

In 1973, the leading light of the Green Guerrillas, the young artist Liz Christy, established a garden on an abandoned site on the corner of the Bowery and Houston Street, which was notorious for alcoholics and homeless people. The city authorities accused Christy and the Guerrillas of trespass and tried to have them evicted. Christy mobilised the media to show how wild gardening could transform a city that had been devastated by financial crisis and arson. A year later, the city backed down and leased the site for $1 a month. The success sparked imitators. In 1978, the city launched Operation GreenThumb which legitimised the guerrilla campaign by leasing derelict lots to volunteers. By 1982, 150 acres in the South Bronx and Brooklyn were seeded with rye, fescue, clover, wildflowers, raspberries and blackberries. The **New York Times** hailed 'an inexpensive and beautiful way to heal a scarred urban landscape' which had begun with Liz Christy's direct action a decade before. Christy died of cancer in 1985, but her garden on the Bowery still blooms, as does her legacy. By the early 1990s, 850 derelict sites in New York City had been greened, seventy of them in the Lower East Side.[28]

This work displayed evidence of changing attitudes to wild spaces in cities. Such sites were no longer universally condemned as eyesores. People were beginning to see beauty in them. There was also a realisation that the forgotten, marginal places in cities were where true biodiverse treasures lay buried. Wasteland, dereliction, abandonment, weeds – such words connoted failure. But, as sensibilities began to shift, they could also conjure up visions of flourishing nature.

The great urban writer Jane Jacobs argued in the 1960s that it was in the unregulated, informal, unplanned parts of the city that innovation was most likely to occur. The same could be said of nature: forget the parks and gardens – it was the feral areas of the city where ecological wealth thrived, unbidden and unasked for. They lacked the order of regulated greenery. To put it bluntly, they were messy.

Visitors to Berlin accustomed to tidy cities might perceive this kind of messiness. This is a city where spontaneous vegetation is tolerated. Tramlines, roadsides and the edges of buildings have copious wild plants which, in other less enlightened cities, would be condemned as weeds and face eradication. This relaxed, unfussy attitude is in large part due to Berlin's unique history. The urban wastelands – the **brachen** – stemming from the Cold War gave West Berliners an unusual amount of wild green space in a claustrophobic metropolis. Added to that, thanks to Herbert Sukopp and others, few other cities had such detailed and scientific knowledge about the ecological importance of ruderal sites. As chairman of the city's 'Advisory Board for Nature Conservation and Landscape Management' (Sachverständigenbeirat für Naturschutz und Landschaftspflege Berlin), Sukopp was able to advocate for the preservation of **brachen** as a component of urban planning. But even as interest in them was mounting, **brachen** were disappearing in the face of advancing urban regeneration.[29]

Protestors dressed as animals and plants invaded planning offices in January 1984. They were there to save a disused railway marshalling yard called the Südgelände. Abandoned since 1952 as a result of the city's division, nature had reclaimed the Südgelände to such an extent that one-third of all plant species found in Berlin – some 334 ferns and flowering plants – had made a home there among the rail tracks and rusting infrastructure, along with falcons, foxes, previously undiscovered beetle species, and spiders which were until then only known to inhabit caves in southern France. These surprise arachnid guests were believed to have hitched a ride on freight trains during the war. This area of outstanding biodiversity was threatened with the chainsaw like so many in 1980s Berlin, because it was about to be revived as a rail depot.[30]

The Südgelände was defended as a unique and valuable spot in the midst of a city, where people could harvest mushrooms, pick fruits, appreciate wildflowers and 'enjoy a wide horizon and the warmth of the dry meadows'. It allowed children to play in a wild way, liberated from the repetitiveness of conventional playground equipment. The Südgelände exhibited 'an extraordinary landscape that no garden architect would be able to shape', a serendipitous oasis in the middle of a city that embodied within it not only the resilience of urban nature but a vivid history lesson illustrating a century of war and division and the rise and obsolescence of once-futuristic technologies. Another site threatened with development, the Lennédreieck – an empty triangle near the Brandenburg Gate that officially belonged to East Berlin but lay on the west side of the wall – was a classic left-over space created by Berlin's division, described as a 'wild, undeveloped metropolitan paradise'. Nearby on Lützowplatz, another triangular ruderal bombsite known as the Dörnbergdreieck was, simultaneously, a camp for homeless people, a meeting place for prostitutes and their clients, an informal

playground for children and one of the most studied urban ecological sites in the world.[31]

These were 'novel ecosystems' – places shaped
and determined by human activity but then left
to natural processes. Campaigners fought to save
these precious sites throughout the 1980s. Wild,
unregulated spaces appealed directly to the spirit
of anarchism in Berlin, and they chimed with the
growing influence of green politics in the city. The
Südgelände became the subject of a massive pub-
licity campaign, which used striking photographs
and scientific reports to drag it into prominence.
Herbert Sukopp argued that the Dörnbergdreieck
and other rubble sites should be preserved as nature parks. In 1988, protestors squatted on the
Lennédreieck for several months in a rancorous battle for the future of Berlin.[32]

Opened in 1999, the Südgelände is today a forty-
five-acre inner-city nature park. The conundrum
of turning an abandoned site into a public park
without undermining its biodiversity was solved
by putting in metal walkways one metre above
ground level so that visitors did not trample on
the vegetation or disturb ground-nesting birds. In
some parts of the park, woodland is allowed to develop independently of human intervention, as if
the marshalling yard had remained abandoned indefinitely; in other parts, natural succession is restrained by mowing and grazing sheep to provide

grass and shrub habitats for rare and endangered plants and animals. The decommissioned airport at Johannisthal, meanwhile, was converted into a sixty-four-acre dry grassland reserve. Elsewhere, a strip of the once-ubiquitous wild vegetation that grew either side of the Berlin Wall was preserved in 2004 as the Park am Nordbahnhof. Such places, in Berlin and elsewhere, are historically significant because they marked the extent to which attitudes towards urban nature had shifted. The ugly and unlovely were worth fighting for because their eco-systems were unique.

But most of the haunts of wildness have gone. The exuberant wildlife of the Lennédreieck has been replaced by glimmering office buildings and hotels that symbolise Berlin's spectacular post-unification regeneration. The Dörnbergdreieck, once so important in the development of urban ecology, now hosts the Sheraton Grand Hotel Esplanade. Many such places where nature was permitted to run rampant for a few decades were re-urbanised from the 1980s onwards.

The history of Berlin provides a fascinating lesson for cities around the world. Even in that city, where government policy and grassroots activism alike fought to preserve wild spaces, the loss of biodiverse brownfield sites continued apace, particularly after reunification. Those that remain do so thanks to years of lobbying and expensive investments. Yet the story of Berlin shows how quickly certain types of urban plant flourish in disturbed environments. Over a few decades, the Südgelände matured into a place of startling abundance just by being left alone. This kind of example was instrumental in opening people's eyes to the potential of cities to support biodiversity in places that hitherto had seemed either unlikely or unacceptably scruffy. The conversion of neglected spots in Berlin into nature parks – the result of scientific consensus and sustained popular pressure combining – showed how unattractive brownfield spots could be incorporated into cities and made accessible to the public.

Another lesson from Berlin is that spontaneous urban vegetation is transitory. Just as cities are in a constant state of metamorphosis, so too is their non-human nature. Wildlife flourished and then waned in Berlin because of geopolitical factors. In a similar way, economic ups and downs have a major impact on biodiversity. At the time of the Great Depression, when the building boom came to a shuddering halt, significant amounts of the surface area of American cities – 20 per cent in San Francisco, Flint and Salt Lake City; 50 per cent in Chicago, Cleveland, Detroit and Milwaukee – were left with stalled or abandoned building works. De-industrialisation in American and European cities from the 1960s punched holes in the urban matrix for plants and animals to exploit. The misery of the city was manna for wildlife. There were 25,000 vacant lots in New York City by the 1970s and 29,782 in the 2010s, collectively occupying the same space as Central, Prospect, Pelham Bay, Van Cortlandt, Marine, Bronx and Forest Parks – New York's most famous official greenspaces – put together. In countries around the developing world, disused factories and other redundant industrial buildings created prominent ruinscapes from the 1960s.[33]

Nature, at its insurgent best, reclaimed this terrain. In twenty-first-century Detroit, over 40 per cent of the city consists of abandoned factories and homes, leaving the shrinking city bedecked with wild plants. The visual impact of widespread dereliction indicated decline and social breakdown, particularly in overgrown and neglected inner city areas. But it also fostered a vogue for the 'post-industrial picturesque', an aesthetic of decline. The ecological by-products of recession popularised a new form of nature writing that feasted on the ruinscape of de-industrialisation and brought to wider attention the findings of biologists such as Sukopp. Richard Mabey's **The Unofficial Countryside** – published, in 1973, the year of the foundation of both the Green Guerrillas and the Institute of Urban Ecology in Berlin – explored inner city canals, rubbish tips, quarries, industrial estates and car parks in de-industrialising London. The magic conveyed in Mabey's book is not so much botanical information as an alternate way to appreciate both nature and the city. Weeds, he wrote, 'green over the dereliction we have created'; their ability 'to grow in the most hostile environments – a bombed city, a crack in the wall – means that they insinuate the idea of wild nature into places otherwise quite shorn of it'. In their lyrical evocation of marginal terrain, writers such as Mabey showed that as much wonder could be found in everyday or neglected urban places as in pristine wildernesses.[34]

The romance of post-industrial dereliction and feral edgelands has enchanted writers, photographers, painters and filmmakers since the 1970s. This post-industrial picturesque has been domesticated in permanent form, most prominently in the Natur-Park Südgelände in Berlin, Landschaftspark Duisburg-Nord, Rainham Marshes in London, Freshkills Park on Staten Island and the High Line in Manhattan. In all these examples, decaying infrastructure is entwined with natural growth; heavy industry and wildlife merge into one another. They institute permanent reserves of wildness in the concrete jungle and celebrate the unexpected cornucopia of novel ecosystems.

But most of the **terrain vague** picked over by people like Sukopp and Mabey have gone. It is subject to the cycles of growth and decline that are part of a city's life. Decaying industry doesn't decay for ever; such sites are gentrified or regenerated, smartened up and landscaped. During the urban renaissance of the late twentieth and early twenty-first centuries, brownfield sites became the prime locations for house building. Yet as disturbed sites are paved

over, new ones are created in the endless building
and rebuilding of cities. Even in good times, eco-
nomically speaking, 10 per cent of the surface area
of a city in Europe, and between 12.5 per cent and
25 per cent in the United States, will likely be derelict, albeit temporarily. In fast-growing cities and
during recessions, it will be a lot more.[35]

The prominence given to spontaneous vegetation during the bombing campaigns of the Second
World War was just a bigger and highly dramatic
version of what is going on in cities all the time.
The ongoing process of destruction and re-creation
provides the space for opportunistic vegetation,
ceaselessly on the lookout for habitats, to strike.
Young sites, before the succession process matures,
have the highest diversity with competing pioneer
species, so the continual turnover of derelict plots
is beneficial for biodiversity.

Just as the no-man's land created by the Berlin
Wall gave shelter for habitats to emerge, even a
chain-link fence provides an edge for opportunistic
vegetation to cling to when it is away from trampling feet and traffic. Cities provide plenty of such
edges for nature to thrive in – roadsides and road
meridians, alleyways, railway lines, walls, roofs, canals, gutters and gaps in paving stones. Although
these places are ubiquitous in cities, they are studied
relatively little compared with parks, wastelands and
urban forests. One thing is for sure – they are profuse with wildlife. A study published in 2019 found

more than 300 species of urban plants sprouting out of the pavements of the French city of Blois, which had recently phased out glyphosate weed-killer. Species richness and plant cover were greatest in streets with older, permeable pavements and in lightly trodden industrial areas. A similar study of Berlin found 375 street-living plants, a full 25 per cent of the floral inventory of the metropolis. This is the unseen, underappreciated, pavement-level urban ecosystem that our feet pound over.[36]

You don't have to do much to transform the grey city into a green urban jungle. As the example of Blois shows, limiting herbicides and breaking up, to some degree, hard surfaces promote rapid vegetation growth. Urban areas proliferate with pauses between human use. Often, their potential as micro-ecosystems is ignored or underutilised. A little creativity can transform these grey voids. In Berlin and Zurich, the vegetation alongside and between roads on roundabouts and under street signs and trees, is frequently left unmown, creating annual wildflower micro-meadows. Webs of rail lines, with their wide, inaccessible margins, provide connective corridors for animal, insect and plant species. In many cities, hundreds of miles of embankments and railway linesides are abandoned to nature or actively conserved as **de facto** nature reserves. Walls, if they are managed well, can be unexpectedly healthy ecosystems. Some 200 species of vegetation have been recorded on the walls of Zurich. The Roman walls of Colchester were designated as a local wildlife site in 1991 in recognition of their unique specialised flora. A layer of mosses and liverworts provide substrata for over 160 plants, including several miniscule flowering species, some of them rare and endangered, that complete their lifecycle within a few weeks during spring.

But, in the main, visible marginal space is still sprayed with chemicals, mown and tidied up to remove all those organic symbols of dereliction. Look about your city as you travel through it: acre after acre of vacant or underused land, rather than being left to wildlife or mown once a year, is brutally hacked back for no other reason than to look tidy. Urban ecosystems very obviously clash with our idea of what nature is or should be – the entanglement of humans and nature is regarded as ugly and unnatural. The kinds of plants that thrive best in the city are those associated with disaster; perhaps something deep inside us revolts at those plants that reek of failure and degradation. As a species we seem to prefer innately wide open vistas that we can control and which have the appearance of being abundant. Yet if we want to maximise biodiversity in cities, we should look again at weeds.

Salt trucks kill off much of the vegetation alongside the road. But for the seaside goldenrod (**Solidago sempervirens**) in the United States, and Danish scurvy grass in Europe, salt trucks have created a sodium-enriched highway taking them, year by year, from their native coastlines into cities. The tons of salt required to keep us on the move during icy winters have created strips of habitat alongside roads that resemble dunes, cliffs and salt marshes. These maritime adventurers are moving into town.

New York, from the vantage point of ragweed, replicates the eastern areas of North America immediately after the last Ice Age, when the land was a rocky glacial till. Having retreated to a few small niches in the subsequent millennia as other, bigger species took over, the plant ran riot in New York from the nineteenth century, forming 'jungles' throughout the poorer parts. New York, for the ragweed, was merely a new glacial till. For the notoriously invasive and prolific tree of heaven, a wall or railway track is akin to the dry limestone hills of China from which it originated. Rosebay willowherb treats the city the same way it does a forest that has just burnt down. Mugwort and curly dock have decamped from European acidic grasslands and found that the high pH levels of masonry-strewn sites in cities around the world perfectly replicate their home soils. In the U.S., they have become the trademark weed of derelict lot meadows, while walls and brick surfaces are ideal for the tiny, pretty whitlow-grass (**Draba verna**), which evolved for arid rocks and mountains. When you look at your city from a plant's point of view, you discover a wealth of stories – not just about the plants themselves but about us, too.

Salty, rocky, acidic, dry, impervious, compacted, polluted, hot – that is the environment we have created. We should be grateful when we see a weed poking through the concrete and be thankful that it is with us at all. The kind of vegetation we get reveals what we have done to the planet. In building our cities we uprooted and paved over primeval nature, extirpating all that was native, burying the soil under layer after layer of rubble, concrete and asphalt. It is little wonder that the plants that characterise the urban ecosystem are those hardy pioneers that colonised the silt, sand, gravel and boulders churned up by the retreat of the glaciers at the end of the last Ice Age. Urbanisation has presented them with a huge new opportunity.

If we looked at our cities as the landscape of a glacial till, an inhospitable coastal cliff, a volcano or an avalanche, we might treat weeds in an entirely different way. Such rough, tough plants are the true urbanites. They have travelled across the globe to live among us because they love the disturbed terrains we are so good at producing. From an ecological perspective, a city is a disaster zone. Only vegetation capable of withstanding continual stress, drought, pollution and degraded soil and resilient enough to survive even the most determined efforts at extirpation can survive in this hostile, polluted environment. The plant life that has found a home in this blasted site is the vegetation that has been humankind's long-standing camp-followers. And they represent the future: they are adapted to living in our disaster-strewn wake and are capable of withstanding climate change. They are entwined with our lives.

Next time you see your local authority strimming, mowing and spraying vegetation – not in the name of safety but for reasons of tidiness – you have a right to be indignant that you are being deprived of essential ecological services. Every unused spot in the city, after all, presents an opportunity for maximising biodiversity. The war against weeds is dauntingly costly in taxpayers' money and pollutes the wider environment with harmful chemicals – more than enough reason to tolerate 'unofficial' growth. The despised ruderal plants skulking on the edges and wastes are the workhorses of the urban environment. They sequester carbon and soak up excess rain, and some species – called hyperaccumulators – help decontaminate polluted soil. They are the pioneers that prepare the soil for eventual succession by other species. And they spread everywhere: they are not needy or particular like their fragile ornamental cousins in the park. The tree of heaven has spread itself across major metropolises such as New York. Because it is considered a 'weed' it is not counted in the inventory of the urban forest, but it is there doing its tree thing all the same, providing ecological services without being asked.

One thing is for sure: we will never be able to eradicate weeds; they are too tough for us. How much we choose to embrace them is up to us. Some invasive plants need to be removed when they do damage. But many more do no worse than offend the eye. Often ugly, they have always been harbingers of recovery after catastrophe: perhaps that is why we should learn to love them a little more in this age of crisis.

Perhaps we are beginning to do so, albeit slowly. When the cities of Dessau, Hanover and Frankfurt began a wilding project on disused urban land in 2016, it was called 'Städte wagen Wildnis' – 'cities daring wildness' – an acknowledgement that unregulated nature is a major challenge to entrenched notions of urban tidiness. In Dessau, the controversy over allowing nature to take over newly acquired municipal land was mitigated in part by the simple expedient of information boards explaining that what looked like abandonment was in fact a conscious plan to maximise biodiversity. If older people saw mess, officials discovered, children found places of adventure. In 2021, seven out of every ten English councils deliberately left public land unmown in the spring and early summer. Road verges, public land and patches of previously manicured parks took on the colour and profusion of rural meadows; unexpected plants poked out where once there had been green deserts of cropped municipal turf. What would have been labelled as messy and neglected in previous years became seen as micro-wildernesses full of pollinating plants. English cities changed in front of people's eyes: rougher, wilder, more colourful. When we understand why certain type of growth supports wildlife, we tend to accept shaggier landscapes. Science – particularly urban ecology – is beginning to shift attitudes.

Even St Louis – the city that prosecuted Smith Patterson Galt for his wildlife garden – has changed its attitudes in response to plummeting butterfly numbers. Its 'Milkweeds for Monarchs' scheme has seen the creation of 250 butterfly gardens planted with exactly the kinds of pollinating flora once stigmatised as invasive pests and regarded with hostility by law-enforcement officials and the courts: goldenrod, black-eyed Susan, butterfly weed and several varieties of milkweed. Weeds are suddenly good. The greenades thrown by the Green Guerrillas contained the seeds – once considered invasive weeds – that are now becoming important in city planning. Give weeds a chance; they are the urban flora of the future.

Our aesthetic preferences are shifting, albeit gradually. This has a lot to do with our acknowledgement of the crimes we have committed against biodiversity. Wildness suddenly seems more satisfying and life-giving, while manicured gardens broadcast their artificiality and the lengths we have gone to in order to maintain them. Solving the riddle of making ecologically productive plantscapes acceptable to city-dwellers who hold entrenched notions of what kind of nature is appropriate has preoccupied the British ecology professors Nigel Dunnett and James Hitchmough. Through much of history, gardening has involved adapting specific sites to the needs of the plants that have been chosen. Dunnett and Hitchmough do the opposite: they select plants that will thrive in pre-existing urban conditions without the need for extensive human intervention. Many are the hardy, drought-tolerant, non-native species that have proven their ability to flourish in disturbed, acidic, nutrient-poor environments. Dunnett and Hitchmough's method of creating naturalistic landscapes follows the science of urban ecology pioneered over the preceding decades by experts such as Sukopp.

When Sheffield Council reduced a four-lane inner city road to two lanes, it employed Nigel Dunnett to transform the reclaimed space into an urban meadow. Today, the street has a wild character rarely seen in cities. Dunnett chose tall, herbaceous, perennial species and grasses that would have a high visual impact but minimal need for maintenance. The result is 'designed ecology' – densely planted meadows that appear to be wild but are crafted to be self-generating, biodiverse habitats. Tall prairie and steppe vegetation, which is definitely not native to the UK, does well in urban terrains, as do many mountain, meadow, coastal and woodland species that were not typically included in the inventory of city plants.

The visual effect is of spontaneous vegetation, yet it is designed to appeal to city-dwellers through the choice of colourful plants and creative landscaping. Here, then, is a substitute for high-maintenance, thirsty, unproductive flowerbeds and sterile municipal lawns, a form of nature explicitly based on the science of urban ecology. It reinforces the idea of cities as human-controlled, novel ecosystems that have replaced those that existed before and need to be managed to a greater or lesser extent. If native plants can't hack it in the metropolis, their place should be taken by specialist species drawn from around the world that find niches in the various microclimates of the concrete jungle. We should be less squeamish about 'invasive' plants and a bit more honest with ourselves about the reality of the humanmade ecosystem we have built, welcoming vegetation pre-adapted to this most artificial of environments. The plants of future parks and public land will be these kinds of cosmopolitan urbanites, chosen for their ability to survive on their own, withstand climate change and enrich the ecosystem, as opposed to fragile ornamentals or natives that can't stick it out or do little in return for all the pampering they receive.

Dunnett is motivated by the belief that people need wildness in their lives. His urban meadows bring that experience of natural processes right into

the heart of the city, creating startling visual juxta-
positions of exuberant wildlife and the built environment that resemble Berlin's **brachen** more than
conventional cityscapes. His projects also remind us
that wildness has to be nurtured to some degree. The
Südgelände and Freshkills Park may possess strong
flavours of wildness; but they are the result of human
activities and can only be maximised in terms of biodiversity by ongoing interventions such as grazing.
Perhaps most importantly, Dunnett's designs make
us reconsider what kinds of plants offer the greatest ecological returns. If urban meadows take hold
internationally, it will mark one of the most significant historical developments in the concept of **rus in
urbe:** tidiness out, messiness in.

In Australian cities, there is a sustained push to
replace mown grass on the verges between houses
and streets with native grasses, tussocks and wildflowers. These 'nature strips' are municipally owned
but have to be maintained by householders. In
Melbourne, nature strips – including roundabouts,
meridians and the like – account for 36 per cent of
public greenspace and 7 per cent of the metropolis's
surface area, a colossal amount of land that can be
partially wilded to become habitats and corridors for
mammals and insects. The Dutch have developed a
farsighted policy of **Tijdelijke Natuur** – 'Temporary
Nature' – which permits construction companies to
abandon inactive building sites for a set period, allowing habitats to establish themselves spontaneously

on wastelands. In the past, developers had every incentive to keep endangered and protected species out of their sites lest they had to fork out cash to compensate for the eventual loss of habitat when their buildings were completed under the strictures of the Nature Conservation Act. By releasing builders from the rigours of the law, **Tijdelijke Natuur** allows temporary habitats to flourish. The policy acknowledges cities as places that continually create, destroy and recreate areas of outstanding biodiversity.[37]

Wildness happens in the city, whether as weeds colonising a derelict site or meadows blooming alongside the road. It occurs most healthily in messy places. What matters is the extent to which we let it flourish and the creativity with which we exploit every inch of unused space, be it tucked away between buildings, draped alongside roads or sitting idly on top of buildings. Ecological science has corrected the notion that urban nature happens only in parks. It is the feral, derelict sites and rough meadows that permits species richness. Whether we can learn to love the kinds of vegetation that denote disaster is another matter.

Left to itself, in many cities around the world, nature would revert, ultimately, to woodland. The urbanised species of plants and grasses would give way to dense groves of trees dominated by a few woody species if rewilding was taken to its logical conclusion. But as eight decades of urban ecology have shown, truly rewilding cities is impossible; wilding cities, however, is perfectly within our range if we are open to it. We have to manage cities actively to provide the botanical mosaics that augment their environments and provide resources for pollinators and other creatures, or else 'wildness' simply means trees. As it is, trees have been marching into town at an accelerating rate over the last two centuries. They are now integrated into the urban ecosystem. There is good reason for this: we seem to have an instinctive reverence for trees in a way that we don't for smaller plants and shrubs.

4.

The Canopy

Just twenty minutes from the blaring car horns, four-lane expressways and glitzy new skyscrapers of Delhi, the world disappears into a truly remarkable, deep, wooded valley. In the rainy season, this precious forest, called Mangar Bani, turns from parched brown to vivid, joyous green. It is a verdant jewel set amid the endless city and the dusty, scrubby semi-desert.

The crest of the hills is thick with dhau, the life-giving tree of the region. Perfectly adapted to this tropical dry forest, it spreads its shrub across the rocky ground like a thick, tangled carpet. After a few years, if it is not nibbled back too far by grazing animals, it begins to climb upwards to the height of ten or fifteen metres, and its roots expand outwards through the ground, forming a colony of trees on the barren terrain. Its bark is silvery, and its dense foliage of small leaves turns from green to purplish brown during the dry season. This is a communal, co-operative species: the subterranean network of roots allows dhau on the moister valley floor to transfer water up to the arid cliffs. In exchange, those high on the exposed sunny slopes send back nutrients to the darker, denser depths of the forest.

The forest contains other trees that are now scarce or have disappeared from the Delhi region: kali siris (**Albizia odoratissima**), with its fragrant, pale orange flowers, and salai (**Boswellia serrata**), which produces Indian frankincense. Mangar Bani is full of colour and aroma in the wet season: the yellow, orange and red of the desert rohida tree, the draping gold of the Indian laburnum, the delicate creamy white of the vallaris, and the papery green fruits of the Indian elm. For sheer vivacity, nothing beats the bright red of the dhak tree, or flame of the forest. There are 600,000 trees in Mangar Bani, which provide habitat for rare species of flower, birds and animals such as leopards, hyenas, civet cats, jackals, blue bulls and ninety endangered species of butterfly. The flora and fauna of the forest serve as an important reminder to the people of Delhi: all life here must adapt itself to one burst of intense rainfall a year after an interminable period of drought.

'Last forest standing': that's what Mangar Bani has been called. Most of the forests on the Aravalli ridge that once shielded Delhi have been rendered barren and scarred by urban sprawl, logging, landfill and mining. In place of vital native trees adapted to the harsh local climate, such as the miraculous dhau, has come the Mexican mesquite (**Prosopis juliflora**), first planted by the British and subsequently used by forestry departments as a quick-growing replacement on denuded slopes. The ubiquitous mesquite has been a horror story for the native biodiversity of the Delhi region. The iconic tree of the Aravallis – the resilient dhau – is vanishing fast. Yet this is the tree that could save the city. Its ability to colonise unpromising, rocky ground and survive prolonged drought makes it an ideal street tree for twenty-first-century Delhi.[1]

Most concerning of all, in sacrificing its green wall, Delhi has opened itself up to gusts of heat and dust emanating from the Thar Desert, which is moving ominously closer to the city, threatening desertification. Deforestation also exacerbates the toxic winter smog, the result of vehicular and industrial emissions and stubble burning, which envelops the city every year, and the searing summer temperatures that make the Indian capital almost unliveable. The loss of its forests is apocalyptic and a terrible warning to fast-growing megacities all over the world. It has made Delhi and its 30 million inhabitants vulnerable to water shortages as groundwater levels fall precipitously. Mangar Bani's ecosystem services, in the form of recharged fresh water, is valued at $2 billion.

Reasons enough to preserve the last forest standing, Delhi's green jewel. Not so. Wedged between New Delhi, Gurugram – 'a suburb on steroids' – and Faridabad, another expansive city, Mangar Bani became prime real estate as it fell out of common ownership and was parcelled up into small plots. Offered tempting sums by investment companies in the 1980s, many villagers sold their parcels of land. What had been village commons were fenced off and earmarked for development.

Only one thing stood in the way of the chainsaw. Many centuries ago, Mangar Bani was home to a baba, a holy man revered by the local Gujjar herdsmen. One day, the hermit disappeared into a cave, never to be see again. In reverence of Gudariya Baba, generation after generation has honoured his memory by becoming guardians of Mangar Bani, regarding any extraction from the saint's forest – including a leaf – as a violation. 'We believe if you break even a twig in this forest for your personal need, misfortune strikes you,' a ninety-year-old village elder, Fateh Singh, told the **Washington Post**. 'That fear has kept the forest alive for nearly 1,000 years.' In the late twentieth century, their protective duty motivated some villagers to fight back.[2]

Over the decades, and through bitter legal struggles, real estate speculators were just about kept at bay. 'It is like a mini war situation out there,' said one activist, as illegal encroachments were made on the forest and fences thrown up. When the region's development plan of 2011 failed even to mention the forest, the government was bombarded with applications to redesignate it as farmland, the first step towards paving it over with housing estates, malls and highways.[3]

Born in 1990 in Mangar village, Sunil Harsana was disabled by polio as a child. Hobbling on a wooden staff, he sought solace in the wood and took upon himself the sacred, multigenerational duty of protecting Gudariya Baba's forest. Many of Harsana's fellow villagers had been drawn into the vortex of the city to do menial jobs, losing their connection with the forest. Harsana devoted his life to re-engaging the village's children with their sacred ancestral grove. He became the spokesman for Mangar Bani, achieving a degree of national prominence. Most importantly, he formed connections with scientists and was able to show, through numerous surveys, how critical the forest was to Delhi's biodiversity. The very existence of Mangar Bani hung in the balance until 2016, when the state government finally responded to intense lobbying from local people led by the young Sunil Harsana and environmental activists, declaring it a no-construction zone and throwing a 1,200-acre buffer around it.

It is a stay of execution, however, as ownership of the lush wilderness remains unresolved. Efforts to protect the Mangar village area have not stopped repeated encroachments by developers and loggers in the years after 2016. A headline in the **Times of India** proposed a solution: 'Saving Mangar Bani: why returning grove to original custodians may be only solution'. As the article points out, it was only the power of an ancient, sacred belief system that had preserved Delhi's last remnant of native deciduous forest from the ferocious market forces that had obliterated the rest of the regional ecology. '[I]f Mangar Bani is not saved,' concluded the article, 'not only will Delhi and the National Capital Region, already facing a host of environmental threats, lose an old and valuable green lung, the traditions of custodianship of the forest will, unfortunately, likely go the way of all the other local customs.'[4]

Gurugram, the satellite city of Delhi and uneasy neighbour to Mangar Bani, represents the future of India. Before the 1990s, it was an obscure backwater on the Southern Delhi Ridge of the Aravalli range. Today, it bristles with state-of-the-art skyscrapers, luxury condos, bars, restaurants and golf courses that broadcast its transformation into India's second IT hub (after Bangalore) and third-wealthiest financial centre. Gurugram symbolises the triumph of twenty-first-century urbanism, but also its deepest failings. The young city suffers from a deteriorating environment, poor air quality and water shortages. It is one of the most polluted cities in the world. Deforestation has deranged the natural hydrology; India's 'Millennium City' is hit by catastrophic flooding during the monsoon.

From the village in the nearby forest, Sunil Harsana is well positioned to see that the hypermodern city needs trees. 'It is because of these hills that Gurugram sustains itself,' he says. 'If the city is aware of their importance, only then will the Aravallis survive. And if the Aravallis survive, so will the city.'[5]

Sunil Harsana is right. Few other living things provide such a range of services to us as trees. Like Mangar Bani, many urban trees owe their existence and survival to our spiritual and instinctive connection to the canopy.

The oldest known human-planted tree in the world stands in the ancient city of Anuradhapura, Sri Lanka. In 288 BCE, the Buddhist nun Sanghamitta Maha Theri travelled to the city carrying a branch from the sacred Bodhi tree on the banks of the Neranjana River in Bodh Gaya, India, under which the Buddha achieved enlightenment. The branch was a gift from Emperor Ashoka to King Devanampiya Tissa. The king planted the cutting, and it grew to become the Jaya Sri Maha Bodhi. It has been tended and revered for millennia and thrives to this day.

The Bodhi tree under which the Buddha sought shade is a fig tree – **Ficus religiosa,** or peepal – one of the world's most important urban trees. Figs are good at establishing themselves in cities, capable of surviving in disturbed areas where other trees would wither and die. Like the spontaneous ruderal vegetation we have already encountered, they exploit tight crevices and degraded land because their seeds are capable of germinating in stone. And they have a high capacity to tolerate air pollution. In return, with their height, girth and broad canopies, they absorb great amounts of particulates and provide shade for street activities. Their fruit is rich in vitamins and fibre, while their bark, latex and leaves provide medicines. They also nurture a far higher number of wildlife species than any other kind of fruit tree: each fig is a mini biodiversity hotspot, known to biologists as a 'keystone resource' in the ecosystem.

The fig was sacred to the ancient Egyptians and the Indus Valley Civilisation. The **Ficus Ruminalis,** a wild fig tree, provided shelter for the babies Romulus and Remus when their cradle washed ashore on the banks of the Tiber. The tree – supposedly the very one from the legend of the founding of Rome – was tended at the Lupercal at the foot of the Palatine Hill until the beginning of the first century CE as a symbol of fertility. Fig groves were grown and tended in ancient Rome, including in the forum and around important civic and religious buildings. When, in 58 CE, during the reign of Nero, a sacred fig, the **Ficus Navia,** growing in the precinct of the Comitium, appeared to be dying, it augured ill for Rome. Confidence was restored when it revived and put forth fresh shoots.

In India, the fig is revered not only by Buddhists but by Hindus. The mighty banyan tree – **Ficus benghalensis** – is a symbol of immortality because its aerial roots, which grow down from its branches, anchor it to the ground and give it a longevity of centuries. Brahma resides in the roots, Vishnu in the trunk and Shiva in the perpetually quivering, dancing, heart-shaped leaves. Invested with sacred meanings of fertility, life and resurrection, banyan and other figs were forbidden from being cut, while planting them was an act of piety. A large banyan resembles a forest in its own right. Villages and cities grew around the capacious sociable space provided by the tree's shade and shelter; the largest banyan in the world can accommodate 20,000 within its embrace. Vadodara, Gujarat's third-largest city, means 'in the belly of the Banyan'. The very name of the tree has an urban connotation: 'banyan' derives from the 'Baniyas', a community of traders. It commemorates a tradition of outdoor meeting, buying and selling that survived long into modernity: in the 1850s, the Bombay Stock Exchange began life under a banyan tree when a group of brokers began trading beneath its canopy.

'Oh Ashvatha [the peepal tree], I honour you whose leaves are always moving,' reads a line in the Bhagavad Gita. Krishna declared that of all trees, he was the peepal. Trees – particularly the fig – and urbanisation are tied together in Indian history from the Indus Valley Civilisation onwards. The revered peepal, under whose branches Vishnu was born and Krishna died, and within which gods dwell, was planted in Hindu temples, in open-air sacred groves (called **kattes** in Bangalore) and along streets. The sacred fig grows to lofty heights, spreads wide and has destructive roots; it is not necessarily compatible with urban density. Yet many Indian neighbourhoods and street plans grew around the spacious fig, not the other way round. Numerous verdant temples, **kattes** and individual trees serving as wayside shrines broke up the hard texture of the city; they were protected in their lifetime and replaced after their death. The fig was the keystone tree of religious devotion and of urban streets, but it grew with other trees of sacred significance – neem, parijata, tamarind and coconut – which augmented urban life with their shelter, fruits and medicines.

The peepal tree is sometimes called the 'people's tree' because it was the tree of Indian village centres, street-sides and urban neighbourhoods. For much of history, the presence of trees in cities was connected to religion. But in most cases, they were restricted to defined sacred spaces, such as the fig groves of ancient Rome. In Japan, forested Shinto temples (**Chinju-no-mori**) scattered through the cityscape contained over fifteen species considered sacred, including impressive towering cedars, camphors and tabunokis. Such vast trees are known as **Goshinboku,** inhabited by **kodama,** their spirits. Pine trees are called **Matsu,** which means 'waiting for god's soul to descend from heaven'. The devotion to trees has meant that ecologically rich oases in cities have been preserved for hundreds of years with light management.

Right in the centre of Japan's third most populated metropolitan area, Nagoya, sits a tangled, ancient, fifty-acre, broadleaf forest at the Atsuta Jingu shrine. Starring among its numerous, venerable, moss-covered trees is the one known as **ookusu,** which translates simply as 'big camphor tree'; it has been worshipped for 1,300 years.

Much more recent, but no less impressive, is the Meiji Shrine in central Tokyo. Walk through it, and it feels like an ancient 170-acre virgin forest. It was planted, however, from 1913 with 122,000 hardy native species. As in other, older **Chinju-no-mori** shrines, the forest has to be self-sustaining. Trees regenerate naturally, without supplemental planting; plant litter, branches and fallen trees are allowed to decompose, enriching the soil for fungi. This is quite unlike the majority of urban woodlands, where the understory is kept tidy. The Meiji Shrine forest ecosystem, in contrast, has been left to itself for over a century, in adherence to the sacred principles of Shinto shrines, creating a wild forest in the middle of the metropolis.[6]

When the Portuguese burst onto the Indian Ocean and the South China Sea from the late fifteenth century, armed to the teeth, they encountered large trading cities such as Calicut in India and Malacca

158 Urban Jungle

on the Malay Peninsula, which appeared to be set within forests of palm and fruit trees. These were within a network of metropolises strung across Asia that had been shaped by Buddhism, Taoism and Hinduism, religions for which trees have a particular significance. Beijing, Bangkok and hundreds of others were well endowed with foliage, particularly in shrines. In south-east Asian maritime trading cities – among the wealthiest in the world – there was a manifest preference for rusticity in urban settings, a blurring that was alien to Europeans.

Such arboreal metropolises contrasted sharply with European cities. Dense, walled cities with narrow streets and alleys did not permit much room or light for trees. The European cityscape was devoid of canopy.

Today, European cities are unthinkable without their tree-lined streets, their boulevards, avenues and malls. Those three words synonymous with urban trees tell us when and why European cities got their canopies.

Boulevard derives from the Dutch word **bolwerk** and the Italian **baluardo,** both meaning 'bulwark'. The introduction of trees into cities was tied up with military technology. Advances in siege gunnery forced military engineers in Antwerp, Amsterdam and Strasbourg from the 1570s to defend cities with massive, mounded earthworks instead of walls. Other European cities – including Lucca, Gdansk, Vienna and Hamburg – adopted the technique and planted avenues of trees along the length of the earthworks to prevent erosion. The by-product of this military engineering was the creation of agreeable **allées** along the walls for promenading in times of peace. The double-planted **allée** was inherited from the then-fashionable Italian garden design.[7]

In Paris, the widest section of earthen ramparts defending the city was known as the Grand Boulevart, a corruption of the Dutch word. In 1670, in an act symbolising France's military invincibility, Louis XIV had the ramparts of Paris pulled down. Or, rather, they were cut down to become raised carriageways sixty feet wide, with two rows of elms on either side, flanked by another twenty-foot-wide **allée** for pedestrians promenading alongside. They were nicknamed **les Boulevards** and became some of the most sought-after residential districts in Paris.

City walls and trees were connected in other ways. The Italian game **pallamaglio** – known as **le jeu du mail** or **palmail** in France and pall mall in England – became popular at the same time that city walls were getting a green makeover. The game, much like croquet, was played by the upper classes on lawns surrounded by **allées** on the periphery of cities. The association of tree-lined spaces with ball games is why we still talk of 'bowling alleys', which comes from the French **allée.** Beautiful sylvian malls appeared alongside the walls of Paris in the 1590s; they were copied in Dutch cities soon after. Berlin got its version, Unter den Linden ('Under the Lime

Trees') in 1647, a kilometre-long former hunting trail running through sandy fields outside the city walls, planted with parallel rows of 1,000 limes and 1,000 nut trees. Pall Mall and the Mall on the western outskirts of London date from the same time, when kings and nobles played pall mall under the shade of trees far from the throbbing metropolis. Such malls were also used as bowling **allées** and archery ranges.[8]

Another Italian fashion – promenading in carriages along the Corso outside Florence on the banks of the Arno – caught on as well. Nostalgic for the Corso, Marie de Medici, the Italian wife of the French king Henry IV, had the Cours-la-Reine constructed in 1616, a wide carriageway with four parallel lines of elms alongside the Seine on the edge of Paris. The Paseo del Prado was laid out in Madrid in the 1650s as a fashionable boulevard in imitation of the French **cours.** The word 'avenue' originated from the French **avenir** – to approach. Avenues were planted on the approaches to Paris in the seventeenth century, creating grand entry routes into the capital reminiscent of landscaped hunting parks and the formal drives leading to Italian country houses. The most famous avenue in the world, the Champs-Élysées, began life as the Avenue des Tuileries, a suburban approach road lined with elms, horse chestnuts and planes running through fields and market gardens.[9]

Boulevards and avenues are now the most characteristic sites of city trees the world over. They began life in Paris in the seventeenth century much like city parks – as settings on the edge of town for the exclusive leisure of courtly elites whose wealth and world views derived from the countryside. Note that it was on the periphery of cities. Only in Amsterdam and other Dutch towns were trees incorporated into the heart of the city. In 1641, John Evelyn described Amsterdam as 'appearing like a city in a forest'. '[N]othing can be more beautiful', he added, than the sight of uniform houses facing canals fringed with limes; it was a 'ravishing prospect'. The effect was remarkable because it was so new; a French writer said that he could not tell whether Amsterdam was a city in a forest or a forest in a city. It resembled a characteristic south-east Asian city in that respect.[10]

Trees were easier to integrate into new cities, particularly in North America. There, colonial cities were reconceived as combining the best of rural and urban, avoiding the mistakes of European urbanisation. Writing in 1748, the Swedish professor Peter Kalm extolled the street trees of downtown Manhattan, commenting that the beautiful appearance, scents and shade of sycamores, black locusts, limes and elms made it 'extremely pleasant to walk in the town, for it seemed quite like a garden'. These New York trees gave home not only to a large number of birds, but to 'very clamorous' frogs: at night 'they frequently make such a noise, that it is difficult for a person to make himself heard'. Loved by the people, trees were treated with suspicion by the Common Council, which decided to remove them in 1791 because they were a traffic nuisance.[11]

By the mid-nineteenth century, Savannah, Georgia, was known as the 'Forest City' because it was lavishly embowered with evergreen oaks and chinaberry trees, the legacy of its colonial and post-revolutionary sylvian proclivities. Street trees were integrated into Savannah from its foundation in 1733. As a city ordinance had it: 'Experience has fully proved that great advantages are derived to the Inhabitants of the City from trees being planted in the streets and squares, from the shade they afford, the heat of a very sultry climate is lessened . . . Council being desirous that the Inhabitants should meet every advantage that Trees planted in our streets and squares can afford, have resolved to extend its protection to all trees standing at this time in our streets, lanes, squares, or which may be hereafter planted either at the public expense or by Individual.' A visitor to Philadelphia basked in the 'freshness and purity' of the city afforded by the long avenues bordered with Lombardy poplars and other species. President John Quincy Adams had elms planted along Pennsylvania Avenue in the 1820s.[12]

Back in Europe, Amsterdam and Paris set fresh

standards of urban beauty. As cities expanded, they enfolded suburban boulevards, malls and avenues into their social and cultural fabric. Places that had been peripheral to cities became their focal points, with trees bequeathing them their ceremonial majesty. Trees went from being amenities for aristocratic recreation to statements of power: Unter den Linden is anchored by the Brandenburg Gate; the Mall by Buckingham Palace; and the Champs-Élysées by the Arc de Triomphe and the Place de la Concorde. Avenues create vistas that direct the eye to monuments and key edifices; they form landscapes of order. Trees made the formal avenues of modern cities resemble, as Lewis Mumford wrote, parade grounds.

They were an architectural embellishment, sought after by the well-off to soften the harsh edges of the city and impart the grandeur of their country estates to the urban environment. Leicester Square in London became the first urban plaza in Europe to be planted with 'walks' of neatly lined trees in the 1660s. By the end of the eighteenth century, London's fashionable squares were thick with trees taller than the surrounding houses. When new streets were created in the wake of expansion or were carved into the existing city, at least in the glitzier districts, trees became an, if not **the,** essential aspect of their design in places such as Paris, Toulouse, Lyon and London. In the wake of the Napoleonic conquest of Europe, boulevards were introduced under French influence across the continent, in cities such as Brussels, Turin and Düsseldorf.

But it was the rebuilding of Paris by Haussmann in the 1850s that seared boulevards, avenues and squares (**places** in French) into the imagination of city planners. Haussmann cut long, straight, broad boulevards into the heart of the metropolis, providing ample room for the 600,000 trees he had planted. The capital had lacked a canopy when it was a rabbit warren of cramped medieval streets. Framing buildings along straight streets, trees created instant beauty.

Paris became the modern template of how a city should look and feel. From Haussmann onwards, trees became indispensable to the urban landscape. Paris's boulevards inspired public authorities in American cities to soften and beautify the geometrical regularity of the grid system. Commonwealth Avenue Mall in Boston, for instance, was planted with a quadruple row of elms, zelkovas, maples and green ashes in the 1880s, transforming a residential street into a Parisian-style grand boulevard. In the same decade, Washington D.C.'s avenues were planted out with pin oaks, elms and limes.

Trees came marching into town. They were planted in central boulevards and suburban avenues; they adorned the new municipal parks of the late nineteenth century; and they became the unmistakable

feature of urban cemeteries. When Japan began
to modernise after the Meiji Restoration in 1868,
stately ornamental trees became a feature of city
roadsides. European-style buildings in Ginza, Tokyo
were complemented with black pine, cherry, maple
and black locust. By the eve of the Second World
War, there were over 270,000 street trees in Tokyo,
predominantly the London plane and the magnificent ginkgo biloba, most either planted since the
1870s or replanted after the Great Kanto Earthquake
(1923). In an age of intense urbanisation, treescapes
had become one of the leading signifiers not only
of modernity but of global prestige. After the reunification of Italy and the restoration of Rome as the
capital, trees were planted throughout a city which
had been notably ungreen. The stone pine was favoured because it had strong associations with ancient Rome. Pines and cypresses, so redolent of a lost
or imagined past, were used to showcase archaeological monuments which had previously been barren;
holm oaks, reminiscent of the Italian countryside
and Renaissance gardens, graced public squares. The
Italian conquest of Libya in 1911 resulted in a massive planting of palms in Italian cities: the street tree
was an everlasting reminder of imperial triumph.[13]

One of the most delicious urban canopies you can
experience is that which turns the streets of what was
once the French Concession in Shanghai into cool
green tunnels. They were planted from 1887 to give

the Chinese city the feel of a Parisian street. They are a reminder that the arboreal greening of cities was an imperial project, conducted in Australasia, Africa, Asia and the Americas. When the British planned New Delhi in 1912, the unmistakable hallmark of modernity and imperial control was the canopy. 'Trees will be everywhere,' stated the report of the planning committee, 'in every garden however small it be, and along the sides of every roadway, and Imperial Delhi will be in the main a sea of foliage. It may be called a city, but it is going to be quite different from any city that the world has known.'[14]

Not only were trees the central feature of the new imperial capital, but over 1,000 acres of the Central Ridge were reforested as a topographical feature emphasising the sylvian perfection of the new capital. Observed from the ridge, New Delhi is indeed lost in its sea of foliage, true to the intentions of its designers. From the right vantage point, the domes of the Rashtrapati Bhavan – India's presidential palace, formerly Viceroy's House – and other government buildings poke out of an immense, uninterrupted, emerald canopy. The administrative city – with its geometric pattern of shaded avenues – anticipated new town design and suburban developments throughout the twentieth century. Readily apparent is the connection between power and greenery. Look at satellite images of Delhi and the greenness of New Delhi stands out from the monolithic grey of the rest of the megacity: as in suburban arcadias all over the world, the privilege of living in an urban forest is reserved for the wealthy.

It is little wonder that the British wanted trees in their imperial showcase; they are by far the most significant regulators of the urban microclimate. According to New York City's commissioner of health in 1872, street trees were badly needed to save lives from excessive summer temperatures. It was an early recognition of the urgency of using urban ecology to mitigate the urban heat island. In tropical cities, trees attenuate solar radiation by 76.3–92 per cent and significantly reduce heat through shade and evapotranspiration. A street tree can reduce a person's 'physiological equivalent temperature' (PET) – a measure of thermal comfort – by 10–25°C, depending on a city's climate. They also offer biogeochemical processing services: in other words, they filter and clean the air. Chicago's trees have been estimated to sequester 5,575 metric tons of air pollution and 315,800 metric tons of carbon a year, offsetting the emissions of 42,106 households. There is a reason why the proximity of trees can increase property values by between 5 per cent and 20 per cent: they improve quality of life, mental wellbeing and physical health. Singapore transformed from a polluted colonial city to the hypermodern Garden City from the 1960s, with the strategy of attracting investment and wealthy expatriates. The long-serving prime minister Lee Kuan Yew said in 2000 of the reforestation of the city state with 5 million trees and shrubs that 'no other project has brought richer rewards to the region'.

Our cities are getting hotter. Kuala Lumpur now has a heat island effect of between 4.2°C and 9.5°C. Temperatures in Louisville, Kentucky – America's fastest-warming city – can be 10°C hotter in the centre compared to the suburbs. Air quality is also deteriorating as urbanisation ramps up. The last decades of the twentieth century and the first decades of this millennium have seen concentrated efforts to get more trees into cities as a means of mitigating the searing intensity of climate change. Where once trees were there to prettify the city, we now need them for our very survival as an urban species.[15]

Multiple cities around the world – as diverse in size and climate as New York, Edinburgh and Accra – have, since the first decade of the twenty-first century, signed up to the Million Tree Initiative, a mass planting project. The urgency of the present tree-planting surge is evident throughout much of the world. It is intended to counter not only imminent danger but an existing threat. In 2013, Beijing suffered its 'airpocalypse', when pollution levels were thirty times higher than that deemed safe by the WHO: it would have been safer to breathe the air in the smoking lounge of an airport than in the streets of the city. The response in the capital and elsewhere in some of the most vulnerable

and polluted cities on the planet has been 'forest city'
campaigns in 170 Chinese cities, which aim to increase canopy coverage to 40 per cent of urban areas.
'Let the forest enter the city and the city embrace
the forest,' went the slogan. Fuzhou – nicknamed
the 'City of the Banyan' – created one hundred new
boulevards lined with banyans, camphors and golden
rain trees.[16]

No one went so far as Bo Xilai, the Communist
Party secretary of Chongqing between 2007 and
2012. Bo Xilai aimed to make Chongqing the
National Forest City of China – one of the most
ambitious street tree-planting campaigns in history. Every day in spring, the streets of China's
fastest-growing city were crowded with trucks
bringing in stacks of ginkgos. They included some
specimens that were over one hundred years old and
cost $45,000 each. These magnificent, transplanted
trees were planted thickly around the city, lining
street after street. 'Chongqing's Breath of Fresh Air',
rhapsodised the press in the heyday of afforestation
as they celebrated the city's swift green makeover
that saw canopy cover increase to 38.3 per cent. So
great was Bo's passion for ginkgos that he was spending $1.5 billion a year on them. In doing so, he not
only took thousands of banyans to the chainsaw
but pushed Chongqing to the brink of bankruptcy
before he was removed from office in disgrace.[17]

Bo's arboreal megalomania exemplifies in an

extreme way the urgency of turning cities into forests not just in smoggy China but on all continents. In Guangzhou, an attempt in 2021 to chop down some of the 270,000 massive banyans that make up its forest in order to make the city more 'visually permeable' was thwarted when five senior city officials were severely penalised by the Central Commission for Discipline Inspection. People love trees; the officials had already faced public backlash in the form of online petitions and performance art. One resident declared: 'Those trees were the first inhabitants of the city.'[18]

Metropolises that are full of trees and green spaces are not just more resilient against climate change but, in the twenty-first century more than ever, attractive places for businesses and investment. The costs of **not** having an adequate number of trees are becoming apparent.

Louisville is experiencing spiralling temperatures because it has an abysmally low coverage of trees – just 8 per cent in its downtown area. In 2012, it was revealed that cities in the U.S. were losing 4 million trees a year to development. It is sad to consider that India – once famous for its historic urban forestry and sacred groves – has denuded its cities of trees. It is no coincidence that Indian metropolises are among the most vulnerable to climate change and are experiencing a rapidly deteriorating quality of life. Bangalore, a city that once attracted immigrants, colonisers and businesses alike because of its cool microclimate created by its thick foliage and lakes, has lost 88 per cent of its vegetation to construction and road widening. Thousands upon thousands of trees, including vast sacred banyans and peepals that stood on polluted roads offering shade to street vendors, playing children and socialising adults, have been felled at a time when the city's temperature is projected to increase by 10°C. The City of Banyans itself – Vadodara – has lost half its canopy in recent years. 'Where have all the peepal trees gone?' read a headline in the **Hindu** newspaper. Where indeed.[19]

The solemn funeral cortege wound its way towards the state assembly building in Mumbai. Then, the 'body' was revealed – part of the trunk of a slain banyan tree, one of thousands felled to make way for the new metro system. When the authorities wanted to cut down four massive trees that shaded 2.5 acres in the middle of Bangalore in 2017, the protests were highly emotional. A year earlier, 8,000 Bangalorians formed a massive human chain to prevent the construction of a steel flyover that would have required the murder of thousands of peepals, banyans and other beloved trees. 'This steel flyover was not a steel flyover,' according to Priya Chetty Rajagopal, a citizen activist. 'It was a Godzilla that basically could damage the heart and soul of Bengaluru.' In both cases, the community won, saving their canopies from rampant development. In 2018, plans to chop down 16,000 trees in Delhi sparked furious protests in a city where 112,169 trees had already been felled legally since 2005 and an unknown number illegally. Campaigners employed social media to organise sit-ins, candlelit vigils and twenty-four-hour patrols to block the chainsaw. They also took the matter to the high court. On 4 July that year, the court banned any further felling, saying it would 'not allow Delhi to die at the cost of the redevelopment projects'.[20]

The ancient spiritual connection that Indians have with trees has spawned a proliferation of citizen groups dedicated to resisting the onslaught against nature in cities. Time and again in this book we have seen ordinary people turn out to demand the kind of wilder, greener city they wanted in the face of unthinking expansion: the Londoners who fought for their rough heaths, the Green Guerrillas of New York, the protestors in Berlin who battled to save the forests and meadows that had sprouted in the derelict centre of the city. There is a conflict always between the kind of nature planted from 'above' and that which is relished by individuals and communities. In India, reverence for trees has given birth to an unprecedented grassroots movement that is proliferating in the 2020s. It is a battle for the soul of the city.

So intense has the onslaught against nature been that many urban trees have already been converted into lumber, and the task of regreening Indian cities is a matter of community action. As a young man,

Shubhendu Sharma, then working on the assembly line at a Toyota factory in Bangalore, met the Japanese botanist Akira Miyawaki. After the meeting, Sharma stopped making cars and started making urban jungles. He founded a company called Afforestt in 2011; within eight years, he had created 144 tiny wild forests in fifty cities and shared his story with the world via TED Talks.

Decades earlier, Akira Miyawaki studied the **chinju-no-mori** – the densely forested shrines – and found they contained a huge amount of native biodiversity squeezed into small, often urban patches. They were, to him, like time capsules, an undisturbed layering of indigenous species consisting of main tree species, subspecies, shrubs and ground-covering herbs. They taught Miyawaki to plant a selection of native tree seedlings at unusually high densities – between 20,000 and 30,000 per hectare – in prepared soil. According to the Miyawaki method, for two years, the site is weeded and watered. Meanwhile, the closely packed shoots compete for light and water, stimulating fast growth. After two years, the mini-forest is left entirely to itself. A Miyawaki forest grows fast: while a natural one in Japan could take 150–200 years to mature through a process of ecological succession, his takes just fifteen to twenty, by which time the taller trees have grown to twenty metres. Since the 1970s, Miyawaki has planted 40 million trees around the world, often on degraded land. The micro-forests act as urban cool islands in dense cities. They absorb up to thirty times more carbon dioxide and particulates than conventional plantations.[21]

At disused locomotive diesel sheds in Bangalore, a Miyawaki forest of 4,100 trees from forty-nine species grows on 1,250 square metres. Planted in 2016, it is one of many appearing on small patches in tree-denuded Bangalore and other Indian cities. Forests don't have to be on public land; gardeners are taking matters into their own hands. Appalled at the conversion of Bangalore from garden city to concrete jungle, retired IT engineer Nataraja Upadhya turned his inner-city terrace into an evergreen micro-jungle. In order to show the city how tiny spaces in a grey city can support dense vegetation, he planted 300 varieties of plant, including one hundred trees; vines and trees emmesh his house and spill out into the street. Throughout India, people are fighting back against the simplification of the urban landscape, turning back to the cool, tree-filled gardens of the past. 'Prim manicured lawns are being put to pasture,' the **Hindu** newspaper reported in 2021. 'In their place, sassy urban jungles are springing up across the country, ablaze with fruit trees, flowering shrubs, water bodies and verdant greenery.'[22]

If public authorities don't care about trees, the community responds: people like Nataraja Upadhya, Shubhendu Sharma and countless others are fighting to restore India's lost urban canopy, one small patch at a time. Their lonely fight should inspire others: the Miyawaki method offers a chance for greening the poorest and most crowded areas of tree-starved, sweltering megacities in quick time.

Trees are adept at surviving in cities. We are perfectly capable of finding space for them within the built environment. They have changed the way we experience cities over the last couple of centuries. Imagine a city with all the buildings, roads and railways gone, but the trees left standing: that's what MIT's Senseable City Lab has done in a project known as Treepedia. Using Google Street View, digital maps of thirty global cities have been produced showing every individual street tree. The results are beautiful images of the familiar outlines and street plans of cities made manifest only in vivid green dots standing out against a black background. This is the city as you've never seen it before – something approaching a forest. Tampa, Florida, with a roadside canopy covering 36 per cent of its urban area, is revealed as a luminous grid of forest.[23]

If you added in the trees growing in parks, gardens, cemeteries and railway lines, you would see an even larger forest emerging. Imagine the city like this and you see the intricate aerial network of branches and leaves providing continuous corridors for species of all kinds. Each tree is an ecosystem in its own right, maintaining habitats for insects, animals and birds.

A study of Warsaw found 2,000-3,000 invertebrates within one cubic metre of tree canopy, supporting populations of birds and bats.

According to the definition of the UN's Food and Agriculture Organization, a forest is an area that has a tree coverage of at least 20 per cent. In London, there are almost as many trees as Londoners – 8.4 million – providing an umbrella that covers 22 per cent of the metropolis. New York has an almost identical proportion, and in Atlanta, Georgia, the share of space belonging to magnolias, hickories, Southern pines, dogwoods and water oaks (among others) is estimated at 48 per cent. America's 'city in a forest' is described in Tom Wolfe's **A Man in Full** (1998): 'He looked away from the buildings and out over the ocean of trees . . . the trees stretched on in every direction. They were Atlanta's greatest natural resource, those trees were. People loved to live beneath them.'

Cities have evolved into large, humanmade forests. In the global north, this has been a recent and rapid experience. According to Paul Wood – the author of **London is a Forest** – in 1921, some 60 per cent of London's trees were planes. Today that species makes up just 3 per cent of London's urban jungle. The gigantic, stately planes have not been cut down in great number; rather, they have been joined by millions of other trees over the last hundred years. It is a startling figure, testament to a century's worth of planting not only in London but in cities around the globe. Numbers of trees have grown hugely, but so too has diversity. London now has between 350 and 500 tree species and cultivars.

Trees help mitigate the effects of climate change. They cannot cure it. Cities need their street trees and micro-forests to cool them and filter their air. But even more importantly, they need actual, large, intact forests.

'[I]t's the color that overwhelms at first – the fecund, verdant green that fills the gaze in all directions and swallows you whole. Then, the smell, of peat and petrichor. Then, the sound of branches swaying and leaves rustling and water rushing and the occasional **crunch** of something moving, unseen, in the tangles and shadows.'

'In the near distance are aging neighborhoods and the city's expanding center, endless ribbons of concrete, the ceaseless bustle. But all that seems a forever away beneath this canopy of hardwoods, this accidental paradise of thousands of acres . . .'

These are the words of journalist Robert Wilonsky in 2019, describing the underappreciated and little-known Great Trinity Forest, a 6,000-acre ancient woodland that slashes through the centre of Dallas, Texas, the most corporate of corporate cities. It happens to be the United States' largest urban forest. 'This place', wrote Wilonsky, 'is where I go to feel like a stranger in the city of my birth.'[24]

It is a large hardwood bottomland forest, saved

from the expansion of the metropolis because it lies in the floodplain of the Trinity River. Much of the original forest was denuded in the nineteenth and twentieth centuries. But as the city suburbanised northwards, the area was neglected and the trees sprouted again. Water bubbles up from urban Dallas's last remaining spring, known as Big Spring, into a lake; there are giant burr oaks that started life before the Mayflower set sail; ponds, swamps and meandering creeks break up the canopy. From Piedmont Ridge you look over the green leaf roof and see only the skyscrapers of downtown Dallas. This forest is the product of neglect; no one knew what to do with this wild leftover in the heart of Dallas, so it became a shabby, half-forgotten place, a dumping ground for an estimated 2 million cubic tons of illegal trash and pollution, the site of illicit mining, hidden marijuana farms and meth labs, and homeless camps. When the abused river floods, it brings up tons of plastic and waste. The forest is Dallas's secret hiding in plain sight, at once a miracle of nature and a place permeated with the sinister. Some of the forest is so impenetrable that no one ever goes there; and so it harbours white-tailed deer, coyotes, feral hogs, turtles, toads, beavers, otters and alligators.

The Great Trinity Forest is an accidental resource of nature, a forest forgotten by time. Most of the urban forest is a poor kind of forest: trees that stand lonely in asphalt or a desert of lawn devoid of a dense understory. The Great Trinity Forest is different; it supports a teeming forest-floor ecosystem. Dallas is lucky to have it; it may well be critical to its future. So too are other cities that have large areas of forest that were spared as the city grew around them. Overton Park, preserved amid multi-lane highways in the middle of Memphis, contains one of Tennessee's few surviving old-growth forests; it dates back to the end of the last Ice Age. New York has retained 10,542 acres of forest patches containing 5 million trees, including stands of native maritime coastal forest at Inwood Hill Park.

During the Second World War, bombing destroyed many of the 200,000 trees in Berlin's Tiergarten park; the survivors were chopped down because of coal shortages in the post-war winter, and emergency vegetable gardens were grown in their place. In 1945, just 700 trees remained. On 17 March 1949, Ernst Reuter, mayor of Berlin, planted a linden; West German cities donated a further 250,000 trees. Under the aegis of the landscape architect Willy Alverdes, the park's original baroque elements were not widely reconstructed. Instead, Alverdes looked further back to the past, when the area was a boggy, riparian forest, in order to reconstruct the 'wildness' that the modern 'city-dweller was instinctively in search of'. Today, it is an unusually dense forest for the heart of a city, a heavily layered, wild thicket. The largest urban forest in the world at 98,000 acres is Tijuca National Park in the centre of Rio de Janeiro, the refuge of sixty-seven endangered species.[25]

In his article on the Great Trinity Forest, Wilonsky quoted Ben Sandifer, Dallas accountant by day and tireless defender of the forest in his spare time. 'There is an immense, rich history that speaks to Dallas itself,' he said of the forest. 'People wonder why we're here, in the middle of this blackland prairie, and the answer lies on the other side of the levee in the forest. It's easy to figure out the attraction people had to this area.' Sandifer points to an important truth: for most of our history, cities were dependent on their forests. The survival of Dallas's eerie forest is a reminder not only of the city's origins but of the vital relationship between trees and cities through time.[26]

When the Romans founded London in the first century CE, it was surrounded by forests and marshes, a landscape largely unchanged since the end of the Ice Age. Over a millennium later, William Fitzstephen described the Great Forest of Middlesex – which stretched twenty miles northwards from meadows adjacent to the old Roman wall, covering most of what would become the northern part of Greater London – as 'a vast forest, its copses dense with foliage concealing wild animals – stags, does, boars, and wild bulls'. Writing a little later, the chronicler Matthew Parris said this impenetrable wood of sessile oak, hornbeam, beech and service trees harboured not only wolves but robbers, fugitives and outlaws. On the other side of the River Thames, another large oak forest – the Great North Wood – stretched all the way from the riverbanks southwards to Croydon. The modern suburban district called Penge derives from the Celtic **Penceat,** which means 'edge of the wood'. Penge, along with Norwood, Gipsy Hill and Forest Hill, hint of their past settings as villages of the peri-urban forest.

Nuremberg, in common with all other European cities, needed its encircling forest, the Reichswald, for its very survival. Owned and maintained by the municipality from 1427, it fattened the citizens' pigs. It yielded firewood and charcoal for fuel that not only kept urbanites warm but supported metal- and glass-working industries and lime-burners, not to say bakers and brewers. It provided clay for bricks and quarries for sandstone. The bees of the thickets produced honey (Nuremberg is still famous for its Lebkuchen gingerbread) and wax for candles and polish.[27]

Big population centres in the medieval period therefore needed forests as much as they needed fields. And they required trees closer at hand than crops because timber was expensive to transport. The counties ringing London were more wooded than anywhere else in the country because the population of the English capital –100,000 people – dwarfed all other urban centres and required, in the early four-teenth century, a forested area of 800 square miles to provide 141,000 tons of wood per year. London structured ecosystems with a radius of roughly sixty miles around the city, within which forests were maintained to supply the capital. Madrid and other urban centres in Europe relied on forested areas of a similar magnitude. Paris, a far larger metropolis than London and Nuremberg, suffered from a chronically insecure food supply system because it needed, from its immediate hinterland, the produce of the forest.[28]

London's great primeval woods, however, had dwindled by the early nineteenth century to a pitiful collection of dispersed copses and isolated woodland collectively making up just 3,000 acres in Middlesex. Because London was a port, and because it had easy access by ship to the coalfields of northeast England, it had no need for forests as a source of heat. The intimate connection between civilised city and wild wood was severed by king coal from the early seventeenth century.

By contrast, at the beginning of the nineteenth century, the Nuremberg Reichswald remained large at 124 square miles because the city had not yet re-placed wood with coal as a source of fuel. The city states of the Holy Roman Empire, Flanders in the Netherlands and parts of Italy had owned extensive municipal woods for centuries. Frankfurt secured its Stadtwald in stages between 1221 and 1484, pur-chasing forestry from the emperors and the Teutonic

Order; Rostock got its 30,000-acre Rostocker Heide ('Heath') in 1252. While deforestation was rampant in the countryside, the intense pressures of urbanisation resulted in a significant **increase** in woodland and hedgerows on urban margins between the sixteenth and eighteenth centuries as municipalities and rulers seized control over adjacent woods and managed them sustainably. In Hanover's Eilenriede, its municipal forest, watchtowers were manned to prevent wood theft. Frankfurt's mayors were required to serve as forest managers after their term of office expired, taking responsibility for afforestation. From the eighteenth century, the Stadtwald was managed by full-time staff led by the chief forester.

Venice, hungry for timber with which to build the maritime city, construct its mighty arsenal and put its ships to sea, possessed massive, highly managed, state-owned forests on the mainland upon which its very future depended. At a much later date in the mid-nineteenth century, but for similar reasons, the bottomland forests of the Trinity valley in Texas provided the preconditions for urbanisation. Forests spelt water and life; they yielded fuel and building materials for infant Dallas. No forest, no city.

And, in many cases, no city, no forest: trees survived to serve the needs of smelters and smiths, bakers, brewers and builders. If you went back in time to European and many Asian cities of the pre-industrial age you would have found them nestled not in landscapes of fields but in the wombs of forests. The same was true for New York where, according to an early Dutch visitor in 1624, the 'land is excellent and agreeably full of noble forest trees and grape vines'. Extensive stands of oak, tulip, chestnut and beech covered the majority of Manhattan Island until the last years of the eighteenth century. The vast wooded tracts fell victim to war and climate change. During the American Revolution, while the British were occupying New York, deforestation was intense during the exceptionally cold winters of 1779 through to 1781 when Upper New York Bay froze to the extent that people could travel by sleigh to Staten Island. Trees were felled for fuel in these arctic months but also for mile upon mile of defensive fortifications. Surveying Manhattan Island from New Jersey in 1782, George Washington observed that 'the island is totally stripped of trees; low bushes . . . appear in places which were covered with wood in the year 1776'. That denuded shrubland covered three-quarters of the island, where once a great forest stood. New York's timber needs had to be satisfied at higher cost from further afield.

Coal killed the peri-urban forest in England very early; it also provided the conditions for London's swift population and spatial growth from the late sixteenth century as it oozed into the countryside. London was thus freed, relatively early, from its dependence on a key natural resource: this was a harbinger of things to come. Once fossil fuels became the predominant source of energy, the tangible benefits of the nearby forest disappeared and the bond between tree and city was broken.

But in many places, it took on a new form. Today, 14 per cent of Frankfurt's area is occupied by its vast municipal forests. The largest wooded area is found to the south of the River Main, but the entire city is dotted with the legacies of its medieval life-support system – ancient urban woods surrounded by modern city. Leipzig is more or less bisected by one of Europe's largest alluvial hardwood forests. Nuremberg's city-owned Reichswald – today almost one hundred square miles – encloses the Erlanger-Nürnberg-Fürth conurbation like a crescent moon. The forests of dozens of German cities are indomitable green walls that have restrained and shaped urban development for centuries, even after they outwore their economic usefulness. Cities in Germany, Switzerland and Austria have grown around the woods. Today, some of humanity's most extensive urban forests are found in those countries. They provide a model of sustainability that should inspire the rest of the world.

They were not sold off to the highest bidder, as they were elsewhere to make room for urban growth, because forests took on a new kind of usefulness in the industrial nineteenth century. In Germany, municipal forests had long been woven not only into the urban fabric but into the urban imagination. Forests were bound up with national identity and Germany's concept of its deep past. The depiction by the Roman historian Tacitus of primordial Germany as a vast landscape of dense forests, populated by fearsome Teutonic warrior tribes invincible against the legions, predominated in the nineteenth century. In an age of urbanisation, industrialisation and nationalism, the existence of forests close to cities sustained the German connection with its mythic past; lose them and you would sacrifice German-ness itself. If the Greeks and Italians had classical ruins where they could reconnect with ancient values and virtues, the Germans had their equivalent time portal in the form of semi-sacred groves which were akin to organic temples and living monuments. As one nineteenth-century writer had it: 'The forest was the setting of our ancient history, the forest is the setting of our native legends, and even the last descendants of those legends, our fairy tales, take place largely in the forest.'

Urban forests were essential to the physical and psychological strength of the heirs of the Teutons, balancing 'the nerve-shattering unrest of the cities' with places of fresh air, relaxation and exercise. Urban forests were more important than rural forests because they were where, for one paleo-botanist, the 'original nature of our homeland' was still accessible to the majority of the population. For the liberal-left scientist and educator, Emil Adolf Rossmässler, urban forests were political. Urban workers had a

right to nature, to the wild sylvian commons that encircled cities. As Rossmässler had it, forests were bound up with social and political equality. Every German should have the right to walk from congested city straight into a wooded wilderness. For all kinds of reasons, from the political to the spiritual, trees were sacrosanct.[29]

In Berlin, people fought long and hard to secure their right to the forest. The imperial capital of Germany was one of the densest and least green cities in Europe. But on its fringes were forests, including the 7,400-acre Grunewald just six miles from the Brandenburg Gate, which was immune from urban development because it was a royal hunting preserve. By the 1890s, the growth of Berlin from a moderately sized city to the second-largest metropolis in Europe meant that the thousands of trespassing urban picnickers and weekenders mooching about the trees of the Grunewald and swimming in its lakes were rather getting in the way of the pomp and splendour of the royal hunt. They walked or, from 1879, came by train to the Bahnhof Grunewald. The unruly people of Berlin, bent on recreation in a wood they saw as theirs, forced the Kaiser out of his forest to more distant reserves untarnished by the grubby hand of the city. Berliners voted with their feet, their picnic blankets and their beer kegs: the Grunewald became a place for weekend excursions to play, drink, eat, swim and sing once the Kaiser was abruptly displaced. With no use for hunting, however, the Grunewald became a state asset: it could generate income as it was sold off, bit by bit, for expensive suburban villas.

The impending destruction of the Grunewald met sustained opposition from the working class of Berlin, the liberal press and city politicians in the first decade of the twentieth century. The forest, they argued, belonged to the people of the city. In 1904, the **Berliner Volksblatt,** the city's working-class, socialist newspaper, issued a rousing 'declaration of protest against the destruction of the Grunewald'. The liberal-left **Berliner Volks-Zeitung** and the **Berliner Tageblatt,** the highest-circulation German newspaper, banded together to formally address the government to save the wood. Battle was formed between public opinion and speculative developers. Workers at a large meeting at the Viktoria Brewery vowed to rise in protest if the Grunewald was violated. For working-class Berliners, the Grunewald belonged to them; it was woven into their family lives and their experience of being urban. They were fully prepared to fight against 'forest slaughter'. The campaign to save the forest and retain the right to nature was emotional and hard-fought. It was one of the first mass environmental campaigns in history, a precursor to the ecological activism of later generations of Berliners.[30]

After a decade-long battle with the Prussian state,

the city finally purchased the wood in 1911, following in the footsteps of cities such as Frankfurt and Nuremberg which had invested so much in forests long ago in the Middle Ages. The state pledged to maintain the Grunewald, along with an additional 16,000 acres of forestry it acquired at the same time, in their 'natural state', along with the lakes and bogs that made up the glacier-formed landscape of the Brandenburg region. Things did not stop there. The creation of Greater Berlin in 1920 increased the area of the city thirteenfold to 340 square miles, absorbing much of its rural and suburban hinterland. It engrossed peripheral towns such as Charlottenburg, Spandau and Schönberg, giving the capital a whopping 46,950 acres of public green space, more than a fifth of the entire metropolitan area. Two-thirds of this public land was forested, preserved in perpetuity as wild terrain fringing Berlin. Today, the Landesforstamt Berlin manages 112 square miles of urban forest within the boundaries of the metropolis. The magnitude of this can be gauged by comparison with other cities: New York has sixteen square miles of dispersed woodland and London twenty-seven.

The city forests of Germany have had a turbulent history. Overexploited at times, many were replanted with fast-growing pines. They suffered severe damage during the Napoleonic Wars and, more grievously, the Second World War, when they were used for military purposes, bombed by the Allies, stripped for firewood and dumped on with rubble. Only from the late 1970s were they taken in hand and managed to maximise their biodiversity. But they still exist, treasured as a precious resource in marked contrast to cities that bulldozed their forests as they expanded. Germany was way ahead of the rest of the planet. Cities such as Dresden, Nuremberg and Berlin show not only that dense, populated cities are compatible with sizeable forests but that the quality of urban life is enhanced by them. Forests bring protection and pleasure. Germans can thank generations of their forebears who prized their urban forests and, at times, threatened retribution on those who dared violate the trees.

There are signs that the rest of the world is catching up. In 2020, Madrid announced plans for the Bosque Metropolitano, a forty-seven-mile forest belt around the city, to improve its poor air quality. Beijing is in the midst of a monumental afforestation programme on its periphery, creating what is called its 'green necklace'. The city planted 54 million trees on 173,000 acres between 2012 and 2016 alone as a barrier against the Siberian winds that sweep across the Mongolian Plateau in winter, bringing with it sand from the Gobi that puts the megalopolis in danger of desertification. The dunes creep closer to Beijing every year, while sandstorms combined with pollution make the air quality hazardous. Faced with landslides, Lima is turning some of its surrounding hills into forest parks. These plans sound radical. But it is a return to a historical norm in which cities needed trees on their fringes for their survival. Forget green belts: cities need forest belts. If we treated forests like oceans – places where it is impossible to build upon even if we wanted – our cities would grow round them or stop at their edges.

Yet many cities, particularly in environmentally critical or vulnerable areas, are on a crash course with forests. Of the nineteen cities in Brazil that doubled in size between 2000 and 2010, ten are in the Amazon. Cities are encroaching on the Atlantic Forest, the Congo Basin and the Indonesian rainforests as well. Yet there is growing awareness that cities need the embrace of forests as a matter of urgency. In September 2019, the UN Food and Agriculture Organization announced a 'Great Green Wall for Cities'. The project aimed to fund and facilitate 500,000 hectares of new urban forests and the preservation of 300,000 hectares of existing forests ringing ninety cities in Asia and Africa by 2030. Once completed, the wall should capture between 0.5 and five gigatons of CO_2 a year.

Whether this ambitious project is financially or politically feasible is open to question. But it is a powerful acknowledgement that cities need forests if they are to survive the climate emergency. A forest with thousands of trees releasing moisture into the air is the best air conditioning you can get. Not only do peri-urban forests provide a host of eco-system services, but they act as a bulwark against sprawl, one of the leading causes of climate change and environmental damage. No forest, no city: that was discovered in Rio de Janeiro in the nineteenth century. The destruction of the Tijuca Forest on the edge of the city for sugarcane farms in the seven-teenth century and coffee plantations in the eigh-teenth meant Rio was facing disaster; its water supply was drying up and it was experiencing flash floods. In 1861, Emperor Pedro II of Brazil was forced to estab-lish federal control over the land and restore its func-tioning ecosystem. The enormous present-day forest in the middle of the metropolis is almost entirely the result of natural regeneration, a showcase of ecologi-cal restoration working alongside urban growth.

New York City's most important forest lies not within its borders but 125 miles away in the Catskill Mountains. When New Yorkers get a drink of tap water, they are getting the produce of a forest. Since 1915, the city has been drawing water – one bil-lion gallons a day – from the lakes and reservoirs of the mountains. Critical to the city's survival is the forest that makes up the greater part of the one million acres of watershed. New York's tap water is unfiltered; the ecosystem does the work of purifying it. Trees protect the soil, filter the water and reduce runoff after storms. The health of the forest deter-mines the ultimate health of New York. Since the

1990s, the city has invested billions in buying forests in the watershed and protecting the ecosystem.
According to Tom Tidwell, chief of the U.S. Forest
Service, between 2009 and 2017: 'Investing in forest
management upstream saves money on water treatment downstream.'[31]

Here is another lesson for the world. Cities ultimately depend on ecosystems beyond the horizon
not just for their long-term existence but for their
daily needs. Mostly, this goes unacknowledged. The
majority of the world's population lives downstream
from forested watersheds; whether they know it or
not, people's lives depend on the ecological vitality
of these areas. The loss of 6 per cent of forest cover
in watersheds between 2000 and 2015 is estimated
to deprive 700 million urban dwellers of adequate
drinking water and to cost $5.4 billion a year in
water treatment. If Rio de Janeiro – already facing
water shortages – followed its nineteenth-century
precedent and restored 3,000 acres of native forest today, it would save an estimated $79 million
over thirty years and spare itself the need to treat its
water with millions of tons of chemicals.[32]

Trees store and filter rainwater; but they also ensure it falls in the first place. We tend to think that
rain comes from water evaporating from the oceans.
That is the case for coastal regions. But in continental interiors, a significant amount of precipitation comes from arboreal transpiration: trees suck

moisture from the ground and release it into the air where it forms 'a river in the sky'. Rainfall is recycled in this way many times. A study of twenty-nine of the world's megacities found that the water supply of nineteen of them were reliant upon evaporation and transpiration from vegetation. Gigantic cities such as Karachi, Shanghai, Wuhan, Chongqing, Kinshasa, Kolkata and Delhi are vulnerable to disruption to their water cycle, not to say their local climates, through deforestation. In 2015, São Paulo suffered soaring temperatures and severe drought as a result of felling. As in German cities or New York, cities need actually to purchase forests to ensure their survival. No forest, no city: that should be the motto of every modern metropolis.[33]

When we substituted wood for coal, gas and electricity, and when we got our water pumped into our homes through pipes, we lost an intimate, tangible connection between city and forest. Cities can't float free from their natural environment: deforestation in Jakarta's hinterland has put the city in mortal danger. As the megacity expanded into agricultural land, it pushed farms further into previously untouched forests. Much of the upper watershed has been denuded. Without trees, the capacity of the land to hold stormwater and only gradually release it into the Ciliwung and other rivers has been compromised. Jakarta suffers catastrophic flash floods as water cascades from its degraded watershed. The loss of trees on the edge of the rapidly expanding city has also harmed the ability of aquifers to recharge properly. Their depletion is compounded by increasing human demand on groundwater in Jakarta: there is simultaneously too much water and too little, the result of grievously wounding the natural hydrology. There are sewage-filled floods and empty aquifers. The city is sinking at an alarming rate as the aquifers empty, opening it up to annihilation in the face of rising sea levels and storm surges.

Jakarta is a warning to the rest of the world. The ability of cities to survive rising seas and unpredictable storm events is in jeopardy. Mumbai has sacrificed most of its natural defence against the impacts of climate change: its mangrove forests which buffer it against the waves and release monsoon rainfall back into the sea. For a long time we have been used to the idea that hard engineering can solve our problems. The lesson of climate change is that our urban way of life is tied up with nature. Trees, with their ability to intercept and store water (between 18 per cent and 48 per cent of precipitation, depending on tree species and landform) and prevent runoff and erosion, are among our best defences against the power of the elements. Cities have a lot of trees already; but they need a lot more both inside and, crucially, outside to shield us from our mistakes. There can never be enough.

Trees are a lynchpin in a wider ecosystem that includes wetlands, rivers and lakes – vital components of the green infrastructure that cities will come to rely on in the twenty-first century and beyond. The story of Mangar Bani and its defenders should inspire us. The generations who preserved this outpost of native vegetation have preserved an invaluable gift for modern Delhi. Like them, we should see such groves as sacrosanct.

5.

Life Force

'. . . the water's gotta go somewhere . . .'

It gave life to a semi-arid desert and made it the ideal site for a great city. A trickle for nine months of the year, the rainy season turned it into a mighty vital force. Floodwater filled the river and spread out into enormous marshes, lakes, ponds and streams. It dumped rich deposits that made this broad alluvial plain first the most densely populated indigenous area of the continent, then the most agriculturally productive land in the country, and, soon after, one of the world's great metropolises. The Spanish colonists who scouted it in 1769 encountered a territory 'so green and lush it seems as though it has been planted' – an Edenic riparian ecosystem of giant oak forests, roses, grapes, willows, syca-mores, alders and cottonwood trees that thrived de-spite low rainfall. Very little water made it into the ocean; instead, it seeped into the dry land. A 'very pleasing spot in every respect', the river and its ex-panse of freshwater wetlands permitted the founda-tion by Spanish colonists in 1781 of **El Pueblo de Nuestra Señora la Reina de los Ángeles.** In 1900, the population of Los Angeles – by then 102,000 – was still being sustained by the river.[1]

Today, the L.A. River is an unhappy symbol of what cities have done to their life-giving waterways. It is a river in name only. The miserable trickle in the huge concrete drainage ditch consists of industrial discharge, oily street runoff and human sewage. Following heavy precipitation, rainfall is flushed within an hour straight into the Pacific. Not so much a river as a flood management scheme, devoid of any traces of the riparian habitat it once nourished. It is ugly and largely ignored, an embarrassment screened off from view by chain-link fences, barbed wire and walls. Yet it is simultaneously one of the most famous urban rivers, used as a bleak location for TV series, pop videos and car chases in films such as **Terminator 2, Grease** and **The Dark Knight Rises.** In **Chinatown,** the private detective Jake Gittes – played by Jack Nicholson – doesn't believe anyone could have accidentally died in the L.A. River, because it would be like drowning in a teaspoon.

Having made the city possible, the river became a nuisance as Los Angeles mushroomed. A wild and unpredictable river, it changed course with every flood. The expansive wetlands were drained and the floodplain forests felled to make way first for farms, then factories and tracts of housing, while much of the water was extracted for domestic, agricultural and industrial use. When it rained, it could no longer cope with the torrents running off the mountains. From 1913, the L.A. River ceased to have much practical use when William Mulholland's great aqueduct began to bring water from the Owens Valley through 215 miles of conduit. Destructive floods following savage storms in 1914, 1934 and 1938 spelt the end for the river. Some 278 miles of streams and watercourses in the L.A. River system were encased in concrete. The river died so the city could grow.

Los Angeles detached itself from the ecosystem that gave it life. That process – true for all modern cities – is expressed at its clearest in the relationship between urbanisation and water. The sorrowful sludge entombed in its concrete coffin at the heart of L.A. is a visible reminder of what city-building has done to the planet: what was free and flowing is now constrained and artificial. The victory over water comes at enormous cost. The paving over of wetlands, streams and rivers, and the hardening of the surface of L.A., resulted in extensive urban run-off that poisoned its beaches.

The history of cities is that of a hubristic attempt to bend a powerful element to our will. The present-day L.A. River symbolises our fear of the power of the natural world and our desire to dominate it. We have buried rivers and turned them into sewers. We've drained wetlands, paved over floodplains and constructed dams and mighty sea walls, rearranging entire regional hydrological systems. In doing so, we have wrecked some of the planet's most valuable ecosystems. But in the end, water is going to bend **us** to **its** will.

Three large causeways connected the island city of Tenochtitlan to the shore of the saltwater lake called Texcoco; an aqueduct brought fresh water to the 250,000 people who lived in the Aztec metropolis. Tenochtitlan coexisted carefully with water. Sitting in the Valley of Mexico, Lake Texcoco was one of five large, shallow bodies of water. The three lakes to the north were salty; the southernmost two, freshwater. These latter freshwater lakes sustained the people of the valley. They built **chinampas,** highly fertile floating gardens made from soil from the lakebed, held together by walls of reeds and given stability by tree roots.

The nutrient-rich **chinampas** yielded four harvests a year, providing a wealth of food – maize, squashes, chillies, corn and vegetables – that fed the entire valley. But they were vulnerable in flood season, when brackish water from the northern lakes washed down. To defend their precious fresh water, the people of the southern lakes built a long dyke to keep out the salt. From the mid-fifteenth century, this system of managing the water got even more ambitious. The dykes of Nezahualcoyotl and Ahuitzotl were constructed north to south across Lake Texcoco, creating an artificial lagoon that made the brackish waters around the great city of Tenochtitlan drinkable, expanding the area available for **chinampas** so that they could feed one of the world's largest metropolises. That wetland agroecosystem created the most productive agricultural system on the planet at the time.

Tenochtitlan itself was a floating city. The Aztecs cut canals running east to west through the urban island to enhance the natural flows of water in the lagoon. The causeways reinforced the protective function of the dykes and prevented the city from flooding. The people of Tenochtitlan took waste very seriously. Leftover food and human excrement were collected to fertilize the **chinampas;** urine was used for dyeing fabrics. Other used materials were burnt at night to illuminate public buildings. The Aztecs lived with water, traversing the city and the outlying **chinampas** by canoe. They were able to maximise and then augment the natural biodiversity of the aquatic environment in which they lived through advanced engineering: the life-giving lake supported food production and provided an abundance of fish and waterfowl.

Wetlands are biodiverse supersystems; they are as rich as rainforests in terms of the range and interconnectedness of the habitats they accommodate. One-third of all vertebrate species on the planet live in wetlands. Estuaries, deltas, marshes and swamps support much of Earth's life systems. The Aztecs' ability to balance city life with their wet environment helped make their capital supremely powerful. It also recalls the longer human history of urbanisation.

All was chaos – a chaos of water and mud – before order was imposed on the swirl. That is the foundation myth of numerous religions, in particular that of the ancient Mesopotamians and of the Old Testament. The world's first cities emerged on islands in the deltaic marshes of southern Mesopotamia around 5000 BCE. They appeared in similar boggy landscapes in the second millennium BCE in modern-day San Lorenzo, Mexico, and the alluvial plane of the Yellow River in China during the Song Dynasty. The earliest urbanisation in sub-Saharan Africa occurred in the swamplands of the Niger Delta at Djenné-Djenno.

Productive agriculture was not a necessary precondition of early urbanism: the ecological bounty of aquatic landscapes gave people extraordinary surpluses of high-protein food resources, encouraging permanent structures in the soggy, shifting terrain of the marshes. Harnessing the gifts of the wetlands and constructing settlements had to be a collective and collaborative endeavour. The range of foods that could be gleaned from swamps freed people from the drudgery of subsistence agriculture to build, engineer and ultimately organise, trade, invent, fight, enslave and rule. Cities built on brick or stone platforms in the marsh represented the control of chaos, victory over the caprice of floods and erosion. These heavily engineered landscapes depended on deep understanding of local ecologies; humans worked with, and adapted to, floods and seasonal rainfall patterns. Early urbanisation happened in inhospitable places where water had to be managed, cajoled and coaxed. Mesopotamia, the cradle of urban civilisation, is hot, windy, dry and arid; life came to this region unpredictably, in great muddy floods or hardly at all, depending on variable rainfall patterns in the distant Taurus mountains. Only by harnessing this dangerous power and turning it to profit through networks of irrigation ditches, canals, locks and reservoirs could urbanisation happen at all. The salt flats and marshy swamps of southern Iraq were transformed into a landscape of farms and huge, highly complex cities. The life force of water and silt, mud and reed, provided the preconditions for urban life.

Shanghai, Lagos, Paris, London, Dhaka, Amsterdam, St Petersburg, Singapore, Toronto, Berlin, Boston, New York, Los Angeles, Mumbai, Wuhan, New Orleans, Washington, Chicago, Calcutta, Bangkok – these are among the large number of key modern metropolises that were constructed, like their ancient forebears, on extensive wetlands. Before Paris there was the Roman city of Lutetia Parisiorum, deriving from the Latin word **lutum,** which means 'marsh'. Of the various explanations for the naming of London are the Celtic **londinjon,** 'place that floods or sinks', and the Ligurian **lond,** meaning 'mud' or 'marsh'. Berlin's name comes from an old

Slavic word for 'swamp', **berl.** Whatever the origins
of their names, these cities certainly emerged atop
an ooze of slime and mud.

'Lutetia, the city of mire', was buried beneath
modern Paris, the city of light, according to Victor
Hugo. In order to capture Lutetia in 53 BCE, Julius
Caesar had to negotiate its defensive encirclement
of swamps. As late as the reign of Henry IV, over
1,650 years after Caesar breached the barrier of
mud and water, 'Paris had wide stretches of barren
terrain – fields, prairies and swamps'. There's something about marshes: the topography of pre-Roman
London consisted of two gravel hills (now known
as Ludgate Hill and Cornhill) surrounded by sedge
and willow-strewn marshes that were watered by the
numerous streams and rivers that flowed into the
Thames. During the Roman invasion of CE 43,
the defeated Britons sought refuge in the impenetrable swamps of Hackney.

Like Paris, London could not shake the primordial mud from its boots. A Venetian visitor in the
seventeenth century said there was 'a soft and stinking mud which abounds here at all seasons, so that
the place more deserves to be called **Lorda** [filth]
than **Londra** [London]'. The opening of Charles
Dickens's **Bleak House** depicts the primordial
slime reasserting itself over the modern metropolis
as crowds of pedestrians slip and slide through the
mire: 'As much mud in the streets as if the waters
had but newly retired from the face of the earth, and

it would not be wonderful to meet a Megalosaurus, forty feet long or so, waddling like an elephantine lizard up Holborn Hill.' And like a marsh, the sinister London of **Bleak House** is shrouded in vapour.

The edge of London was, for Dickens, a liminal zone of eerie marshes with its sinking houses, rotting detritus and dubious characters. Much of the East End of London – the notorious slum of the nineteenth century – was built on tidal marshland that had been reclaimed over the course of centuries. For many writers, the dank, fetid slums were forever rooted – physically and morally – in the primeval swamp from which they emerged. Balzac wrote that nineteenth-century Paris had its 'foundations plunged in filth . . . making the famous name Lutetia still appropriate. . . . Half of Paris sleeps nightly in the putrid exhalations from streets, back-yards and privies.'

Humans are drawn to build on swamps, despite the incompatibility between slimy liquid and solid stone buildings and despite our loathing for what were long seen as unproductive, insalubrious, boggy wastelands. There is good reason for this apparent contradiction. Marshes are highly defensible, as Caesar found when he went to subdue Lutetia. Bangalore was strategically founded in the middle of a wilderness of lakes, forests and marshes, because these natural obstacles provided excellent barriers against enemy invasion.

But more attractively, marshes mean water, and

water means trade. Rivers are conduits of commerce. Deltas and estuaries provide us with ports. These prime locations are by their nature soggy. Wuhan emerged from several urban settlements clustered around the confluence of the Yangtze and Han Rivers in central China, key inland ports linking the world's largest transport system before the invention of the railway. The boundless possibilities of trade bequeathed by the riverine network made these cities risky places: the rivers changed course and regularly flooded. Wuhan – like New Orleans, Bangkok, Kolkata, Lagos and many others – is sited in a dangerous but lucrative netherworld of swamps. This worldwide preference for wetlands as places of settlement pits cities against water and puts them on a crash course with some of the planet's most valuable ecosystems.

The Aztecs of Tenochtitlan revered their swampy lakes and turned them to immense profit. The Spanish **conquistadors** who captured and razed this stupendous metropolis in 1521 did not attempt to understand the balance between urbanisation and hydrology that the Aztecs developed. They abandoned the **chinampa** agroecosystem in favour of haciendas; they travelled by horse, not canoe. If the lakes were a way of life for the Aztecs, they were, for the Spanish, a problem to be engineered away. They destroyed the dykes and causeways and began to drain the lake by diverting and damming rivers. Mexico City, built over the ruins of Tenochtitlan

and its dried-out lake, was therefore prone to horrendous flooding, which was in turn exacerbated
by deforestation on the hills. The inundation of
1629 killed over 30,000 people; the survivors had
to celebrate mass on church roofs. Only in 1635
did the waters recede. In response, the authorities began work on a trench to drain the lakes, a
task that would take 165 years and claim 200,000
workers' lives. On several occasions in the sixteenth
and seventeenth centuries, the Spanish put serious
consideration to moving the capital. But the site
of Aztec Tenochtitlan retained a powerful symbolic
resonance. The city brazenly stayed where it was
in defiance of geography. The consequence was a
never-ending war against nature.[2]

Flooding was only one part of the problem. Stagnant water, polluted with excrement and dead animals, brought cholera, malaria and gastrointestinal
diseases. Heavy modern buildings were beginning
to sink into the soft lacustrine soils of the former
lakebed. In the nineteenth century, after Mexico
achieved independence, a series of canals, tunnels
and aqueducts was constructed to solve the water
problem. But the lake always wanted to reassert itself: the drainage systems overflowed, turning much
of Mexico City into a giant and dangerous puddle.
By the mid-twentieth century, underground pumps
were ceaselessly at work removing the last drops of
liquid. Mexico City's remaining forty-five rivers
were buried underground in giant concrete pipes

used as drains for stormwater. The lakebed is now very dry indeed: Mexico City is, at the same time, running out of water and as flood prone as ever. It has sunk by thirty feet.

What the Spanish, and later the Mexicans, did to Tenochtitlan did not differ from the ways Western city builders treated their wetlands and rivers. Water became dangerous and undesirable in streams, ponds and bogs. The rivers and streams that flowed through London to the Thames became toxic soups of disease and death as they were filled daily with excrement and pollution, particularly butchered animals. Only in 1854, during the cholera epidemic, did the physician John Snow link polluted water to disease. Until then, conventional wisdom held that infection was spread by miasmas – toxic vapours that emanated from putrefying matter, contaminated water and marshes – rather than waterborne pathogens. In 1560, a doctor wrote of the 'stinking lanes' around the Fleet River where 'there died most in London and were soonest inflicted [with disease], and were longest continued'. Jonathan Swift depicted the river in 1710: 'Sweepings from Butchers Stalls, Dung, Guts and Blood, / Drown'd Puppies, stinking Sprats, all drench'd in Mud, / Dead Cats and Turnip-Tops come tumbling down the Flood.'

The Fleet became a byword for squalor and death; no one would live near it but the poorest who had no choice in the matter. Beginning in 1737, the river was bricked over until no trace of it remained above ground save for the valley it had carved through the metropolis and the thoroughfare called Fleet Street. A natural river became part of the underground sewer network, concealed, controlled and disciplined. So it went with London's numerous rivers, and indeed rivers in cities everywhere, particularly in the nineteenth century when the bill for desecrating rivers was paid in thousands of annual deaths from cholera. Dickens wrote that 'through the heart of the town a deadly sewer ebbed and flowed in the place of a fine fresh river'. As a result of the flushing lavatory, London's great artery of commerce and the source of its domestic and industrial water, the Thames, filled with raw excrement. Michael Faraday wrote to **The Times** in 1855, 'Near the bridges the feculence rolled up in clouds so dense that they were visible at the surface, even in water of this kind. The smell was very bad, and common to the whole water; it was the same as that which now comes up from the gully-holes in the streets; the whole river was for the time a real sewer.' Three years later, exceptionally high summer temperatures and low rainfall brought about the Great Stink, a stomach-turning, unbearable stench of human shit rising from the Thames.

Pestilence and pollution fundamentally shifted the balance between cities and nature. Infrastructure and technology took the place of natural flows. Subterranean sewage systems, pumping stations and water treatment became cardinal features of cities: they were drained as never before. Water came at considerable cost from outside the city – often far outside the city. The engineering of urban hydrology was a response to a self-created ecological catastrophe. These titanic projects aimed at the ultimate goal of nineteenth-century urbanism – the sanitised, hygienic city – saved millions of lives, but they also severed the link between city and nature.

Turn on the tap or flush the lavatory, and the flow of the city seems entirely artificial and humanmade. The city appears to operate independently of natural processes. We tend to think of urbanisation conquering green space. But it is far more destructive of the blue spaces – rivers, marshes, lakes, coastlines and beaches – that contain the bulk of a city's biodiversity. Banish the rivers and wetlands, and you hobble the ecosystem. The decision to get rid of insalubrious and life-threatening rivers and marshes made sense when they had been poisoned by human abuse. But cities have paid a high price for it – to the point that they will become unsustainable in the near future. And none more so than cities that perch on the edges of oceans.

The welfare of the 13 million residents of New York and its wider metropolitan area is bound up with the vitality of the Hudson River Estuary. New York needs to revert to 'more natural hydrology and hydraulics by creating more resilient shorelines, streambanks, and wetlands that can better withstand flooding and strong storms associated with climate change'.[3]

This call for a return to nature did not come from utopian environmentalists. It was the culmination of an investigation, decades in the making, conducted by the U.S. Army Corps of Engineers and published in 2020. The report did not hold back when it said that what had begun as incremental urban expansion had escalated into total 'overdevelopment, exploitation, and degradation' of the estuary to the extent that not only had the regional environment suffered, but the future prospects of its human inhabitants had been compromised. The lesson for the rest of the urbanising world is clear: New York pushed far beyond its natural limits in the quest for endless growth, and it is facing submersion by the end of this century.[4]

Before the coming of the Dutch to the Hudson Bay area in 1609, the edgelands of New Amsterdam, later New York, were liquid: sea on three sides and marshland to the north. The city was set amid an estuarine ecology of unparalleled biodiversity: the New York-New Jersey shoreline was close to 1,000 miles, with forests, intertidal mudflats, meadows, white cedar swamps, and wetlands 'so big that one cannot see across them', prolific with grasses and flowers. These ecologies supported a stunning profusion of wildlife: wading birds, ospreys and eagles; oysters, lobsters, crabs, clams, mussels and turtles; whales, sturgeon, shad, carp and perch; beavers, otters, wild turkey, bears, deer, wolves and foxes. The wetlands of the Hudson River Estuary were a prime stopping point in the Atlantic Flyway, the great migration path of North American birds. This terrain did not suit agriculture; but its biodiversity provided an enticing menu of foodstuffs that had long supported the Lenape, the indigenous inhabitants of the Bay. New York, like all other North American cities, was a small speck amid wildness. In this case, it was a wilderness of wetlands that nurtured ecosystems richer than a jungle or a savannah.

And this wet, muddy environment provided a valuable service for human beings. Hundreds of square miles of oyster reefs, barrier islands and wetlands protected the Hudson Bay estuary against hurricanes for millennia and made New York an inviting harbour for ships. They are the first lines of defence, acting as buffers against the sea, dissipating wave energy and absorbing floods.

Water, water everywhere, and not a drop to drink. The marshes and mudflats presented a barrier to growth, not a means of sustenance. The water New Yorkers depended on came from wells dug into the ground on the tip of Manhattan Island. Insufficient to sustain the city, this subterranean supply was augmented with rainwater collected in cisterns. By the mid-eighteenth century, even horses wouldn't touch the stuff, so polluted was it by cesspools, privies and runoff from the street. All that was left

as a source of life was the Collect, a deep forty-
eight-acre pond that sat to the north of the city
located in what is now Chinatown, between two
large wetlands and at the foot of a 110-foot hill
called Bayard's Mount. These bodies of water sealed
off colonial New York from the rest of Manhattan
Island, preventing northward expansion. But by the
end of the eighteenth century, the city-sustaining
Collect Pond had become 'a very sink and common sewer' thanks to the runoff from breweries,
slaughterhouses and tanneries. A source of yellow
fever epidemics that threatened New York's future as a major seaport, pressure mounted for the
Collect to be eradicated. Between 1803 and 1811,
Bayard's Mount was levelled and dumped into the
pond. The landfill was built upon, but it could not
shed its dank origins: it became the notorious Five
Points, a damp, muddy, mosquito-ridden, crime-
infested slum made famous for modern audiences
in **Gangs of New York** (2002).

Filling in the pond neither slaked New York's
thirst nor eased its sanitation crisis. In 1832, dread
cholera arrived in the city. The public demanded
technical solutions to the disasters of industrial
urbanisation. From 1842, New York enjoyed the
highest per capita consumption of water anywhere
in the world. Gallons of it were brought along a
forty-one-mile aqueduct from the Croton River
in Westchester County on the mainland. The island metropolis lost its dependence on local water

sources. They could be buried and built over at will. And New York certainly had a lot of water that could be converted to real estate.[5]

In the late eighteenth century, a substantial salt marsh that occupied present day Soho was drained through a canal to the Hudson River. The same fate befell the Stuyvesant salt meadows on the other side of the island, the largest such ecosystem on Manhattan Island. The geologist Issachar Cozzens recalled the meadows in the 1810s as a wondrous spot on the edge of the city 'covered with beautiful native oaks and other trees . . . on its beach I used to catch an insect called the cicindela [tiger beetle]. These meadows were nearly a mile long on the shore [of the East River], and more than half a mile in width, now [in 1842] they are almost all filled over with the earth of the surrounding hills, and built upon.' The marsh became the East Village, Alphabet City and Gramercy Park.

The watery world is still there, buried beneath concrete, asphalt and skyscrapers; on a normal day, the New York Metropolitan Transport Authority has to pump out 13 million gallons of water to keep the subway working and double that after storms. If the water was not removed on a daily basis, Manhattan's asphalt surface would quickly crater and break apart. As the city expanded northwards in the nineteenth century, hills were razed and used to fill in bogs and swamps. By 1900 – by which time the city's population had swollen to 3.48 million people from 33,000 in 1790 – a collective total of just one square mile of marshes on Manhattan Island remained. Yet despite the growth of the city and the eradication of wetlands on Manhattan Island, there were still 300 square miles of largely untouched, biodiverse tidal wetlands within a twenty-five-mile radius of the Statue of Liberty in the first decade of the twentieth century.[6]

The gargantuan garbage dump at Freshkills is a monument to the fate that befell this vast ecosystem over the course of the twentieth century. As we saw in chapter one, New York's aquatic edgelands were subsumed by development, the marshes and meadowlands filled with rubble and trash. Of the 300 square miles of 'life-enhancing tidal marsh' that still existed in the Hudson River Estuary in 1900, 85 per cent had been urbanised by the turn of the twenty-first century in a whirlwind of geological reordering. In addition, the city sacrificed 99 per cent of its 350 square miles of freshwater wetlands. Of the 1,000 miles of gently-sloping natural shorelines, 75 per cent had been converted into humanmade structures such as bulkheads, rip-raps and piers.

In place of the soft barriers of oyster reefs, coastal marshes, beaches and dunes that shielded New York from the sea came walls of concrete, steel and rock. As with sewers and the undergrounding of urban rivers, engineering took the place of natural processes, and the metropolis became a kind of stone fortress thumbing its nose at the power of water. The engineering of the city altered the regional hydrology beyond recognition. Tidal marshes act as vital purifiers of dirty water, trapping nutrients and heavy metals coming from the land. Water sent to the city from the Croton River and then the Catskill Mountains was being flushed – along with rainwater, sewage and industrial waste – straight into the bay. By spewing high-nutrient water straight into the seawater, the city caused an oxygen crash. Lack of oxygen depleted fish and crustacean populations and the birds that fed on them. Sediment and plankton, attracted by the abundance of nutrients, blocked out sunlight and killed the sub-aquatic seagrass – the 'ecosystem engineer' of the seabed that provided indispensable nursery habitats for numerous species. Seagrasses are the lungs of the oceans, producing oxygen through photosynthesis. The 'kidneys' of the ocean, meanwhile, are oyster beds that filter nitrogen and sewage bacteria from the water and feed on phytoplankton; and 200,000 acres were destroyed by dredging and pollution at exactly the same time. Remnant patches of marshland left untouched by development were fragmented by the release of raw sewage, high-nutrient water and oil, which led to declining root density. The massive ecosystem and its biodiversity, on shore and at sea, had been crippled.[7]

The transformation of New York's estuarine ecology to a humanmade ecology is illustrative of a wider global trend. During the course of the twentieth century, as the global urban population soared, we destroyed 60 per cent of the planet's wetlands. That precious biome is the fastest-disappearing ecosystem on the planet, going three times faster than forests.[8]

Coastal ecosystems are in an endangered state in this age of rapid urbanisation. The Yellow Sea coastal wetlands defend 60 million people from storms and sea level rise. Yet 65 per cent has been lost in the last five decades. Flood-prone, low-lying Lagos, Nigeria – built on a huge tropical swamp forest – saw its mangrove wetlands decrease from 88.5 square kilometres to 20 and its swamps from 345 square kilometres to 165 between 1984 and 2006 as it became one of the largest megacities on the planet. The destruction of mangrove forests to pave the way for urban growth is prevalent around the world, and it is deeply troubling. Mangroves are home to an astounding array of wildlife, for a start. They clean the aquatic environment, trapping heavy metals and pharmaceutical waste. Most helpfully, they draw down carbon dioxide four times more efficiently than other forests and store the carbon in their soggy soils for millennia. Mangroves are the front-line defence against incoming waves, coastal erosion and rising sea levels. Mumbai needs more and more mangroves to protect itself against the Arabian Sea and flash floods; yet it is losing them at a sickening rate. It is not alone: almost a million hectares of coastal mangroves were destroyed on the Mexican Gulf Coast between the 1970s and 1990s.

The story is the same in other fast-growing mega-lopolises: the poor who live in unplanned, informal settlements find themselves in damp, insanitary conditions on recently reclaimed land denuded of natural protection such as mangrove forests. Our faith in re-engineering marshes, rivers and entire hydrological systems remains undimmed, at least when we are bedazzled by fast growth and quick profits. We have been doing it throughout history; now it happens at a monstrous rate.

The gamble can only go on so long. The heroic age of engineering is coming to an end. In its place we are looking back to natural solutions to the coming water crises.

'I can't comprehend the wholesale destruction of these marshes,' Sergius Polevoy said in horror in 1960, as he watched ecological carnage unfold. Polevoy, the state game protector for Richmond County, Staten Island, told the **New York Times** that 'garbage is literally taking over' the south-west portion of the island. He reported that 5 million tons of garbage had been used to fill 90 per cent of Oakwood Marsh to harden the ground for suburban houses.[9]

Go to Oakwood today; those houses, built in a fit of confidence, have gone or are in the process of being dismantled. You can still make out the outlines of homes that used to line the streets and cul-de-sacs; but in their place, meadows of wetland wildflowers and shrubs are growing, grazed by deer and geese. Here, at Oakwood Beach, the tidal wetlands, the low and high marshes, and the maritime scrub habitats that served the time-honoured role of protecting Staten Island from the sea are being allowed to return. Oakwood Beach is undergoing managed retreat, ceding ground back to nature, sacrificing itself to defend the rest of the city. Its abandonment and reversion to marshland marks the first tentative steps in the human retreat from its hubristic attempt to obliterate the entire wetland ecology of the Hudson Bay estuary in the name of progress. The desolate scene at Oakwood will become more familiar as we are at last forced to acknowledge the value of tidal wetlands – New York's blue belt. If, as is predicted, New York's sea level rises six feet by 2100, there will be more Oakwoods throughout the twenty-first century as the city is forced to withdraw. By 2100, as many as 13 million Americans living on the east coast may have had to move inland. Mud always wins. The question is when.[10]

The need for Oakwood's managed retreat became painfully obvious in October 2012. Hurricane Sandy developed in the Caribbean Sea on the 22 October and seven days later hit New York City and New Jersey. Supplemented by a spring tide, the surge was 12.65 feet above normal levels. Water poured into marshland in Staten Island and Long Beach just as it should have done; only these wetlands had become housing developments that were, like Oakwood Beach, defenceless against the tide. Water breached the concrete walls of New York, filling parts of lower Manhattan Island that had once been the Stuyvesant and Lispenard salt meadows but are now some of the most valuable real estate in the world; it poured down Canal Street and settled where the Collect Pond used to be.

The financial centre of the world reverted to its boggy past. Water ran over the seawalls that had replaced tidelands, inundating Jersey City and Hoboken. The blue on the flood map, when overlaid on the familiar street plan of the city, revealed its lost creeks and buried rivers, filled marshes and forgotten wetlands, as water temporarily recreated much of New York's forgotten primordial topography, killing fifty-three people, causing $19 billion of damage and releasing 10 billion gallons of raw and partially treated sewage into the bay. The likelihood of such a catastrophic event used to be reckoned to be at 1 per cent each year – a once-a-century superstorm. In the near future, it is likely to become common and – combined with rising sea levels – more deadly. By the end of this century, New York might be dealing with a Sandy-type hurricane every three years.[11]

Looking to defend New York over the remainder of this century in response to the devastation wrought by Sandy, the U.S. Army Corps of Engineers de-manded 'enhanced ecological conditions' in the es-tuary to 'partially or fully re-establish the attributes of a naturalistic, functioning, and self-regulating system' as a matter of urgency. 'A healthy estuary is . . . essential to the regional economy.' And at the heart of a healthy estuary is a healthy popula-tion of oysters, bivalves that clean the water and protect against surging waves: the Billion Oyster Project, founded in 2014 by Murray Fisher and Pete Malinowski, is attempting to restore New York Harbour's key species.[12]

Having spent most of its history, between the ar-rival of the Dutch in 1609 and the 1990s, attempt-ing to eradicate and replace the natural barriers of marshes, New York has at last awoken to their value. How much are they worth? One estimate puts them at close to $1.5 million per acre, a figure that would shock generations of city boosters who regarded them as worthless blots on the landscape. In the words of the army, the priority must be to 'restore and sustain a mosaic of habitats within the human-dominated landscape . . . The need for the proposed action comes from recognizing that valu-able natural resources have declined to a point that the ecosystem may no longer be self-sustaining without immediate intervention to impede signifi-cant ecological degradation.'[13]

Oyster and coral reefs, wetlands, mangrove for-ests and barrier islands cannot come back on their own in heavily anthropically altered estuaries and deltas where sediment flow and hydrological processes have been irreversibly altered. In New York, this means actively restoring 1,000 acres of coastal and freshwater wetlands in the short term, and an additional 125 acres per year thereafter; 500 acres of maritime and 500 acres of coastal forests; and 2,000 acres of oyster reef habitat. Recreating a fraction of the pre-1600 estuarine ecosystem identified for action by the U.S. Army Corps of Engineers would come at a cost of $588,745,000. That is in addition to the $1.1 billion that had already been spent on ecological restoration of wetlands and reefs in the preceding seven years.

Ferocious storms such as Sandy and Katrina have awoken us to the fact that cities do, after all, rely on natural processes. We still need humanmade walls and barriers, but the lessons of recent storms teach us that they work best when they are combined with local ecosystems.[14]

Where there were factories, warehouses and enormous gantry cranes serving the then-busiest port in the world, there is now a wetland. The hard edge of Hunters Point in Queens, N.Y.C., has been softened with trees, grass, bioswales and artificial wetlands that create both a public park and a buffer against future storm surges. Close by is Newtown Creek, as polluted an urban river as you could find. Before European colonisation, it consisted of

1,200 acres of tidal wetlands. By the twentieth century, it was one of the busiest watercourses in the city, lined with warehouses, freight depots, chemical works and oil refineries. The first kerosene works in the U.S. was founded here in 1854; Vaseline was produced from petroleum jelly; and by the 1880s, John D. Rockefeller's Standard Oil was processing 3 million gallons of crude oil a week in over one hundred refineries. The river became an outlet for the sewer system, a toxic stew of urban runoff, raw sewage, oil and industrial wastewater. Newtown Creek was the site of the largest oil spill in U.S. history; between 17 million and 30 million gallons of oil and petroleum leaked into the area over several decades. By the end of the twentieth century, the stagnant tidal river had the sheen and stench of petroleum; its bed was a 4.6-metre layer of congealed sludge.

Today, this vile urban river is being replanted with salt marsh habitat along its forbidding grey bulkheads. Thanks to the hard graft of local volunteer groups, wetland plants and mussels are colonising the bulkheads; blue crabs, eels, fish and waterfowl are beginning to return. Imagine the whole waterside of New York – or any coastal city – transformed like this, with its concrete outer armour softened with mud, marsh, grass, trees and vegetation. Such efforts aren't going to save cities from climate change-related flooding on their own. But they are the first stages in restoring the health of the wider aquatic urban ecosystem by re-establishing the biodiversity that makes it tick. Softening the hard carapace of cities – making them porous – is becoming an urgent priority in this century not just for vulnerable coastal cities like New York and New Orleans, Shanghai and Singapore, Lagos and Mumbai, but **all** cities, including those inland.

Having attempted to turn cities into highly engineered humanmade machines, we are beginning, like New York, to seek natural solutions to the problems of flooding and drought. Because we need it, because we dread it, water is the most potent force reshaping cities across our dangerously unstable planet.

Chulalongkorn Centenary Park is a sponge in the centre of Bangkok. Opened in 2017, it has been designed to absorb one million gallons of rainwater over its eleven acres during savage downpours. Its creator, Kotchakorn Voraakhom, set it on a three-degree angle so that gravity draws rainwater via water tanks from its highest point – a 5,220-square-metre, low-maintenance roof garden on top of a museum – down to a retention pond, a shallow, bowl-shaped lawn, woodland and a series of wetlands. Sitting on the deltaic floodplain of the Chao Phraya River, Bangkok is called the 'City of Three Waters' – rivers, rain and sea. A metropolis of canals and paddies, it used to live in harmony with its three waters; a semi-aquatic city that had adapted to the monsoon. Long accustomed to flooding as a part of life, its people directed excess water through artificial and natural channels to feed orchards and rice fields. The Aztecs would have recognised this delicately balanced urban agroecosystem.[15]

But today, like many Asian metropolises, Bangkok has a serious water problem, having filled in its matrix of canals and paddies and sprawled across the floodplain. The city has ceased to be porous; its acres of concrete and buildings block water trying to reach the sea. As a result, along with other water-threatened cities like Jakarta and New Orleans, it is one of the most vulnerable human settlements on the planet. Bangkok is sinking into its bed of alluvial mud and will soon be below the present sea level.

Chulalongkorn Centenary Park is an attempt to show how modern Bangkok and other at-risk cities can mimic natural hydrology and topography to mitigate torrential downpours. It looks back to south-east Asia's long history of water-based urbanism. Bangkok needs to relearn the lessons of its own history. Voraakhom's park can't deal with all the water falling on and around the city. The wider metropolis needs the park's features to be expanded on the biggest possible scale: more roof gardens, rain gardens, artificial urban wetlands, canals and retention ponds integrated into the urban matrix to soak up the water.

Go from Bangkok to Dordrecht to see how cities

need to change. There are few more lovely or historically important cities in northern Europe than Dordrecht, which was, in the Middle Ages, the largest and most important city in Holland. It has always lived close to the edge, vulnerable to flooding from the North Sea and the three major rivers it lives alongside. The epochal St Elizabeth's flood of 1421 submerged much of its hinterland, killing 10,000 people, sweeping away around twenty villages and turning the city into an island. A flood of that extent today would cause €4.5 billion of damage to the city.

Cycle into Dordrecht today and you travel through a landscape that has been continually reshaped by fears of that inundation and threats yet to come. There are, most obviously, the defensive dykes. Much of the Netherlands is polder – land reclaimed from the sea and from marshes and peat bogs. The long-term, collaborative endeavour in making land and maintaining dykes is memorialised in the modern Dutch concept **poldermodel,** a consensus-based means of economic and social policy decision making. The Dutch are the world masters of flood planning. They had to be: with over half the country lying below sea level, their history has been characterised by making the soggy land liveable, safe and productive.

In 1953, floods killed 1,835 people. In response the Dutch government invested billions in a highly sophisticated network of dams, pumps, storm surge barriers, dykes and sluices. Severe floods in 1993 and 1995 forced the Dutch to change tack from flood protection to flood resilience. Building more barriers and raising the heights of dykes was not enough when the unpredictable future awaiting us in the twenty-first century was taken into account.

The change of policy can be seen as you cycle through the edgelands of Dordrecht. Much of the periphery, you notice, has been returned to a tidal landscape. Where once there were fields and farms abutting the city, reedlands, willow plantations, thickets and marshy woodland, interspersed with large expanses of open water, reconstituted wetlands and catchment areas now dominate the terrain. This scruffy, semi-wild zone is part of Dordrecht's 'blue-green climate buffer – an area where natural processes are given space in order to increase social and ecosystem resilience against the impacts of climate change', according to the city's dedicated climate change adaptation department.

It is called Biesbosch National Park. **Biesbosch** means 'forest of sedges', a reference to its former and future state. From the Middle Ages until the 1990s, this huge area of rivers, marshes, mudflats and creeks had been progressively claimed from the water. Following the floods of the early 1990s the polders have been gradually removed. The Biesbosch is now one of Europe's largest freshwater tidal areas, a forest not only of sedge but of willows, rushes, marsh ragwort, comfrey and bitter fieldcress that have returned with the maze of creeks. This flood defence strategy has resulted in a thirty-five-square-mile national park, a boom in the beaver, bittern and kingfisher populations, and the triumphant return of ospreys, egrets and white-tailed eagles.

Dordrecht's newly wilded edgelands are replicated throughout the urbanised Netherlands. It is part of the Room for the River programme, which gives rivers space to flood by 'de-poldering' farmland. These manufactured floodplains and swamp forests double as places of recreation amid the outstanding biodiversity that they provide. In July 2021, Europe was hit by devastating floods, killing 220 people in Germany and Belgium. Had the Dutch not worked with nature and given the rivers land to flood, many cities would have been inundated. As it was, they stayed dry, even as the rivers of the Rhine delta swelled around them.

The natural defensive area encircling Dordrecht – its climate buffer – is not simply a place for nature to run feral. It is a place to live, too, but in a very different way now that the river and its tides have been given freer rein. As you cycle closer to the centre of the city, through the rugged terrain of the Biesbosch, you come across a distinct kind of twenty-first-century suburbia. It is intriguingly semi-aquatic. It is an ecotone, where the roughness of the tidal Biesbosch elides with the urbanity of Dordrecht. Houses are built to work with the tides and floods; they sit high on pilings within an expanse of mud and marshland trees and plants. Here, you clearly see the integration of humans, water and nature. Above all, you see a resilient community that no longer fights the power of water.

All very well to drastically reorder the empty edgelands in the name of safety and biodiversity. But what happens downtown, where the buildings are dense and the surface is hard?

Jump from Dordrecht to Copenhagen and you will see how even old and congested cities can be retrofitted. In 2011, the Danish capital suffered a catastrophic storm when 150 millimetres of rain fell in a couple of hours. Rather than wait for another flood, the city responded with its Cloudburst Masterplan. When the heavens open, 'cloudburst boulevards' and green streets, with wide, vegetated strips running through the centre or along the sides, temporarily absorb water in their swales and patches of vegetation. When excess water builds up, it is diverted to V-shaped side streets that follow old river valleys, becoming emergency 'urban creeks' that channel the flow to parks, public squares, rain gardens and underground car parks that have been re-engineered to flood when needed. Rainwater, slowed down and collected in artificial catchments, is slowly released into the sea. We shouldn't fight water: we need to let our cities flood.[16]

Cities turn storms into humanmade disasters.

Peak flood discharges can be 250 per cent higher in impervious urban areas than forested catchments. Underground streams are poor at dealing with the strain: they are slower than natural streams in removing excess water and, because they are biologically inactive, carry a lot of pollution. Little of heavy urban rainfall recharges groundwater. Instead, it is swept into urban streams and rivers, bringing a toxic deluge of pollution and chemical and nutrient overload with it, degrading watercourses through erosion and sedimentation. More seriously, storms overwhelm sewers, releasing stupendous volumes of untreated sewage into the environment and people's homes. Cloudbursts are going to get less regular but far more intense in the coming decades, degrading the quality of urban life.

There is a way of dealing with this flow of water: breaking up the impervious surface of the city. The Saint Kjelds district of Copenhagen, chosen as the world's pioneer 'climate-resilient neighbourhood', transformed 20 per cent of its hard street surfaces into green space to manage stormwater. Many asphalt roads have been replaced with permeable materials that soak up water; parks were relandscaped with undulating depressions to create floodable retention ponds. Fly across the Atlantic and you can see something similar at work. Instead of spending $9.6 billion on grey infrastructure, Philadelphia invested $2.4 billion in a bid to create the United States' largest citywide green stormwater infrastructure by the 2030s. As of 2019, it had converted 1,500 acres (out of a projected 10,000) of previously impermeable land into sunken rain gardens, bioswales, urban wetlands and roof gardens. Some of this was public land; but by using planning laws and tax incentives, the city mandates that businesses and property developers green their sites. An acre of urban wetland absorbs a million gallons of water a year, keeping it out of the sewage system. This kind of green retrofitting in cities is intended to 'optimize and engineer the landscape' so that it mimics a natural hydraulic system even in the centre of dense, heavily populated urban cores.[17]

Fears of floods are forcing cities to become greener. The retrofitting of Saint Kjelds and Philadelphia is introducing a huge amount of greenery into the streets for the benefit of their residents and massively augmenting urban biodiversity in the process. Following a spate of disastrous storms in the 2010s, China is creating 'sponge cities' that maximise green spaces to soak up floods. In a country facing a water crisis, the plan is to make up to 80 per cent of city surfaces permeable and reuse 70 per cent of the naturally collected stormwater for human needs, rather than watching it stream away.

On the microscale, every intervention helps. Courtyards, gardens, patches of spontaneous vegetation (our old friends, the weeds) in unkempt back-alleys, planters, small roof and wall gardens, pocket wetlands, bioswales next to houses and porous pavements all help and collectively add up to a lot of water infiltration and retention, especially in dense inner cities. Even a single tree planted in a small pit in an otherwise impermeable asphalt surface can absorb an astonishing amount of stormwater. We need to think creatively about maximising green space in every nook and cranny, even in unlikely places: they will pay dividends when the dark clouds mass overhead. The happy by-product of sponge features for the human and animal life of the city – built-up areas interposed with wetlands of all kinds and protective canopies – is all too obvious.

But we also need to think on the macro scale. Healthy upriver forests, tidal marshes and mangroves are vital outer defences for a city. But city centres have to protect their blue infrastructure as much as their green. Before it became notorious as the place of origin of Covid-19, Wuhan was defined by its water; it was 'the city of a hundred lakes' with 138 bodies of water. The city lies in the Jianghan Floodplain and in the intermediary zone between the east Asian and south Asian monsoon systems. Most of Wuhan's lakes disappeared in an orgy of late-twentieth-century urbanisation, leaving it more open than ever to the disastrous floods that have always been its curse – and its blessing. Generations of Wuhanese adapted their city and

The ultimate urban tree: banyans running wild in Hong Kong.

LONDON going out of Town ___ or ___ The March of Bricks & Mortar!

The urban edge under attack: 'The March of Bricks and Mortar' by George Cruikshank, 1829.

The emperor in his garden: the Mughal Emperor Babur receives ambassadors in 1528.

Bombsite as ecological treasure house: a couple inspect wildflowers in the ruins of Gresham Street, London, in July 1943.

The **brachen** – or abandoned sites – of Berlin revolutionised the study of urban ecology and provided unexpected social places in the city.

A habitat-rich wild garden contrasts with the sterile neatness of suburbia in Lincoln, Nebraska.

In the 1970s, the Green Guerrillas transformed blighted parts of New York City with wildness.

A crop of feral cannabis harvested under the shadow of the Brooklyn Federal Building in 1951. That year twenty tonnes of wild marijuana were pulled and destroyed from vacant lots in New York City. The plant had been grown to make fibres for rope during the Second World War before going rampant across the city.

The peepal tree is the people's tree of India, providing shade for street life in all its forms.

Nataraja Upadhya's extraordinary evergreen micro-jungle in the heart of Bangalore.

A house in Oakwood Beach, New York City, destined to be destroyed in the wake of Hurricane Sandy to make way for marshland to protect the city from the effects of climate change.

New York City's green defences: emergent marshland takes over from concrete defences at Hunter's Point in Queens.

When Paris fed itself: market gardens in the shadow of the Eiffel Tower in 1918.

Otters lording it over Singapore in 2022.

When cars are removed, lushness returns: modern Amsterdam.

their ways of life to the unpredictable elements, and they learnt to read the river. When it began to turn the colour of copper, they knew it meant that heavy rain had fallen upriver, where the river cuts through red sandstone. It was the signal for the poor to move their reed huts higher up the bank. Wealthier merchants, meanwhile, lived in houses on stilts like many people in low-lying parts of Asia. When it flooded, Wuhan became a floating city, with its junks and sampans converted into temporary market stalls that plied the inundated streets.[18]

Adapting to water like this lasted until the twentieth century, when Chinese cities underwent a rate of growth unprecedented in human history, which generated untold wealth but made them highly vulnerable. In 2016, half of Wuhan's annual average rainfall fell in just one week, forcing the evacuation of 263,000 people and causing $4 billion in damage. The disaster was a wake-up call, leading Wuhan to revisit its liquid legacy and learn the value of aquatic adaptation as the Dutch have over the last three decades. It began building expansive new wetland parks and artificial lakes in its inner city and re-naturalising its river and canal banks. Historically, the city was shaped around water; now it is reverting to an amphibious metropolis by giving space back to its abundant aquatic assets. Having spent most of their history trying to fill in unwelcome bogs and inconvenient lakes, cities such as Wuhan

are battling to make wetlands a central feature of a
revived concept of waterscape urbanism whereby
we live with water and make space for it, rather
than fighting it in a series of losing battles.

In a change of attitudes only apparent within the
last decade, wetlands, along with their diverse habitats, are coming back to cities. There is more rain
falling than cities were designed to deal with: traditional engineering techniques have to be complemented by natural solutions. Since 2015, Beijing has
constructed 27,000 acres of new wetland to work
alongside its afforestation programme. In Dallas,
the river corridor of the Trinity River – of which the
massive Trinity Forest is a part – is being converted
into America's largest urban park at 10,000 acres, a
chain of wetlands and bottomland forest designed
to hold floodwater, provide recreation and improve
the city's biodiversity. Urban water parks have to be
more rugged than conventional recreation grounds,
because they have to be hardy enough to deal with
the dynamic environment caused by periodic inundation. They need to be able to recover from
repeated disasters, like the vegetation of a natural
floodplain. And, as we have seen throughout this
book, lightly cultivated places are good for nature.
Water is helping to sculpt very different cities from
those we have seen before.

Mimicking natural processes, urban wetlands are
becoming the characteristic parks of the twenty-
first century, a vital part of the solution to filter,

treat and store water. The key word is 'mimicking': these are constructed wetlands, as artificial as any traditional urban park. Having built over most of its marshes, Hong Kong constructed a large, entirely humanmade wetland park in compensation. Meanwhile, just fifteen minutes from the centre of London is Europe's largest urban wetland nature reserve, Walthamstow Wetlands, created out of ten water-supply reservoirs. Once, we feared the marshes that fringed cities and sought their eradication; now, from Freshkills to Wuhan, they are places of recreation and ecotourism. Despite their humanmade origins, these urban wetlands mature into viable ecosystems in the midst of the concrete jungle. In the same way, our constrained, poisoned urban rivers can never be set free and returned to their original natural state. They can, however, be revamped with the semblance of naturalness.

The embankment walls that protected Wuhan from the Yangtze are being taken down. In their place are (so far) 45,000 trees, eighty acres of shrubs and ninety-six acres of native grasses that gently slope down to mudflats and emergent marshland, providing a floodable, seven-kilometre-long, green-blue buffer in an era of deluges. Rather than grapple fruitlessly with water, the restored riverfront is intended to 'incorporate . . . flooding as an essential element of the ever-changing landscape', much like at Dordrecht. At a planned final length of sixteen kilometres, the Yangtze River Beach Park

will become the largest urban green riverfront in
the world. By restoring riverine habitat, the project
has obvious ecological benefits. But it also creates a
huge new recreational park that restores the ancient
cultural connection between the people of Wuhan
and their river, which has, latterly, been obscured
by industrial development. The beach park dis-
solves the physical barriers between water and land
that were built up from the end of the nineteenth
century. In that respect, it is part of a larger worldwide movement.[19]

Naturalised riverbanks and waterfronts are becoming the key public spaces of contemporary
cities. We are magnetically drawn to water and to
nature. For the Celts, the River Isar was 'the torrential river', with a constantly changing course and
shifting gravel islands. But for the last hundred years,
it has flowed through Munich meekly, like a tamed,
humiliated beast, via a system of straight canal-like
waterways. Work began in 2000 to give the alpine
river back its independence. Embankments reinforced with sheet piling and stone-filled trenches
were moved further away from the banks and covered with vegetation. This stops the river shifting
too far but gives it room to reshape itself during
floods like a writhing snake. Over the course of
eleven years, the Isar was widened from fifty metres
to ninety in some places; its concrete banks were
replaced with gravel. The citizens of Munich got

better flood defence and a river right in the middle of the city beside which to sunbathe and in which to swim, at the cost of €35 million. The urban river has not been returned to its wild state; it has been given a wilder character that has in turn coaxed wildlife back into the heart of Munich.

Few things augment the quality of urban life more than a fresh river with a lush bank. When a stretch of the River Ravensbourne at Ladywell Fields park in Lewisham, south London, had its concrete channelling removed and its aquatic vegetation restored, visits to the park doubled. Time and again, people are prepared to fight for access to natural rivers. Walk along the River Wandle, a tributary to the Thames in south London, and the city disappears, camouflaged by an almost rural screen of riverine vegetation. A fast-flowing chalk stream, the Wandle was a magnet for mills, breweries, printers and tanneries, making it a vector of pollution and disease. It became heavily industrialised, with thirteen mills in 1086 and over one hundred by the end of the nineteenth century. In the 1960s, it was officially declared a sewer, with much of it culverted. Today, it is among the most improved rivers in England, thanks to the efforts of local volunteers who cleaned the waters, removed weirs, enhanced habitats, added gravel and re-established wetlands in order to filter pollutants entering the stream from urban runoff during intense spates of rainfall.

The trout for which the Wandle was once famous have returned, along with chub, roach, dace and perch. The stream is a world-class example of urban river rehabilitation, a model and an inspiration for similar projects everywhere. Across London, more than seventeen miles of river have been liberated from concrete and exhumed from burial in the twenty-first century, their banks wilded. Along canals and rivers where walls cannot be removed, there has been a programme to establish artificial wetlands – floating planters of reeds, marsh marigold, purple loosestrife, watercress and flag iris that filter dirty water and provide habitats for wildfowl, fish and frogs. The River Lea in east London has been converted in a remarkably short space of time from a culverted drain to a biodiverse river. Many of the English capital's waterways have not been so healthy or vegetated for centuries. They are part of an emerging latticework of ecologically high-value, green-blue corridors expanding throughout the metropolitan core – new kinds of urban public space that are appearing not only in London but in developed countries all over the globe.

The most famous daylighted stream in the world is the park-lined, 5.2-mile Cheonggyecheon flowing through downtown Seoul. Buried under a six-lane expressway in the 1950s, it was disinterred in 2005. Achieved at eyewatering expense, it has proved a beautiful public space that has changed Seoul and become a haven of urban biodiversity:

plant species increased from sixty-two to 308 after completion, fish from four to twenty-five, birds from six to thirty-six and aquatic invertebrates from five to fifty-three. The stream has a microclimate 3°C to 6°C cooler than the rest of the city and has seen a drop in air pollution of 35 per cent. It receives 60,000 visitors a day. Like the Wandle, the Cheonggyecheon shows how quickly biodiversity can be attracted to inner cities. River restoration rejuvenates cities as well. The Saw Mill River in Yonkers, New York, was daylighted in 2010 at a cost of $19 million. It proved a wise outlay: a section of healthy river has beautified the urban core and attracted significant investment.

The Yangtze in Wuhan, the Isar in Munich and the Wandle in London are leading examples of how we can transform the urban environment for the benefit of people and nature. Aquatic ecosystems are at once the most productive in cities, the most popular, and the most vital for our future. In the twenty-first century, we can see all too clearly how forests, meadows, wetlands, marshes, reefs and rivers interact: the entire system needs to work together. It is capable of recovery, even after centuries of abuse.

But the story of water in modern cities reveals another melancholy truth: we trash first and restore only once we have sucked every last bit of value out of natural resources. River restoration comes after de-industrialisation. Most of the world's urban rivers and wetlands are in a shocking state of neglect and pollution. It is better, and cheaper, to preserve rather than to restore later: that should be the lesson for the most fragile and fastest-growing cities around the world today. As advanced, state-of-the-art Chinese cities are discovering, green infrastructure and natural hydraulics are by far the most efficient ways of adapting to climate change. Only when we design around water will our cities be resilient enough to withstand the emergency.

Water has always shaped cities, for good and ill. Which brings us back to Los Angeles. The murder of the L.A. River in the 1930s coincided with the beginning of Los Angeles' descent from paradise into ecological and social nightmare, with its smoggy air, polluted beaches, car-dependent sprawl, poisoned ocean and wildfires, with its racial dysfunctionality, poverty and homelessness.

The L.A. River tells another story about us. Cities are greedy consumers of raw materials: they suck them in from elsewhere and expel them as waste. Water is brought hundreds of miles to L.A. at great cost, not least to the distant ecosystems in the upper watershed. Meanwhile, the rain that falls on dry, drought-prone L.A. is fast-tracked into the ocean through the concrete channel of the erstwhile river, along with all the toxicity that builds up in the city, without feeding aquifers or nurturing soil along the way.

But even this disgraceful emblem of environmental degradation is capable of revival. After decades of campaigning, the river is in the first stages of being revitalised. It will never run wild again. But plans are being put in place to release portions of the river from its concrete encasement, establish riverine habitats, and create a continuous ribbon of green space along its fifty-one miles over the next twenty-five years. The city has been buying up land in order to sculpt several new riverside parks linked by bike and pedestrian trails. The concrete bed of the river will be deepened and lined with natural materials – sand, sediment, gravel, cobbles and aquatic vegetation. The flow of the river will be slowed, and side pools and other habitats put in place. One of the tests of the river's recovery will be the return of steelhead trout, which, before canalisation, travelled upriver from the Pacific to spawn in the mountain headwaters.

If the fall of the L.A. River mirrored Los Angeles's degradation, today it is front and centre of the city's bid for environmental recovery. Restoring a river has knock-on effects that extend far beyond its banks. A healthy and accessible river running through L.A., instead of a fenced-off ditch, would transform the quality of life for the city's residents with an enormous public space and a new focal point. It would bring investment, as people went from shunning the watercourse to seeking it out for leisure, dining and living space. But there are wider ecological implications. If you want a clean river and lavish billions of dollars on it, you need a clean city, otherwise it gets clogged with the same old toxins. A river is more than just the channel of water flowing quietly along, generating income and tax revenue: its wellbeing is determined by the entire watershed. It needs trees, vegetated banks, wetlands, riparian marshes, bioswales and rain gardens to filter and cleanse run off from adjacent land. Restoring a river has ripple effects.

The challenge for the rest of this century is to change how water flows through the city before it becomes a destructive force. That means all kinds of changes to the urban environment, from cloudburst boulevards to cleaner rivers, reanimated wetlands, urban forests and spongey surfaces. It means a move away from hard engineering to natural processes. It means adding substantial greenery to cities in the form of roof gardens, raingardens and street trees and imbuing public parks with ecological, as well as recreational, functions. Above all, it means going in for 'biomimicry' – copying, replicating or restoring natural hydraulic systems. Envisaging a reborn L.A. River helps us to see how water has the power to reshape cities everywhere.

Such a development in our urban way of life will, among other things, reverse a historic trend. When L.A. brought in its water from the faraway Owens Valley, the connection between city and water was severed. To put it another way, the gap between production and consumption became so big that people in the city could no longer perceive the connection between cities and ecosystems. The same thing happened with other key resources, particularly food. The division between city and nature hardened. Climate change is forcing us to break down that division.

6.

The Harvest

Parisians who entered the Tuileries in April 1793 for a springtime stroll discovered that the formally planted flowerbeds and parterres of the royal garden had been ploughed over. In the place of the usual palette of colours were rows of a single plant with a violet flower. This was the crop of revolution and republicanism: potatoes.

The conversion of the Tuileries from royal pleasure garden to potato patch was a minor, but highly symbolic, part of the turmoil of 1793. Louis XVI had been executed that January. Revolutionary France, at war with much of Europe, was deprived of imported grains. The Vendée region was in revolt. Just as the potatoes were beginning to poke above ground, on 6 April, the Committee of Public Safety was established as the executive body of France. The new, austere governors of the infant republic ripped up the absolutist Bourbon city; all uncultivated land in Paris, including royal parks, would be used to grow vegetables to feed the hungry masses during a period of political crisis and food shortages.

The altar of French republicanism, the Tuileries

was renamed the Jardin National, a place of secular ceremonies and the focal point of national public life. Its main crop, the potato, was dubbed the 'Food of the Republic'. The replanting of the royal gardens was the brainchild of the pharmacist Antoine-Augustin Parmentier, as part of a rebranding exercise for the despised spud. Parmentier saw potatoes as the solution to the famines that wracked France, the gift of the New World to the starving Old. The problem was that the French loathed the tuber, believing that it caused leprosy, and refused to eat it. Long before the revolution, Parmentier had lobbied hard to make the potato palatable. In the 1790s, the need to feed France was acute, and Parmentier had his moment; the revolutionary regime ordered extensive cultivation of potatoes and distributed pamphlets exhorting their virtues, alongside a cookbook, **La Cuisinière Républicaine,** with dozens of tantalising potato recipes. In 1802, US President Thomas Jefferson had fried potatoes 'served in the French manner' at a White House dinner: French fries began their journey to global domination.

The potato was political. It was a counter-revolutionary weapon. So too was urban agriculture. The Jacobins saw self-sufficiency as a moral good, on both a national and a local level. They worried that cities were parasites, producing no food while bleeding the rest of the country dry with their greedy demands for staples and exotic luxuries. Eating simply and locally was an imperative.

Ploughing over the Tuileries and the Jardin du Luxemburg symbolised this move from luxury to utility. But it was more than a gesture: the Tuileries crop amounted to an impressive 4,300 bushels, about 120 tons. Some Jacobins urged the government to go further and pull up paving stones throughout Paris to make way for potatoes. The official press exhorted everyone to grow spuds in any available bit of space in the cityscape: 'all good Citizenesses who are motivated by the public good', urged a mouthpiece of the regime, should grow potatoes on their balconies and windowsills instead of flowers. Potatoes weren't merely political; they were patriotic. The city should go green with sprouting crops as Paris remade itself as self-sufficient.[1]

In the summer of 2020, Nature Urbaine, the world's largest rooftop farm, opened in Paris on top of an exhibition complex in the fifteenth arrondissement. Covering 14,000 square metres – the size of two football pitches – it produces just over one ton of fresh, organic fruit and vegetables a day for nearby restaurants during the growing season. The effective growing space is much greater – up to 80,000 square metres – through the use of tall, plastic growing columns and cultivation gutters. Just as the potato field in the Tuileries back in the 1790s was intended to showcase the latent agricultural productivity of urban areas, Nature Urbaine highlights the unused space in cities that can be made fertile. In crowded urban areas, where land is at a premium, vacant ground available for agriculture exists up in the sky, on the flat rooftops that can occupy up to 30 per cent of inner-city areas. It exists underground as well: with car ownership in decline in Paris, redundant subterranean car parks are being turned into mushroom and chicory farms.

Nature Urbaine is not going to feed Paris. But it is part of a global movement to reclaim and employ parts of cities to produce food. In 2009, Toronto passed a by-law mandating that all new buildings have to have green roof coverage. By 2019, there were 640 roof gardens covering 464,515 square metres, or 115 acres of additional green space for the city. Living roofs are a key part of climate change adaptation, reducing rainwater runoff by 60 per cent and lowering the energy requirements of air conditioning by up to 75 per cent.

With so many of Toronto's roofs going green, there have been calls for this space to be turned into aerial farms, something that is only slowly happening. Chicago – another pioneering green roof metropolis – has a similar extent of sky-high greenery and a growing number of rooftop farms, including a 2,000-square-metre site on top of the McCormick Place convention centre opened in 2013. Such urban farms are small and experimental, but they show us what could be possible if we ever decided to put our minds to transforming cities into food production centres. A study of Bologna suggested that if it used all its flat roof surfaces (203 acres) for agriculture, it could satisfy 77 per cent of its demand for fresh vegetables every year, massively reducing the environmental costs of importing perishable food.[2]

Nature Urbaine in Paris shares the moral impulses of the revolutionary potato patch at the end of the eighteenth century. With their demand for fresh produce, modern cities place a huge strain not only on their hinterlands but on ecologies across the planet. Half of the world's habitable land – close to 5 billion hectares – is now given over to agriculture, twice the amount compared to 1900. Pressure of this intensity on the land is driving species extinction. Using empty space is part of a wider movement to eat locally sourced food as much as possible and take the pressure off the world's forests, shrublands and savannahs.

It is not merely a utopian dream. In many ways, introducing highly intensive agriculture to cities would be a reversion to what cities used to be like. The potato campaign in the Tuileries did not last more than three years. The gardens reverted back to a formal public park. But the Jacobins' dream of making Paris an agricultural city was, in the end, realised.

In the nineteenth century, Paris's market gardeners, **maraîchers,** were called 'goldsmiths of the soil' because they were able to coax four, and sometimes as much as eight, harvests out of urban land each year.* Walled market gardens made up around 6 per cent of the city's area in 1844, each one between one and two acres in size. A British visitor described the edge of Paris as 'a series of interminable parallelograms, planted with salads, spinach, carrots, cabbages, horse-radish and haricot-beans'. The French capital of 2 million people was not only self-sufficient in fresh vegetables harvested from just 2,000 acres of gardens; it exported its surplus to England, where consumers were astonished that the **maraîchers** provided them with salads in the depths of winter. Cucumbers and melons were on sale as early as May.[3]

Miracle-working **maraîchers** worked their tiny gardens exceptionally hard. Heat was generated by cold frames and glass bell-jars covered in rye mats; there were 6 million of these bell-jars in use in Paris in 1909. Vegetables were grown close to each other, radishes next to carrots, then – when the radishes were picked – salads alongside the carrots. Not an inch was ever left fallow or underutilised. Realising such high yields was a specialised, labour-intensive business that was only ever achieved in France, although others tried – and failed – to emulate the success of the **maraîchers.** Making such a garden

---

* The word **maraîcher** comes from **marais**, 'marsh', because the first Parisian market gardeners cultivated crops on the bogs that surrounded Paris.

work called for 'unceasing watchfulness, unlimited industry, and a Spartan disregard for the limits of a working day', according to an awestruck foreign observer. The backbreaking labour gave urban farmers wages far in excess of the city's poor: the profits on one acre of urban land were said to be the equivalent of £87,000 in today's money.[4]

The famed **maraîchers** made their plots more productive than comparable gardens in the countryside. This alchemy was the result of exceptionally hard work and skill, to be sure. But they also had a magic ingredient. Their success is less surprising when you realise that cities contain within them more nutrients than any other ecosystem on the planet. Urban areas have the power to make barren land fertile.

He shook the hand of the head of state, and he achieved national fame. Not bad for a man nicknamed 'Mr Shitman' and 'Stinky Shit Egg'.

A refugee to Beijing in the 1920s from rural poverty, Shi Chuanxiang took what work he could find. That work was as a nightsoil man, emptying latrines by hand and carrying away the waste in fifty-kilogramme buckets. He slept in a shed alongside donkeys and fifteen fellow workers, living on coarse grain rather than rice. Not only was this dirty work; it was dangerous, too. **Fenbas** ('shit lords') vied for the most lucrative shit-collecting routes in Beijing, fighting viciously for the profits of filth. Despite being a pawn of these exploitative criminal gangs, Shi was diligent in his duties. After the founding of the People's Republic of China in 1949, his lot improved when he became a member of his district's sanitation workers' committee and a deputy to the National People's Congress. In 1959, he was named as a model worker, proclaimed a socialist hero, and invited to speak at a ceremony at the Great Hall of the People. It was there that he met Chairman Liu Shaoqi and became an overnight celebrity, interviewed on television and in the newspapers, his portrait painted and his life-story dramatised in a play. Shi's speech was greeted with 'stormy applause'; delegates broke into tears at his tales of a life of privation, filth and danger, moved above all by his miraculous moral and material redemption under the new dispensation of Chinese communism. Liu Shaoqi's daughter volunteered to work on Shi's cleaning squad.

Shi deserved recognition. But honouring him was an urgent act of propaganda. In 1959, China was engaged in a national effort to collect more shit than ever from cities as part of the Great Leap of agriculture – a target of 12.5 billion kilogrammes to spread on the fields. 'Everybody get working,' the newspapers exhorted townspeople, 'everybody collect fertilizer, battle for an even bigger and more bountiful harvest!'[5]

Shi's life story is a reminder not only of how cities in Asia and Mesoamerica fed themselves, but of the unacknowledged and despised people who have been crucial in sanitising the city and insuring its supply of food. The amazingly productive **chinampa** system of agriculture in Tenochtitlan relied on the refuse of 250,000 city-dwellers to make it a model of urban sustainability and self-sufficiency. In Japan, China and Korea, there was a long-standing and highly valuable market for urban excreta, which was likened to gold or treasure and could not be wasted. Nightsoil taken from Asian cities was buried in covered pits and mixed with other materials such as rice straw. Under anaerobic conditions, the manure decomposed until it was safe to use as fertiliser. A Japanese agricultural writer noted in 1682 that 'farmland close to a city is blessed with good access to the source of fertility'. As megacities such as Edo (Tokyo) and Beijing – two of the largest metropolises in the world in the eighteenth century – grew and densified, so did their fringe farms become more productive.[6]

The system produced a virtuous cycle of nutrient exchange: the city paid its way by recycling its prodigious outputs. It is known as a 'closed-loop ecosystem'. Cities reshaped ecosystems around them with their waste products, making their edges incredibly fertile. Metropolis and countryside were locked into an intimate relationship based around the most fundamental of human processes, eating and defecating.

During the reign of the Qianlong Emperor

(1736–96) in China, nightsoil collection was called 'the business of the golden juice'. In Japan, the saying went that 'the landlord's child is brought up on dung': owners of tenement buildings made so much money from selling their tenants' faeces (which they legally owned) that they could live in style. Urban shit was graded according to its potential productivity: the deposits of the wealthy, with diets full of protein (particularly fish), commanded the highest prices. Farmers and peasants on the fringe of Edo fought for generations to regulate the dauntingly high prices charged by nightsoil middlemen for a commodity that was indispensable not only for their livelihoods but for the fate of crowded cities. This system continued until the first decades of the twentieth century; in 1908, 24 million tons of human manure were recycled. But by the 1920s, with the rapid growth of cities in Japan, the supply of shit far exceeded demand; the bottom fell out of the market and it was not profitable to do the dirty work of nightsoil collection. Farmers turned to chemical fertilisers. In the 1950s, when Shi became a national hero, urban excrement was more valuable than ever in China, where synthetic fertiliser was not yet widely available or affordable. Until recently, fourteen out of China's fifteen largest cities were self-sufficient in food, supplied by their agricultural suburbs, which were kept fertile by treated human waste.[7]

In European and North American cities, by

contrast, such practices were pooh-poohed. People recoiled with revulsion from the idea of using their own emissions to fertilise their food. Excreta was dumped into streets, rivers and harbours, fomenting the horrendous diseases of the nineteenth century – typhus and cholera. In contrast, Edo/Tokyo – with its commercialised human waste-collecting and recycling system – was cleaner and hence spared the ravages of infection. Unlike in New York, Paris and London, faecal matter – the brown gold of cities – did not enter the water systems of Asian towns. Western metropolises developed expensive engineering solutions to the humungous backlog of crap – sewage and wastewater systems that flushed the problem away, out of sight. For some critics in the nineteenth century, the mass expulsion of **merde** represented a criminal waste of resources. What could have been a closed ecological loop became a linear conveyer belt of consumption and expulsion on a titanic scale.

Karl Marx lamented the rift in 'the metabolic interaction between man and earth' caused by capitalist extraction and conversion of nutrients from the land into pollution. The modern city, he wrote in **Das Kapital,** prevented 'the return to the soil of its constituent elements consumed by man . . . it hinders the operation of the eternal natural condition for the lasting fertility of the soil'. Friedrich Engels called for a 'fusion of town and country', so that the masses 'languishing' in cities could use their excrement 'for the production of plants instead of for the production of disease.' The garden writer Shirley Hibberd, writing in 1884, was almost apoplectic with rage that English towns were 'all busy in devising schemes to waste' what he saw as the most powerful fertiliser going. 'London, especially, might contribute to the soil around her [human] manure worth two-million [pounds] a year, yet the Boards that manage these things are busting their wooden heads to throw it into the sea.'

One thing was missing from this analysis. Human excretions could never command the high prices they did in Japan and China because Western cities possessed a comparable resource on a stupendous scale.

'A great city is the most mighty of dung-makers', declared Victor Hugo. Manure 'symbolises the world and its life', wrote Emile Zola '. . . Paris rotted everything, and returned everything to the soil, which never wearied of repairing the ravages of death'. The miracle-working **maraîchers** were so productive because they fertilised each acre of their market gardens with 400 tons of Paris's most prolific energy by-product – horse dung.

The same principle was true in most cities. When George Washington departed Manhattan and journeyed to Long Island in the spring of 1790, he found fields in 'a higher state of vegetation . . . than any place else I had seen – occasioned in a great degree by the Manure drawn from the City of New

York'. Market gardens in Queens and Brooklyn –
just across the water from Manhattan – bloomed
with the input of horse manure and organic waste
produced in profusion by the city. London possessed 'Dung Wharf' near Blackfriars, where the
city's copious manure and sewage was sent down-
river to fertilise market gardens first in Chelsea
and then in west Middlesex as the expansion of
the city displaced the thousands of market gardens
and orchards that clustered in the urban edgelands,
feasting on the nutrient overload produced in the
city centre.

'The richest soils . . . are those around the
Metropolis', observed John Claudius Loudon. Farms
and fields disappeared on the urban fringe, converted into intensively managed and heavily enriched small market gardens and orchards. The
edges of cities, with their fruit trees, vegetable plots
and commercial nurseries, along with great tracts of
suburban gardens, were **more** biodiverse than agricultural regions. Cherry and apple blossoms, le-
gumes, courgettes, tomatoes, squashes and soft fruits
are insect-pollinated produce: bees did well on the
urban edgelands.

In the 1860s, 10 per cent of the entire market
vegetable produce of the United States was harvested within the present-day limits of New York
City – a staggering level of productivity. Manhattan
Island was the 'dung heap of the universe', making
nearby Flatbush, Brooklyn, the 'Market Garden of

America' as a result. At Covent Garden, London's main wholesale fruit and veg market, carts and barges (and later rail waggons and lorries) carrying strawberries, raspberries, gooseberries, apples, plums, pears, cabbages, cherries, salads, peas, asparagus, tomatoes and other fresh produce converged every night during the growing season. In the early morning, those carts and barges returned, laden with manure that had emanated from the 700,000 or so horses that trotted through London each day. Improved with decades' worth of manure and (later) sewage sludge, the soil in the area around the village of Heathrow, fourteen miles to the west of central London and wedged between its expanding suburbs, ranked among the best in the world for growing fruit, flowers and vegetables up until the Second World War. The city had made this land miraculously fertile with its filth.[8]

Today, Heathrow is still full of fresh produce. The difference is that it is no longer grown in the area's artificially enriched soil but imported thousands of miles to Heathrow Airport, built from 1944 on top of London's fruit and veg basket. The urban market garden hinterland has disappeared in cities all over the developed world during the last sixty years or so. The combustion engine killed the Parisian urban farmer and the London market gardener: no more horse shit to turn soil into gold when streets were full of cars, buses and lorries. In any case, the advent of chemically-intensive, industrial scale agriculture along with technologies of refrigeration and cheap air transport would have seen them off on their own. The highly productive form of city agriculture, based on waste nutrient recycling, collapsed. In the twenty-first century, 81 per cent of the 6.9 million tons of food consumed in London each year is imported from outside the UK.

It is vital to realise just how recent this disconnect between city and food is. Up until the 1940s, 40 per cent of all vegetables consumed within an American city were grown **within** its metropolitan area. No item of food travelled more than fifty miles to Los Angeles. Many settlers in L.A. had come from farming backgrounds in the Midwest; the metropolis was attractive because its climate, irrigation and soil allowed them to combine small-scale domestic farming with blue-collar jobs, supplementing incomes by keeping poultry and/or a cow, and growing fruit and vegetables. During the Great Depression, the federal government financed 'subsistence homesteads'. Over 25,000 small farms ringed L.A. in the 1930s, joined by many more food-producing backyard plots. The same was true of most American cities, where – until after the Second World War – suburbia had the distinct tinge of the farmyard. Urban-edge farming reached a peak of productivity in the 1930s as it grew in lockstep with rapid urbanisation.[9]

By the 1950s, L.A.'s urban agriculture was on its way out. In cities everywhere, market gardens and orchards became suburbs, airports, arterial roads, distribution centres and shopping malls. The advantages of farming perishable goods close to cities, with their voracious markets and generous sources of nutrients, simply vanished. Tighter regulations and zoning ordinances kicked cows, goats and chickens out of suburbia, erasing its jumbled rural-urban character of small farmsteads and backyard horticulture. The burden of food production was shifted to distant, unseen ecosystems as the lawn smothered suburbia like a hungry octopus.

Today, 34 per cent of greenhouse gases and 78 per cent of oceanic and freshwater pollution is caused by food production and distribution. We are highly aware of how significantly we have disrupted the global carbon cycle, but less so of our disruption of the nutrient cycle by pumping vast amounts of manufactured fertilisers into the environment. Humans have doubled the amount of nitrogen in circulation and tripled the amount of phosphorous. 'We are fertilizing the earth on a global scale and in a largely uncontrolled experiment,' the United Nations Environment Programme declared.[10]

'Our hordes of population,' complained a British agricultural periodical in the 1840s, 'instead of being enrichers of the island . . . are absolute impoverishers.' Instead of using the nutrient cycle, European countries were importing guano from South America to use as fertiliser – impoverishing one distant ecosystem in order to fundamentally transform a closer one. Various companies collected and dried human excrement and mixed it with charcoal and gypsum to create a powder called poudrette, which was sold as fertiliser under euphemistic brand names such as 'Alkine-vegetative Powder', 'Alexander's Chio Fou', 'Clarke's Desiccated Compost' or 'Owen's Animalized Carbon'. Poudrette factories were established in France, Britain, the United States, Singapore and Bombay. But the economics of collecting faeces from cities were dead set against such schemes, particularly in the era of municipal sewage systems that flushed away the waste. By the end of the nineteenth century, with the advent of modern synthetic fertilisers, entrepreneurial attempts to harness the power of poo had been abandoned. The American agricultural scientist F. H. King wrote with horror in 1911 that 'a generation has swept into the sea soil fertility which only centuries of life could accumulate, and yet this fertility is the substratum of all that is living'.[11]

Food, energy, water and waste are the primary ways a city impacts on the environment. The accumulation of excess nutrients in cities was most commonly disposed of straight into urban watersheds, inflicting grievous environmental damage on rivers and coastlines. Excess nitrogen wreaks havoc on coastal marshland, turning it into bare mud that offers scant protection against the tides. In 2020, British water companies discharged raw sewage over 400,000 times for a total of 3.1 million hours straight into the country's rivers and beaches. During the twentieth century, sewage was incinerated, buried in landfill or dumped at sea as the metabolic rift between city and countryside grew larger and many times more destructive. In the US, discarded food left to rot in landfills is not only an immense, unused accumulation of organic matter but the second-largest emitter of methane, a more harmful greenhouse gas than carbon dioxide. Rather than being a recycling loop, a modern city commands a one-way flow of nutrients and organic material. This represents a triumph of engineering but a colossal squandering of resources: if we collected all the nutrients in domestic wastewater and organic waste, we could fertilise all the crops needed to feed the world's population. As it is, most nutrients that enter a city accumulate there. Some 60 per cent of the nitrogen and phosphorous inputs into Hong Kong stay in the city, buried in waste dumps and seeping into groundwater. In cities all over the world, the mass expulsion of **merde** kills the tidal marshlands that should form its bastion against water.

Things are beginning to change, albeit slowly. Tougher regulations regarding clean water and bans on dumping at sea, landfilling and incineration have forced countries to find alternative destinations for their sewage. Today, the euphemistic name for anaerobically treated sewage sludge is 'biosolids', and its use is growing as a means of closing the nutrient loop. Britain uses 3.6 million tons of sewage on its fields every year, delivered to farms by 170,000 lorries. That means that 76 per cent of sewage sludge is used for agriculture, a massive increase over the last few decades. The European Union recovers 50 per cent and the U.S. 60 per cent of its sewage for fertiliser. In drought-stricken Australia, human waste used to be pumped into the ocean. Today, treated sewage from Sydney is boosting productivity for cattle farmers in New South Wales; wastewater now irrigates 200 square kilometres of Adelaide's peripheral market gardens and cereal farms. The trouble is that we have poisoned our bodies as well as our land and water. Much modern sewage is full of unwelcome pharmaceuticals, hormones, antibiotics, heavy metals and microplastics. There are some 80,000 humanmade chemicals that can enter sludge. The dark shadow of the city extends over millions of acres of farmland.[12]

Rethinking what we do with our cities' waste is fundamental to considering the place of the city in nature. But so too is the other side of the coin – what the city eats in the first place.

In the past, these relationships were readily apparent, manifest in the malodorous piles of shit and the rings of market gardens, orchards and fields that pressed up against the edge of the city. Now that those processes have become invisible, we have to stretch our minds further to conceptualise the complexities of urban metabolism. The eradication of city food production was very recent and must count as an experiment. Today, in the developing world, city farming is a mainstay of urban economies; in Hanoi, 80 per cent of vegetables come from the city and its immediate periphery. As we count the costs of planetary environmental degradation, we might by necessity have to rethink where our resources come from: ventures such as Nature Urbaine in Paris might one day become widespread as a response to disruptions to our supply chain brought about by climate change, pandemics and other unforeseeable disasters. As the Tuileries potato field illustrates, growing food in cities is often a reaction to a crisis. Cities have been forced to turn to their own resources many times through history, often with surprising success.

In other words, cities have enormous potential to cultivate food. Urban agriculture is sometimes a means of survival. But it is also an enormous pleasure for millions of people. It challenges our notion of what a city can be.

The Roman poet Martial wrote to a friend in the first century CE: 'You have given me, Lupus, a suburban farm, but I have a bigger farm in my window . . . wherein a cucumber cannot lie straight, nor a snake harbour its whole length.'[13]

The poet was referring to a windowsill container

where he could raise a few vegetables. Pliny the Elder commented that 'the lower classes in the city used to give their eyes a daily view of country scenes by means of imitation gardens in their windows'. From ancient Romans growing vegetables in the windows of cramped **insulae** – tenement high rises – to modern allotmenteers, the urge to grow food in cities has always been with us. For some, harvesting an urban crop is a form of nostalgia for the distant countryside and natural processes, a pleasure that contrasts with the greyness of the city. For others, it has been a matter of survival.

An 'oasis in a concrete desert', they called it – a fourteen-acre farm in South Central Los Angeles that juxtaposed the roaring highways and grey expanse of warehouses. It grew on a plot of abandoned, rat-infested land in one of L.A.'s poorest districts, purchased by the city for a waste-to-energy incinerator in 1986. Still unbuilt when the area was badly scarred during the race riots of 1992, the city allowed the Los Angeles Regional Food Bank to create a community garden on the site as a way of repairing this damaged community. It proved an immediate hit with South Central's recently arrived Latino immigrants, who had largely grown up in rural parts of Mexico. In an area short on supermarkets and fresh produce – a quintessential urban food desert – the farm provided the community with varieties of corn, avocado, guava, Mexican wild yams, tomatoes and squashes among 150 different plant species grown on 350 plots in the once-benighted wasteland. It also became a public space for the community to form around, escape from the pressures of the city and reconnect with rural life.

L.A. cops in riot gear, brandishing chainsaws, arrived on 13 June 2006. They were there to enforce an eviction order. The bulldozers followed the police, ripping down sheds and acres of plants as the dispossessed urban famers angrily protested. The original owner had decided he wanted his land back to build a warehouse and distribution centre. The farm reverted back to wasteland, remaining empty for years.

The South Central Farm replayed a story that has been told throughout history. Access to and ownership of land – land that can be tilled and made bountiful – is bitterly contested. Land represents freedom, independence and subsistence. In 1880, a journalist visited what he called the 'Bohemia of the labouring class' – a shanty town located close to Central Park in Manhattan's Upper West Side, between 62nd and 72nd Streets. Here, he found an interzone, a collection of self-built cabins housing rag-pickers, day labourers, junkmen, porters, drivers and their families, living hard against the advancing frontier of millionaires' houses and apartment buildings. They settled there yearning for 'light and air, for the smell of the bare earth and the sight of trees and water'. They exploited this liminal area, keeping goats, cows and chickens and growing vegetables for their own subsistence and to sell to others before the tide of urbanisation pushed them to a new frontier. This kind of precarious edgeland squatter settlement, caught betwixt city and countryside, was typical not only of American cities but of European ones as well.[14]

The journalist found the inhabitants of the Upper West Side shantytown proud, independent and scornful of those imprisoned in tenements downtown. Many originated from Germany and Ireland; living in huts on the edge of cities was, for them, as much a lifestyle choice as a necessity. These edgeland urban villages resisted the living conditions, forms of control and exploitative property market prevalent in the industrial city. On the edge of Berlin, Europe's fastest-growing city in the second half of the nineteenth century, **Laubenkolonisten** – 'garden shed colonists' – occupied and grew produce on vacant land. Many of them – like the Latinos who tilled L.A.'s South Central Farm – came from rural backgrounds to work in Berlin's industrial sector; they deployed their farming skills to supplement their incomes, feed their families and ease the transition to city life.[15]

Their self-created peripheral world of huts and vegetable plots became a feature of the urban landscape, a curiously untidy and shabby one. In 1872, the capital of the newly unified German state experienced an unmanageable influx of immigrants. Squatter camps mushroomed on the edge of the city, as they did in Paris and numerous other big cities. For some, this state of affairs was a disgrace. But many observers celebrated – or romanticised – the orderliness of the shantytowns and the good sense of the squatters in rejecting the inner city in favour of a more natural setting. For one thing, the huts and vegetable patches signified self-sufficiency. The newcomers were, in this version of events, like sturdy American frontiersmen, building communities on their own and embracing self-reliance. Like the squatters on the Upper West Side in New York, they rejected the iron distinction between urban and rural life, blending the two in ways that seemed incongruous with the modern city. The shantytowns that sprang up in 1872 were soon cleared, but the informal **Laubenkolonien,** the 'green slums', continued to house 40,000 Berliners in sheds surrounded by vegetables, fruit and domestic animals at the end of the nineteenth century; by 1933, there were 120,000 people living this quasi-rural lifestyle in the German capital.[16]

In Britain, working-class allotmenteers jokingly boasted of their 'town' and 'country' residences – their homes and their vegetable plots. At a time when the cost of food soaked up 40–60 per cent of incomes, producing one's own food was an economic necessity. But it also brought pleasure, exercise, an escape from the routine of monotonous labour, and congested communities. In heavily built-up parts of the East End of London or the rental barracks of Berlin, vegetable plots were the only available garden space for the poor. Working an allotment (**kleingarten**) or community garden was, above all, an escape from the unremitting urban environment, a truer form of **rus in urbe** than a formal park.

The fight for a small plot on which to grow food marked a battle over the future of cities themselves. Demand for allotments came from the grassroots, from working people who craved land to till and the primal connection to nature that comes with that experience. Allotments provide a rare example of how ordinary, often powerless, people have been able to shape the cityscape. In industrial cities – particularly in the grimmest and most neglected parts of them – there was a desire among locals to green the grey urban environment by their own means. In Berlin, garden shed colonists appropriated municipal land on the edge of the expanding metropolis, voting with their spades to preserve places in which to garden. In the East End of London, in the unlikely spot of Cubitt Town on the Isle of Dogs – one of the dankest slums in the city – a group of 'zealous gardeners' made up of dock labourers, lightermen and boilermen rented disused industrial land and 'had to dig through two feet of old iron in a lumber yard, to clear away two-barge-loads of burnt matches, and from the foundation of a house that was never built to remove . . . forty tons of concrete ere they could lay down their . . . soil'. By the autumn of the following year, these men were able to show off their harvest of cauliflowers, onions, cabbages, carrots, beans and beetroots wrought from the unforgiving city.[17]

In some cases, the working class were aided by philanthropists. From the beginning of the nineteenth century, rural immigrants to German cities were provided, if they were lucky, with **Arbeitergärten,** or 'poor gardens'. Railway companies often rented out unused land alongside tracks to their workers, making allotment gardening highly visible to passengers entering cities. Aware of the virtues and health benefits of urban cultivation, municipalities, factory owners and landlords sometimes rented out wasteland to working people as a means of alleviating urban poverty. But, despite these paternalistic efforts, the right to land was one that had to be asserted again and again by the gardeners.

This desire to cultivate ran contrary to the logic of urban expansion, when land is at a premium and fiercely contested. Working people had to fight hard to protect from development the land they had laboriously cleared and made fertile. Their tenure remained uncertain: any day the garden could be taken away to make way for buildings. The **Laubenkolonisten** of Berlin founded an association in 1897 to protect their holdings. The right to land became highly politicised, drawing in left-wing parties to defend the rights of working people. The first national **Kleingarten Kongress** (Allotment

Congress) was held in Danzig in 1912, demanding
legal and political protection for urban allotments.
In the East End of London, urban gardeners who
saw the tidal wave of urbanisation surging their way
formed a 'solid phalanx to protect and promote their
interests', mobilising as a political movement in order
to protect the land they cultivated and pressure the
municipal council to provide more fields. Growing
food in the city was a radical act. According to the
East Ham and West Ham allotment associations: 'It
may be [the allotment holders who] are effecting a
silent revolution on one of our acutest problems –
that revolution of ideas which alone is calculated to
advance the cause of Democracy.'[18]

During the First World War, when Germany
was under blockade and Britain faced the threat of
U-boats to its food imports, the value of working-
class gardens became apparent almost overnight.
In German cities, the amount of urban land under
cultivation jumped from 3,275 to 26,676 acres.
Allotments doubled in Berlin and grew eightyfold
in Cologne. In Britain, U-boat warfare caused spiralling prices and a dearth of fresh food, resulting in
commons, parks, playing fields, schools, cemeteries
and even palace flower gardens being converted into
allotments. By the end of the war, there was one
allotment for every five households in Britain, and
still 7,000 new applications for a plot every week.
Patriotism motivated people to garden in cities on
a scale unseen before, but they were also animated,

according to one observer, 'by the awakening of a long-latent land-hunger in the hearts of the people' who had discovered the joys of working the city's soil and did not want to relinquish it in peacetime. Unfortunately for the budding city farmers, the passion for allotments was stifled as almost all the urban plots were returned to their pre-war uses, despite loud protests. They were revived when the next world war came along and Britons were once more urged to 'Dig for Victory'.[19]

A by-product of total war was cities turned green as never before, albeit temporarily. By exploiting their land, cities were able to supply 50 per cent of their domestic vegetable needs very quickly; few would have suspected that metropolises could be so productive. Germany managed to cling on to some of the wartime legacy: when Greater Berlin was formed in 1920, it had 165,000 allotment gardens which made up 14,826 acres (7 per cent of the total land area), compared to the 1,853 acres given over to parks, playgrounds and sports fields. The determination of generations of working-class urban gardeners added a significant amount of greenery to Berlin and other cities that would not have been there otherwise.[20]

Today, Berlin's allotments have shrunk to 70,953 plots covering just over 7,000 acres of the city. Even so, that amount of green space given over to gardening is exceptionally large for a city of its kind (over double that of London, for example). As ever in history, the amount of land dedicated to allotments in cities falls far short of demand; in 2019, Berlin had 12,000 people waiting between three and six years for a plot to become available. In London, applications for a plot rose from 1,330 in 1997 to 16,655 in 2011. In Britain as a whole, 87,000 people were on the waiting list for an allotment shortly before the Covid-19 crisis sent demand through the roof. In the past, people grew food out of necessity. Now, when food has been cheap, at least by historical standards, a driving force is, among other things, ecological – a desire to escape the environmental catastrophe of industrial agriculture and eat produce that has not travelled in refrigerated conditions for 2,000 miles. The appetite for growing food in cities is becoming ever more apparent; it remains an elemental desire among many people. Now, as in the past, the challenge is to carve out room in the city to sow the seeds.

The planting of the Tuileries with potatoes in 1793 shows that necessity is the mother of urban horticultural revolution. Or rather, emergencies clear space in the city for people to grow their own food, typically when supply lines are compromised. The Great Depression, the Second World War and other periods of dearth revived small-scale food production in cities. In the United States during the Second World War, the output of 12 million urban and suburban and 6 million rural 'Victory Gardens' matched the produce of commercially grown fresh vegetables – 10 million tons. During the Cold War, 13.5 million East Germans grew vegetables on plots totalling 91,500 acres. Allotments provided badly needed fresh food at a time when agricultural food production was concentrated on staples; and more than that, the veg patch and its hut was a private space away from cramped apartments and the stresses of surveillance. The fall of the Soviet Bloc in 1991 had a devastating impact on Cuba's food, fertiliser and fuel imports. In response, Havana managed to make itself almost entirely self-sufficient in vegetables by turning 12 per cent of its land area into high-yield, organic, urban farms – fertilised, as by the nineteenth-century Parisian market gardeners, with manure and household waste – and squeezing 25,000 allotments into every available patch of land.

Nine meals from anarchy. The oft-repeated phrase was written by the investigative journalist Alfred Henry Lewis in 1906. A century and a bit on, the vulnerability of food supply lines is painfully apparent. In August 2000, when British lorry drivers were blockading fuel depots and oil refineries in protest against fuel duties, government ministers were warned by the big supermarkets that the shelves would be empty within three days – or after nine meals – if deliveries ceased. Looting swept New Orleans after Hurricane Katrina struck and food could not get into the flooded city. In April 2008, riots broke out in cities in thirty-seven low-income countries after oil price spikes forced up fertiliser – and hence food – costs. The invasion of Ukraine by Russia in 2022 placed even greater costs on the production and distribution of food, placing millions under the threat of starvation. Supermarket shelves emptied as people panicked in the face of perceived shortages in the early days of the Covid-19 pandemic. Food security is fast becoming one of the critical issues of the twenty-first century. It is acute in cities, which always exist nine meals away from anarchy.

There is not much empty space between the small dwellings in Kibera, Africa's largest slum, on the outskirts of Nairobi. But thousands of people grow vegetables in sacks filled with manure and soil. Kale, spinach, onions, tomatoes, arrowroot and coriander sprout from the sacks placed on doorsteps and in alleyways. During the Covid-19 crisis, when food supplies were disrupted, sales of slum-grown vegetables surged, providing income for people living in extreme poverty. In Kampala, Uganda's capital, 49 per cent of households engage in urban agriculture (up from 25–35 per cent in the 1990s). The average for urban Africa as a whole is around 40 per cent. The vitality of food production in this city of 1.6 million was invaluable during the lockdown of 2020, supplying 65 per cent of the population with their fruit and vegetables and 70 per cent with poultry products. In Kampala, food is grown wherever there is space, including on the roofs of houses and in sacks, vertical planters, discarded plastic bottles and old tyres. Since the food crisis of 2008, and during a period of rapid urbanisation and increasing prices, finding innovative ways to produce food has yielded new business opportunities in thousands of low-income cities. Add climate change to the list of threats, and the importance of city farmers will only rise as the twenty-first century progresses.[21]

In ancient cities such as Angkor Wat and those in pre-Columbian Mesoamerica, areas of cultivation coexisted with clusters of high-density housing and temple sites. Up until the later nineteenth century, around 40 per cent of Tokyo was reserved for agriculture. Rice paddies were placed next to residential areas not only as a source of food but as reservoirs to soak up floodwater. This kind of multifunctional cityscape is appearing again in the fastest-growing cities of the present day. Continued urbanisation might prove to be impossible without reshaping cities in this way. The shift is happening, in many cases, organically, without central direction. The reason for this is that the bulk of urban growth is occurring on the edges of cities. Low-density urbanisation is enfolding farms into the city, creating a novel form of city – a **desakota** or ruralopolis – consisting of a hybrid landscape of

high-density housing, factories and farmland. This
process simultaneously urbanises the countryside
and ruralises the city.

Dar-es-Salaam, Tanzania, is an example of this
new kind of megacity. One of the fastest growing
metropolises in Africa, it has a population of over
7 million and is projected to be the continent's third-
largest city by 2100, behind Lagos and Kinshasa.
A quarter of Dar-es-Salaam's land area is used for
agriculture. Growing takes place predominantly on
plots smaller than half an acre found (often illegally) in fringe areas, on wastelands, roadsides and
swamps and under power cables. Agriculture is the
second-biggest employer in the Tanzanian capital
accounting for 20 per cent of full-time jobs. This
workforce supplies almost all the city's fruit, vegetables and eggs, as well as 60 per cent of its milk. This
preponderance of locally produced food is not un-
typical in the developing world; in Africa and Asia,
virtually all greens are grown in urban and peri-
urban market gardens, as was the case in London,
Paris and New York just over half a century ago
and still is in Australia and China. Studies have
shown that African cities that can grow nutritious
food have better health outcomes. Across the globe,
urban agriculture is an unacknowledged mainstay
of city life, involving a workforce of 100–200 million people and supplying 15–20 per cent of our
food needs.[22]

I say 'unacknowledged' because urban farmers are,

as they always have been, in a precarious position. Farming in cities has, until recently, been illegal in many countries, and most growers exist in the grey economy without representation or champions. Like the Latino farmers in South Central L.A. or generations of working class allotmenteers, the overwhelming majority do not own the land they cultivate, and it can be taken away from them at a moment's notice. City agricultural production has been associated negatively with poverty, failure and emergencies. Very few African cities include horticulture in their city planning; as a result, it is likely to fall victim to the pressures of development. Yet urban agriculture should not be seen as a relic of the past. It is, on the contrary, an answer to the problems of modernisation and a route out of poverty for many: a third of people in Dar-es-Salaam make an income from micro-gardening and animal husbandry, and the city would have a subsistence problem without them. It also has important ecological consequences in greening and providing biodiversity in megacities that are starved of parks, forests and other open places and which contain many people born in rural areas.

Agricultural land is declining and our hunger for food is rising. Cities are a big part of the problem; they gobble up agricultural land as they grow. Rising incomes associated with urbanisation increase the demand for imported foodstuffs. As we have seen, cities have been, and can be, remarkably

productive landscapes, particularly during times of
crisis. There are plenty of advocates who want to
reintroduce intensive agriculture back into cities or
their immediate peripheries in order to reduce our
food miles and ecological footprint. Given that cities once lived in close harmony with their hinterlands, and still do in many parts of the world, are
we destined to return to that situation? There is
certainly a case for putting local, urban and peri-
urban agriculture at the heart of urban resilience
and climate change adaptation, closing that wide,
ecologically costly gap between food production
and consumption.

Could we go back to the days of the **maraîchers**
or become more like Havana and be nutritionally
autonomous? Around the world, entrepreneurs are
experimenting with ZFarming – zero-acre agriculture in old warehouses, factories and other disused
buildings, a form of cultivation that has no need
of pre-existing green areas. In an abandoned steel
mill in Newark, New Jersey, almost a million tons
of leafy greens can be grown in vertical stacks without soil, sunlight, pesticides or fertiliser. LED lights
allow the micro-greens to photosynthesise; a fine
mist of nutrient-rich, recirculated water continually feeds the roots in a process known as aeropon-
ics. Or, they are grown hydroponically in inorganic
substrates. Similar farms are appearing in cities all
over the world, including a former bomb shelter
thirty-three metres below the streets of London and

a 3.7-acre greenhouse on a former Sears warehouse rooftop in Montreal operated by Lufta Farms. Such rooftop farms are heated by sunlight and watered by harvested rain. An aeroponic or hydroponic ZFarm has a yield up to seventy times greater than a conventional farm, while using a tenth of the water and no pesticides.

We are yet to see whether this revived form of urban agriculture will succeed or become widespread. Maybe unforeseen crises will force the issue. Singapore – where just 1 per cent of land is used for agriculture – is aiming to boost its domestic food production from 10 per cent to 30 per cent by 2030 using these high-tech methods. Cities will never become self-sufficient, however, even if we scale up rooftop farms to the maximum extent and convert hundreds of factories into ZFarms. You can't grow cereals or rice in busy urban centres, let alone find room for herds of cattle and flocks of sheep. But they can become many times more bountiful, especially in soft fruits, tomatoes, chillies, delicate greens, kale and lettuces – exactly the kinds of edibles that incur high transport and refrigeration costs and require lots of chemicals and plastic wrapping. The alchemy of the **maraîchers** could be reborn, only this time in an anonymous warehouse.

All these things will no doubt reduce the ecological footprints of cities. But one of the lasting legacies might be a revolution in the use of space in cities. A project like Paris's Nature Urbaine forces us to confront the acres of unused, sterile ground in cities, just as the world wars forced people to exploit parts of the urban terrain that had been overlooked or underused for generations. If you **really** want food, every surface becomes a potential seedbed. Studies of both Sheffield in the UK and Cleveland, Ohio, showed that if these cities exploited every vacant lot, rooftop and green space, they could become self-reliant in fresh produce. Now, neither city is going to plough up its parks, golf courses and cemeteries to grow greens; but the studies remind us just how much of a city could become vegetated if we wanted. Every year in Germany, 2,500 acres of roof gardens are created. London has added a green area to its inventory larger than Hyde Park – 371 acres – over the last few years just by converting rooftops. Creating habitats like this out of thin air is of huge ecological consequence. We could do more; think of all those barren flat roofs on hospitals, schools and supermarkets suddenly blooming with life. Cities could become three-dimensional jungles, with green roofs, walls, windowsills and other crevices and surfaces.

Only an apocalyptic crisis will make cities self-sufficient. Edible rooftops are important because they motivate people to cultivate the cityscape. The company Urban Organic created a series of large, terraced roof gardens on the top of Coutts Bank in the City of London, some of it squeezed into narrow maintenance walkways. Year-round, they cultivate dozens of different varieties of fruit alongside tomatoes, beans, squashes, salads, herbs and unconventional exotics almost certainly absent elsewhere in central London, such as saffron, samphire, wasabi, kiwis, pepinos, Sichuan pepper and Chilean guava.

Such rooftop gardens – even if they were scaled up – can only provide the barest nibble to satisfy the appetites of the millions who inhabit a large metropolis. But that is beside the point. Our eternal quest for novelty, fresh, exotic food, and the sheer pleasure in the miracle of coaxing crops out of the bleak concrete adds biodiversity and greenness to cities. Many rooftop gardens are not edible; they are there to provide beauty in the form of flower meadows, trees and ornamental planting. But the edible component of skyline cultivation is by far the most exciting and enticing part of this aerial revolution.

Making cities resilient and self-sufficient through urban agriculture has been strongly advocated by some experts and campaigners. But the focus should be on finding as many new ways of maintaining and maximising biodiversity. Vegetables and fruits are just part of the cosmopolitan mix of species found in cities. Cities are not farms; that is one of their great advantages for wildlife. Just ask a bee. An urban bee has a stronger immune system than its rural cousin, has a much higher winter survival rate and produces considerably more honey. There are more bees, and bee species, in cities today than ever before. Analysis of honey from a bee in Boston, Massachusetts, found it had pollen taken from 411 different species of plants; nearby country honey contained traces from just eighty-two. Cities are islands of biodiversity compared to rural monocultures, with a bigger and more diverse source of nectar even than nature reserves and forests; they are not awash with pesticides and synthetic fertilisers.

The realisation that cities are good for bees has led to a very modern form of urban food production. In 2014, Los Angeles City Council relaxed the rules that banned beekeeping in part to balance colony collapse in rural areas. Urban beekeeping has surged in popularity, tripling in London, for example, during the 2010s to reach 7,500 registered hives that produce jars of city-made honey. In Paris, meanwhile, there was a 733 per cent increase in hives in the same period. Honey from an urban terroir can contain less glyphosate than country honey and have a more complex taste.

We need to preserve the diverse patches of natural and semi-natural habitat in cities that benefit bees. As ever, there are competing ecological needs nibbling at us; food production is just one. Parmentier's potatoes in the Tuileries answered a pressing problem; but rows of crops cannot compete with the amazing biodiversity in gardens or the riot of spontaneous growth throughout the urban wildscape. Across the planet, there is a battle between our demands for food and for wilderness habitats. Perhaps cities should not join this battle and instead offer up their open spaces to invertebrates, mammals and birds that are now learning to relish the curious, complex urban environment and the abundance of nutrients we pump into it.

7.

Zootropolis

On a hot, sunny August evening in 2020, just as the sun was setting, I rode my bike out of central Berlin to swim in the Teufelssee, the 'Devil's Lake', in the Grunewald forest. It is joyful to swim in a wild lake in the middle of a city, surrounded by trees and snuffling wild boars. Unbeknownst to me at the time, one of those boars, nicknamed Elsa, had become internationally famous that very day. Accompanied by her piglets, she had picked up and run off with a bather's laptop bag. Photographs of the nude, rotund gentleman desperately chasing the triumphant thief around the beach were going viral as I swam in the darkening waters.[1]

Berlin's wild boars had, in recent years, been claiming large parts of the city for themselves, and their behaviour around humans is getting bolder. They are part of an incredible influx of animals into cities over the past few years.

Koalas are making themselves at home in Brisbane, and endangered Carnaby's cockatoos have taken up residence in Perth. In the same period, peregrine falcons have become urbanised, bee numbers have

boomed in cities, wolves are hanging out in the suburbs of central Europe, and in Minnesota, the largest
concentration of white-tailed deer now resides in the
Twin Cities metro area. Golden lion tamarins are settling in Brazilian cities. Benefiting from cleaner waters and the re-naturalisation of urban watercourses,
otters have been found in Singapore, Chicago and
over one hundred British towns and cities since the
turn of the millennium. Even leopards – secretive
and wary of humans – have infiltrated Mumbai,
slipping through the city by night, generally unseen.
Coyotes have taken to the urban lifestyle since they
started exploring American cities in the 1990s. Now,
they exist in vast numbers alongside other recent city
migrants such as raccoons and skunks. They are at
the vanguard of an invading army of wildlife which
in all probability will soon include wolves, mountain
lions and bears.

Surveying the city from its vantage point high
on a skyscraper, the peregrine falcon does not perceive a compromised environment. It is a landscape
reminiscent of the cliffs and canyons of its natural
hunting grounds, but it is even better than the real
thing, well stocked as it is with prey. A pair moved
to New York in 1983, and four decades on, that
city has the highest density of peregrine falcons
anywhere in the world. They have also moved into
Cape Town, Berlin, Delhi, London and dozens of
other big cities in recent years.

The early-twenty-first-century global skyscraper

boom has been a blessing for peregrine falcons; it has increased the number of cliffs many times over. The tall buildings favoured by globalised capitalism are perfect for aerial dive-bombing. In New York, peregrines exploit the wind channels between sky-scrapers to herd flocks of pigeons out to sea, where they catch them. An increased number of pigeons in Delhi, meanwhile, attracted peregrines, Bengal eagle owls, shikras, kestrels and Bonelli's eagles in the late 2010s to try their luck in the big city. The reign of the peregrine is evidence, perhaps, of a healthy city. It is an apex predator, reliant on a food chain of microbes, insects, small mammals and birds. The peregrine is with us in our cities because they are more biodiverse than ever.

No animal is native to a city. Like us, like the per-egrine, like the rat, all urban species are immigrants trying their luck in a novel ecosystem. Those wild animals that learn to become urban go through a process known as synurbanisation. The peregrine is symbolic of synurbanisation as it rereads the human metropolis as a bounteous landscape. Urbanising animals must possess a high degree of plasticity – that is the ability to adapt a range of behaviours to a bewildering new environment and, crucially, the proximity of human beings. Rats, cockroaches, pi-geons and monkeys have been doing this for millen-nia. Now, they are being joined by an extraordinary array of animals. Like their predecessors, they are undergoing fast adaptations.

As **Urban Jungle** has explored, cities are experiencing significant change as they adapt to the climate emergency and respond to our need for nature. As a result, they have become much more enticing environments for a number of species, with their shaggier parks, increasing canopy and rewilded wetlands and rivers. But things are changing outside the city as well. Urban expansion, the intensification of agriculture, deforestation, heatwaves, droughts and wildfires are forcing numerous species to seek refuge in cities and adapt to their new surroundings. What can we do to make urban centres hospitable to these creatures escaping the baneful consequences of our actions? What will be their fate? The intermingling of animals and humans has never been an unproblematic relationship.

That brings us back to Elsa and the boars of Berlin. Like greedy Elsa, they have rapidly gone from being curiosities to nuisances, turning over rubbish bins and uprooting gardens, parks and cemeteries. The city has to cull 2,000 a year. After otters raided a pond in Singapore and feasted on expensive farmed fish during the lockdown of 2020, there were calls for a cull: they were fiercely defended by Singaporeans and got a personal tweet of support from the prime minister. The Twin Cities of St Paul and Minneapolis pay exterminators $250 per deer destroyed and fork out $700 for each one injected with contraceptives. Because urban fringes are so good for deer (and boars), their numbers explode;

they bring with them a host of nuisances, including Lyme disease. The back gardens of suburbia have become bowline hunting grounds, a form of population control which is legal and encouraged. Complaints about urban badgers are increasing in Britain, indicating that elusive species' increasing presence in the big smoke as well. It has taken little more than a century to go from seeing cities as places of ecological sterility and degradation to moaning about their superabundance of wildlife. Whether we love them, loathe them or fear them, the truth is that we will all have to get used to co-existing with booming populations of non-human creatures. The immediate challenge is to understand how this relationship is going to work.

Ever since there have been cities, animals have been pests. They import zoonotic diseases that can have lethal consequences. But they also provide services, both officially and unofficially. Large-scale urbanisation would scarcely have been possible without vast animal populations providing muscle power and protein. Cities are as much animal as they are human, a point often written out of their stories. The city is a dynamic environment, shifting and volatile. We don't need animals to work for us so much these days; but the cityscape is undeniably becoming wilder. This is a story about the rise and fall, the twists and turns, of animals seeking their fortune in the big smoke.

★

When an Englishman in New York in 1819 described the city's streets as full of 'innumerable hungry pigs of all sizes and complexions, great and small beasts prowling in grunting ferocity', he could have been describing almost any city outside the Islamic and Jewish worlds from much of history. When streets were unpaved and traversed by horses, when rubbish, offal and dung went uncollected, open areas were a kind of urban commons for the poor, where they could turn out their pigs, goats, cows, chickens and dogs to forage among the bonanza of free nutrients. One estimate put the number of hogs freely roaming Manhattan at 20,000 in 1820; along with humans and dogs, swine were the most obvious and characteristic life-form in the city's streets. New York authorities wanted to get rid of the ramshackle state of affairs that gave the city a backward appearance and stank the place up to high heavens. But for the poor, swine not only provided a meal but were 'our best scavengers, as they instantly devour all fish guts, garbage, and offal of every kind', which would otherwise putrefy in the summer sun.[2]

The air around Shepherd's Bush in London was described in 1850 as 'sonorous with the grunting of porkers'. As in all cities, pigs roamed free or occupied back gardens; they lived in rooms with people. In the centre of London were Smithfield, a vast livestock market serviced by innumerable slaughterhouses, and Leadenhall Market for poultry. In

1853, 277,000 head of cattle and 1.6 million sheep, along with hundreds of thousands of geese and turkeys, were driven from all corners of the kingdom into the middle of the metropolis, filling streets as they came. Animals lived in the city as well, cheek by jowl with humans: tens of thousands of dairy cows fed from brewers' grains and distillery swill, countless pigs snuffling through garbage heaps, and chickens packed into buildings. Added to that was the principal muscle power of the city, the horses that kept wheels turning. Animals were used for entertainment: fighting dogs and cocks, dancing bears, exotic species imported to amuse and distract, caged birds and curious menageries. During the plague of 1665, the lord mayor, believing that domestic animals carried the disease, ordered the mass slaughter of dogs and cats. Daniel Defoe reckoned that 40,000 dogs and 200,000 cats were slaughtered at this time, a grim revelation of the extent of the canine and feline zootropolis. Horses, cows, pigs, goats, donkeys, cats, dogs, chickens: this was city as cacophonous farmyard. They far outnumbered humans.[3]

Many urban pets led a feral existence, scavenging by day, returning home at night. Some domesticated animals left home completely, most famously that ubiquitous urban resident, the feral pigeon. Bred from rock doves, the 'city pigeon' found that the built environment replicated the sea cliffs and mountains in which its ancestors had evolved to live. Its proclivity for human refuse gave it a year-round banquet in the stone expanse, without need of ever seeing the countryside. Sparrows possess two genes – COL11A, which allows them to grow large beaks to break open seeds, and AMY2A, which encodes the enzyme amylase – that are essential for digesting the starches found in human beings' staples of wheat, corn and potatoes. Pigeons and sparrows, two quintessential urban species, have evolved over the last 11,000 years to share our leftovers. For many years, a colony of sparrows led an entirely indoor existence inside Terminal 2 of Heathrow Airport, feasting on scraps of packaged and fast food. Their plasticity makes them suited to the urban jungle. Some London pigeons, meanwhile, have learnt to commute from nest to food source by tube to save the bother of flying, getting on at Hammersmith and alighting at Ladbroke Grove.[4]

Wild species benefited from the untidiness – or at least those few species able to adapt to dense, built environments. Deforestation during the later Middle Ages forced a number of avian species to seek an alternative lifestyle in urban areas. Mud-nesting birds such as swallows and house martins colonised the centre of European cities because their unpaved streets yielded a lot of dirt with which to construct nests; swifts, accustomed to using old woodpecker holes in dead trees and crevasses in cliffs, found in cities good alternatives, nesting in cavities in buildings and under open eaves. All that manure produced by horses and livestock taken to market attracted a bonanza of flies, bugs and beetles, perfect for birds who found the novel ecosystem highly attractive. Horse traffic and sparrows went hand-in-hand, the urbanised avian feasting not only on the masses of dung insects but on spillages of seed from nosebags.

Red kites were once the quintessential urban birds of northern Europe. They loved cities – and were tolerated in turn – because they scavenged rubbish and rotting animal carcasses. A visitor from Bohemia in 1465 wrote that he had never seen so many kites in one place as on London Bridge. The secretary to the Venetian ambassador noted that Londoners did not have an aversion to crows, rooks, jackdaws, ravens and kites because 'they keep the streets of the town free from all filth'. Less helpfully, kites had a habit of stealing clothes left to dry on the line and even people's hats during the nesting season. The large raptor was a familiar sight in the medieval and Tudor cityscape, picking its way through piles of rubbish and procuring nesting material. So tame was this city bird that it would take buttered bread from the hands of children.

In Delhi, black kites have always relished city life, capitalising on the Islamic practice of feeding them meat scraps. The black kite breeding pairs that do best in Delhi, according to mathematical modelling, are those that have learnt to anticipate human behaviour, siting their nests near mosques and places overflowing with garbage. Defensive behaviour intensifies in these choice areas. Living with humans in Delhi entails 'fine-grained, context-dependent strategies and trade-offs' among the city's kites. It is a little-known fact that Delhi has the highest concentration of raptors on the planet. The megacity, with its plethora of waste, is a magnet for kites from central Asia which have shifted their migration patterns; tens of thousands of them sometimes darken the sky over Delhi.[5]

Animal migrants hitched a ride to the city. Those species that had a lot to gain from proximity to profligate humans discovered the urban ecology to be highly rewarding if they were capable of adaptations. Originating in south-east Asia, possibly Malaysia, Thailand and Java, the black rat (**Rattus rattus**) spread to European cities in the wake of Roman conquest, and on to the New World and Australasia through subsequent colonisation and trade routes. Good climbers, in the wild they lived in cliffs, rocks and palms. The urban habitat gave them wall and ceiling cavities. Like unloved ruderal vegetation, black rats thrive in disturbed environments; they can adapt effortlessly to new and complex microhabitats and a range of diets. They displace native species as they go. Unlike their less streetwise competitors, black rats are made for the city. Their journey from eastern Asia to every niche in every city on the planet reminds us that cities are novel ecosystems: out go native species – both animal and vegetable – and in come those that can tough it out. Like us, urbanised animals are immigrants.

The uncontested reign of **Rattus rattus** came to an end in the eighteenth century when it was dethroned by another stowaway opportunist, the brown rat (**Rattus norvegicus**), which originated in Mongolia and began migrating with the opening up of trade routes in the later Middle Ages. Industrialisation favoured the brown rat by providing it with miles of sewers, drains and pipes full of tasty faecal matter. The sewers beneath the abattoirs of Smithfield Market, with their liberal supply of offal, were particularly popular with brown rats. Another disaster-tolerant species more than happy to live near as many humans as possible, cockroaches also came to European cities from east Asia in the Middle Ages. The bedbug, meanwhile, made the journey from south-west Asia, arriving in Italy around CE 100, Germany in 1200, France in the fifteenth century, Britain in the sixteenth and the Americas in the seventeenth, hopping from city to city as they traversed the globe's expanding urban network.

Urban infrastructure created a new ecosystem favoured by our most steady of camp followers – pigeons, rats, mice, cockroaches, moths, lice and bedbugs. They flourish in the most drastically modified human environments, colonising it in perpetuity. These familiar denizens of the grey city – as opposed to the green city of parks, rivers and woodland – are common across almost all urban environments, regardless of continent or climate. It is another instance of biotic homogenisation across urban ecosystems, a reminder that cities have more in common with each other in an ecological sense than with their hinterlands. Bedbugs or cockroaches in one building might be genetically different from those in another nearby building because each infestation originates from a different place, maybe from cities in other countries or continents. That goes to show how fully urbanised these species are: their genetic history speaks of millennia-long intercity migrations.[6]

Historically, the urban ecosystem – at least the animal part of it – was far from something to be celebrated; it was fraught with danger. The black rat was the main vehicle for the transmission of the Black Death, via its fleas. The brown rat was feared for its reproductive virility and its aggression as it ravaged food stocks and damaged buildings. Rodents and other urban pests carry a number of pathogens and parasites that have had decisive impacts on human history; they are drawn to our effluence as a source of food. And it wasn't just the unbidden urban colonists that caused trouble. The thousands of animals with which humans – particularly poor humans – lived in tight proximity were vectors of diseases.

'Shitehawks' British colonisers called the scavenging black kites of India and Africa because of their apparently unsanitary urban lifestyles. In **King Lear,** Shakespeare has the king dismiss his daughter Goneril as a 'detestable kite'. Useful as scavengers are, we are repelled by them. On its own, a black-eared kite is a magnificent bird of prey; but there is something disconcerting about flocks of 10,000 gorging themselves on landfills on the outskirts of Delhi. In Mumbai, flamingos have come to the city since the 1980s as a direct result of pollution: high levels of untreated sewage and industrial effluence have warmed the water and increased blue-green algae levels, upon which the flamingo feasts. People have tended to see animals that live among us and adapt themselves to our habits – rats, squirrels, pigeons, seagulls, foxes, raccoons, monkeys – as degenerate, lesser versions of their country kin. But our hatred is really shame: they are only adapting themselves to our vices, our disgusting waste. They represent, above all, mortal threat.

In August 1760, the Common Council of London paid a bounty of two shillings to anyone who killed a dog. The metropolis was gripped with panic: rabies, the deadliest virus on the planet, was believed to be rife among the free-roaming canine population. Young men patrolled the streets armed with cudgels until the virus faded. Dogs, however, did not disappear from the streetscape. New York passed a dog law in 1811 that instituted the post of dog register and collector, empowered to collect a $3 dog tax and kill all canines wandering the city. Met with resistance, often violent, from the working poor, such official efforts to clear the streets failed. Rewards were paid instead to individuals who killed stray dogs, leading to more rancour on the streets as people fought off freelance cullers. There were repeated rabies panics throughout the nineteenth century. In 1886, after twenty-six Londoners died from rabies, 40,158 dogs were killed in Battersea Dogs Home, many of them belonging to working-class people who could not afford muzzles and had no choice but to allow their dogs to scavenge on the streets for discarded scraps.[7]

The common assumption was that rabies occurred spontaneously in canines during the sultry 'dog days' of summer because of heat, thirst and agitation. In fact, it was the degraded urban environment that was to blame, just as it was for the prevalence of pests such as rats and cockroaches and diseases such as cholera, dysentery and typhus. Microbes in rotting offal and contaminated water caused the horrifying rabies virus. Urban ecologies incubated reservoirs of diseases. This was due to the appalling way city animals were treated. Dairy cattle kept in filthy cowsheds, never seeing daylight or munching green grass, were prone to foot-and-mouth disease, pleuropneumonia and other illnesses. Urban milk, from cows fed on the waste products of alcohol production, was thin and blueish. It had to be thickened and whitened with other ingredients. In 1858, the campaigning publisher Frank Leslie ran a sensational series of exposés about the nightmare of urban dairies, asking New Yorkers: 'Are you aware what kind of milk you are drinking? Are you aware that over seven thousand children die every year in New York and Brooklyn from drinking swill milk?' Forcing cows into sheds, feeding them swill and adulterating their milk was a scandal. The treatment of other animals in urban conditions also represented a disaster waiting to happen. In October 1872, a mysterious equine disease escaped from its origin point in cramped, unsanitary stables in Toronto and spread through the entire North American urban network with incredible speed via the railroads.[8]

The Great Epizootic, as it is known, left horses unable to work. Cities across Canada and the United States ground to a halt; there were food shortages and a transportation shutdown. The disaster showed not only how dependent cities were on animals but how abysmally they treated them. There can be little surprise that the late-nineteenth century saw campaigns to regain control over cities from the degraded, disease-ridden animal kingdom. Scavenging dogs, stray alley cats, stinking pigsties, disgusting dairies and offal-strewn slaughterhouses had no place in the urban realm anymore: they were public health hazards and eyesores. Cities enacted ordinances banishing livestock and roaming pets. The unruly, animal city was tamed.[9]

Or was it? In the 1930s, stories began to circulate about enormous alligators lurking in the bowels of New York. Robert Daley, in his 1959 book **The World Beneath the City,** reported the aftermath of an underground visit made by Teddy May, the superintendent of sewers, in 1935. 'He sat at his desk screwing his fists into his eyes, trying to forget the sight of alligators serenely paddling around in his sewers.'

The story is fanciful. No alligator could survive for long in a New York sewer amid the E. coli and salmonella, not to say the cold winters. But that does not mean there weren't **any** alligators. On the contrary, newspapers reported numerous sightings in the 1930s. They were all baby pets, however, abandoned by their owners to a sure and swift death. In March 1984, Parisian firefighters were called to the sewers near the Pont-Neuf. There, in the humid darkness, they came face to face with a metre-long Nile crocodile baring her teeth and thrashing her tail. Later named Eleanore, she had probably been abandoned by a pet owner and lived on rats for a month or so. She went on to enjoy a happier life in an aquarium in Vannes, where she grew to three metres and still lives to this day in an enclosure designed to resemble the Paris sewers.

The persistent urban myth of alligators and crocodiles in the sewer speaks to our fear of nature in the city, a deep-rooted suspicion that dangerous forces lurk beneath the thin façade of civilisation. The legend morphed into stories about sinister, blind, albino gators. Much earlier, in 1850s London, stories circulated of a pregnant sow that had fallen down the sewer in Hampstead. She became the matriarch of a race of ferocious, supersized mutant hogs that fed on sewage and never saw the light of day, traversing the network of sewers and buried rivers that formed an alternate, subterranean London. Even before that, the Romans circulated an already-hoary myth about a gigantic octopus that had swum up the sewers, entered a house and smashed earthenware vessels with its massive tentacles to get at a store of pickled fish. These stories were as bogus as those of swarms of alligators in New York. They were built on fears of animals in the city, particularly of what happens when animals exploit the urban environment and our pollution. They all revolve around the murky world that lies unseen beneath our feet, the shit-filled sewers that we try and banish from our minds. It is a fear of toxicity, of mutation, of animals that will come to bite us.

From swallows to pigs, from kites to goats, the animals that found niches pre-twentieth century were ones that could exploit the forbidding grey cityscape, the actions of humans and the messiness of the urban environment. Ask someone in the nineteenth century about animal life in the city and the answer would focus on beasts of burden, livestock, feral creatures and invasive pests: the city was an ecological disaster zone in terms of animals, water, sanitation and air quality. The move to rid the city of animals coincided with a wider movement to discipline the urban environment: weeds came under rigorous control, water and waste were channelled underground, pigs and dogs were banished. Stories of alligators in sewers periodically resurfaced as reminders of the dangers of uncontrolled urban nature.

Just as many of the animal denizens of the city were being expelled, however, a new set of species were heading to town. The metropolis was about to get a lot wilder.

On the evening of 12 August 1949, listeners of the BBC 9 o'clock radio news were surprised that the bulletin did not start with the customary bongs of Big Ben. Later on, the BBC reported to concerned listeners that the non-appearance of the chimes was due to a mass of starlings perching on the minute hand, slowing the clock.

Starlings were relatively new on the urban scene in the 1940s, having made the move to town only at the turn of the century. They had made their presence known. At sundown in autumn and winter, great murmurations of starlings – a miracle of nature where tens and sometimes hundreds of thousands of birds form mesmerising, co-ordinated, pulsating clouds before they roost – gathered in Trafalgar Square and Leicester Square. A murmuration of 100,000 starlings 'used to wheel, chattering, over queueing London cinema goers'. Why were they there?[10]

At the close of the nineteenth century, starlings discovered that the city was a good place to roost. For
a start, it was warmer in winter than the countryside: the urban heat island effect was becoming apparent. They took a liking to grand buildings with
Corinthian capitals, niches and ledges, such as the
National Gallery, Nelson's Column, the British
Museum, Buckingham Palace and the Royal Opera
House. Addicted to prime real estate, starlings chose
to settle in only the best part of town. In the words of
the London ecologist Richard Fitter, the grand buildings and squares on the north bank of the Thames
from Westminster to the Tower of London 'must be
regarded as one gigantic starling roost'.[11]

Starlings became reverse commuters, sleeping in
city centres at night and heading out to the countryside and suburbia by day to feed. London's starlings
tell a tale about the changing shape of cities. Even
as urban authorities expunged one form of urban
ecosystem at the end of the nineteenth century –
the semi-rural metropolis of market gardens, piggeries, dung piles and garbage heaps – they created
a new one, with parks, thousands of new trees, and
recreation grounds. New York's Central Park provides a stopover for 210 bird species on the Atlantic
Flyway migration route. Migrating birds actually
prefer the city parks to rural areas because they contain more insects as a result of a greater diversity
of plant species. But it was not just the warmth
provided by modern cities and the proliferation of

green public spaces that induced these changes in the animal world: cities were changing shape very quickly. They went from compact patches of grey to massive, complex landscapes in their own right, ideal territory for starlings who could divide their time between well-stocked suburban back gardens by day and Buckingham Palace by night. The story of the red fox explains this process.

Largely unknown in urban areas, foxes were observable in British cities only from the 1930s and relatively common by the 50s. They were, as yet, not present in cities outside Britain. Some people blamed the migration on an exploding fox population in the countryside during the war, when gamekeepers stopped culling them, or the decimation of rabbits by myxomatosis in the 1950s. Outcompeted in rural woodlands, the theory went, the weaker specimens skulked around urban fringes scrounging for food. According to this hypothesis, city foxes were a degraded bunch, forced into an alien environment to scavenge as best they could.

But it wasn't so much that the fox changed its habitat: we changed **our** habitat, flocking to suburbia during the sprawl of the interwar years. Foxes did not come to the city; the city came to **them.** The old city was dense and grey; the new was expansive and greener, with varied habitats in domestic, industrial, recreational and natural spaces attractive to starlings and foxes alike. Gardens in particular are awash with the exotic range of flowering plants and fruit trees we have brought in to brighten up the dull cityscape. In some places, urbanisation can have a positive impact on biodiversity; in the desert region Phoenix, Arizona, species richness increases as a result of urbanisation because of irrigation and ornamental landscaping. Cities are artificial oases of plenty, drought-free (because we water our plants) and brimming with exotic foliage. White-crowned sparrows living in San Francisco have much more diverse gut microbiomes than rural sparrows, indicative of their generous range of habitat. If cities once abounded in pig shit and horse manure that provided food for some species, they now contain a smorgasbord of foliage imported from all over the world. The wealth of flowering plants supports more insects, and in turn birds and smaller mammals, that larger creatures such as foxes and falcons can feast on.

Just as suburban expansion results in a ferociously high turnover of plant species, so does it rearrange the local animal population. First come the cats and dogs, which often equal or outnumber the human population. As in the wild, some species depart, and others – unknown before – enter the scene. In Nassau County in suburbanising Long Island, N.Y., studies of bird populations in the 1960s showed that species loss was being outpaced by new recruits to the changing landscape. Grassland birds such as the meadowlark and grasshopper sparrow were disappearing. But new arrivals included migratory and generalist birds that relished suburban gardens. White-tailed deer, on the verge of extinction in the 1940s on Long Island, boomed to an extraordinary extent in the 1950s.[12]

The deer of Long Island and the Twin Cities, as well as the boars of Berlin, are there for a reason. They are safer in the city than the country, spared from hunters and predators alike. The deer numbers of Ramsey County, the smallest and most densely populated county in Minnesota, add up to 1,200. If this was a rural area, the land could only support 500 of these creatures. As it is, the anthropic environment provides deer with plentiful food sources, just as messy Grunewald picknickers, tasty domestic gardens and overflowing bins swell Berlin's wild boar population. The increase in the populations and diversity of city animals over the last sixty years is proportional to the growth of global suburbia and the maturity of that environment, as the trees and shrubs grow and spread in the years following the shock event of construction.[13]

We changed the environment, but **we** changed too – perhaps the crucial factor. We stopped shooting mammals and birds on sight. Most cities are, for good reason, no-hunting zones. Instead, we like to feed our mammalian and avian neighbours, relishing rather than fearing wildness. The British spend £200 million and Americans $4 billion a year on bird food. So enticing is this offer that the Eurasian blackcap warbler has changed its usual migration route from central Europe to Spain and north Africa, heading to British suburban gardens to join the bonanza. And then there is the rubbish – all that discarded food left out for the picking.

Speedy, lithe, rangy and elusive, the fox proved highly adaptable to this emerging environment, navigating it at will like a parkour runner, squeezing through small gaps and jumping obstacles, clambering over bridges and scaling walls, disappearing into drainage pipes, taking shortcuts along railway tracks and hiding in tiny patches of wild vegetation, remaining hidden most of the time. **Vulpes** is one of the most adaptable and geographically distributed wild carnivores, successfully exploiting habitats varying from arctic tundra to deserts and everything in between. Using these skills, they pushed ever closer to the centre of cities from their edgeland entry points from the 1930s, learning and passing on new skills as they explored, year by year, the labyrinthine maze they now call home. In 2011, a fox was found on the seventy-second storey of the partially completed Shard skyscraper in London, happily living off scraps of food discarded by construction workers.

Fortune favoured the bold – and the adaptable – in the conquest of the urban ecosystem. In North America, coyotes have begun to behave like British foxes. They are recent arrivals, having moved into Chicago only in the 1990s. Since then, their numbers have surged by 3,000 per cent, infiltrating every available nook and cranny of the metropolis, from leafy suburbs to the mean streets of down-town. They now occupy nearly all North American metropolises.[14]

Like the rat and the macaque millennia before them, foxes and coyotes – brilliant, opportunistic generalists both – proved to be synurbanisers **par excellence** as the twentieth century wore on. The metropolis had a lot to offer a mammal on the make. As we have seen, cities are warm and brimming with nutrients. The living can be easy if you can access the treasure trove of resources. Foxes, raccoons and coyotes are among many species that build up greater densities in cities than in the countryside, where they often lead longer lives. Chicago raccoons travel less far for food than their country relations, produce more offspring and are in better physical condition. That is true of other large mammals, which also tend to wean their pups later, giving more opportunity for juveniles to learn unintuitive life skills.

They move to the suburbs, settle into the neighbourhood and enjoy the good life, living longer into old age. Investing more time in bringing up their families, they become less aggressive and take to monogamy. Urban coyotes are changing fast, moving away from their rural origins with incredible velocity. Individuals with greater plasticity are more likely to enter the city in the first place, and then survive its evolutionary pressures. Compare an urban fox in Britain with its country cousin. City-dwelling foxes and coyotes are accomplished synurbanisers, learning to shape their behaviour in complex, artificial habitats. They can learn new tricks and pass them down to their offspring. But something permanent is happening too. Urban foxes are developing shorter, wider snouts and smaller heads; and they are becoming bolder and smarter.

Foxes with shorter snouts have a larger nasal region, allowing them to sniff through bins full of rotting food. No longer reliant on hunting voles, mice and rabbits, they do not need the fast jaw-snapping speeds conferred by long snouts. Instead, they need stronger bites to access food bins and crunch through packages and bones. Females appear to be doing better in the urban environment than males: their crania have shrunk faster, as their reduced range while nurturing pups intensifies their dependence on bins. With their diminished adrenal glands and the wealth of available nutrients, urban foxes are becoming less territorially aggressive. Will we end up with metrosexual male foxes, more similar in appearance and temperament to females, as vixens select for mates that best navigate the city? With their changing features, perhaps marking the beginnings of domestication, they look cuter to human eyes; soon, they will be instantly distinguishable from rural specimens, even by the casual observer.[15]

Phenotype change happens quickly in the city. That is to say, the observable characteristics of species alter as a result of the interaction between genes and the environment. Take the dark-eyed junco. A few dozen pairs of the mountain bird moved to San Diego in the 1980s and underwent an extraordinary and rapid transformation. In the mountains, male juncos focus on aggression and sex, competing hard during the short breeding season. However, because San Diego provided so much food all the year round, they did not have to be aggressively territorial. Females began to spurn macho mates in the easy-going Californian metropolis. Instead, they selected for males with lower testosterone levels – those dedicated to childcare and raising several clutches a year rather than the one they managed in the forest. Monogamous family men pass on their genes to their offspring, which are more numerous than those of their aggressive competitors. White tails are a sign, in the junco, of high testosterone, a valuable trait in the forest but unwelcome in the city. San Diego's male juncos have duller plumage and higher songs, communicating that they will concentrate on rearing young. Females, meanwhile, have stopped ground nesting and moved up to buildings and trees. Like many other urbanised birds, they have given up the migratory habit, preferring the warmth and food resources of the city. City-living changes songbirds like the junco in deeper ways, however: it rewires their neural pathways.[16]

When researchers took young juvenile juncos

born in both San Diego and their ancestral forests and raised them in identical conditions in an indoor aviary, they found that the offspring of the city juncos were far bolder and more explorative. Their innate inner-city brashness was the result of lower levels of the stress hormone corticosterone, something they had inherited at birth. Other urbanised birds, such as blackbirds and great tits, have variant serotonin transponder genes, which make them much more prone to risky, but highly rewarding, novelty-seeking behaviours. Caution does not help the urban avian; being relaxed and uninhibited is a key component of living among humans, traffic, loud noise, artificial light and novel food sources. The urbanising process has fundamentally altered information processing in their central nervous system. Behavioural change is not just a matter of nurture; with the juncos, it is genetic, the result of evolution that took place during their forebears' colonisation of the city barely three decades ago. The reason San Diego's dark-eyed juncos are so important to us is because such experiments, involving wild urban animals that examine both behaviour and physiology, are, so far, rare.[17]

To country-bred birds, their urban cousins look crazily impulsive. But they act in ways that allow them to thrive in their new environment. Perhaps, like foxes, only the boldest go to the city in the first place, where they mate exclusively with other urbanists and pass on their genes to their offspring, becoming a city-specialist population very quickly in the process. Hormonal and genetic changes are observed in numerous other urbanising species. Coyotes in Chicago are bolder and more exploratory than in non-urban environments, suggesting that, like San Diegan juncos, they develop lower hypothalamic-pituitary-adrenal axis activation after being exposed to stress. Salamanders in New York City are bolder and less aggressive. Small mammals such as shrews, bats, voles, mice and gophers experience a jump in brain size as they cope with the bewildering blizzard of cognitive demands in the cityscape. Brain size is not just about intelligence; it confers greater behavioural flexibility, surely a requirement for fitting into a new, highly challenging and unpredictable habitat. Numerous animal species – including tropical agamid lizards, Australian myna birds, rhesus macaques and North American raccoons – prove better at problem-solving tasks in laboratories if they were born in cities.[18]

Brains and behaviour change, but so too do bodies. Urban anole lizards in Puerto Rico have longer legs and stickier toe pads in order to hold on to slippery city surfaces. Cliff swallows that choose attractive roadside nesting sites have evolved shorter wings – better for rapid vertical take-off and aerial pivoting to avoid colliding with cars. Those with longer wings remove themselves from the gene pool in the form of roadkill, just like Puerto Rican lizards that can't hold on tight. House finches in Tucson, Arizona, now have longer and wider beaks than those in surrounding desert habitats because selection favours those that can chow down on sunflower seeds from garden bird feeders, food that is harder and larger than that of their natural diet. Some animals are able to evolve in response to pollution and toxins. Atlantic killfish living in New Jersey estuaries have evolved with incredible rapidity to survive in the toxic water. The white mice population isolated in Central Park have aberrant genes that allow them to digest fatty junk food and neutralise aflatoxin, a carcinogenic fungus that grows on nut-based snack bars.[19]

The Manhattan mice are important for helping us understand why animals are evolving so quickly in cities. Once upon a time, their ancestors were part of a population that roamed around the forests and grasslands of Manhattan Island. Now they are marooned in islands within the island: parks cut off from other parks and hence the wider gene pool of white-footed mice. Each park in New York now has a group of mice with their own unique genetic signature. It is known as genetic drift or, in everyday language, in-breeding. It sounds negative, but isolation and genetic drift have allowed Central Park's fast food-guzzling white-footed mice to adapt very quickly to the specific requirements of their micro-environment. Natural selection favoured those that possessed the aberrant gene that allowed them to digest fatty foods and eat mouldy snack bars. The pressure of living in highly modified environments has induced evolutionary changes on an astonishingly miniscule timescale. The mice would have to wave goodbye to their junk food if their isolation came to an end and other mice entered the Central Park gene pool.[20]

Reduced gene flow resulting from habitat fragmentation is one major reason that cities are powerful drivers of evolution. Another is sexual selection. Many species have a preference for the habitat in which they were born: they stay and mate with fellow urbanists. Great tits living in Lisbon have more in common, genetically speaking, with great tits in Glasgow than with those living in the adjacent countryside. That is true – and becoming truer – for lots of species of plants and animals that are showing signs of splitting between urban and rural versions. Rural species show far greater genetic variety; those that choose a metropolitan existence (or have it thrust upon them) tend to become more genetically diverse as they adapt to the specificities of their urban niches. San Diego juncos exist as a tiny population of around eighty breeding pairs. Many of those creatures that evolve quickly in cities do so because they possess, within their populations, pre-existing genetic variations that can be highly beneficial when they encounter a radically different environment such as a city. Individuals with these variant genes suddenly become desirable sexual partners. Long-limbed lizards – rare in their ancestral habitat – suddenly become not so rare in the city: their success in the cityscape means they pass their genes down. The same goes for short-snouted foxes, junk food-eating mice, toxin-resistant killfish, laid-back juncos and bold blackbirds.[21]

Not all animals can adapt to urban life or close proximity with humans. Most cannot; when we heavily modify their habitats, we doom them to extinction. But it is becoming clear that many more species than we ever thought possible are finding a home in the anthropic environment, changing their bodies and brains in the process. Like them or not, these are the species best-placed to survive the pressures of the Anthropocene and the mass extinction of species. They are the organisms that are fighting back against the disaster we have caused. Animals that are able to do well in cities are pre-adapting to warmer climates and human-modified environments.

Our metropolises could very well be where we conserve a significant chunk of global biodiversity during upcoming decades when living systems are put under severe pressure. We owe it to these animals to make our cities even more welcoming. We have seen numerous species evolving very quickly within our lifetimes to claim a perch in the city. All this has happened in a blink of an eye. The majority of animals are at the very beginning of a journey. How can we make room for even more?

They are quite a sight flying over the city as dusk falls in dense swarms. The grey-headed flying fox is an Australian megabat with a wingspan of over a metre, an orange furry collar and dark, beady eyes set in a grey face. During the day, this enormous mammal sleeps upside down, its giant wings wrapped round its body. Every night, these bats fly in search of nectar from eucalypt blossoms, rainforest fruits and one hundred species of native plants. They are a keystone species, fulfilling a vital role in the south-east Australian ecosystem. As they forage, they pollinate the rainforest and spread seeds – as much as 60,000 each per night – over distances of fifty kilometres. When an area is devastated by fire, they bring recovery. But the grey-headed flying fox is an endangered species, its habitat wrecked by climate change, agricultural expansion, bushfires and urbanisation.

But if the city is the problem, it is also part of the solution. In 1986, between ten and fifteen megabats established a colony in Melbourne. Its population increased to 35,000 by the 2020s. Another 'campsite' (as their roosts are known) was established in Adelaide in 2010 and swiftly grew to 17,000. Why did the bats move 400 kilometres from their usual

colony sites all the way to Melbourne? It has everything to do with how we have changed the urban
environment. Before Europeans settled Melbourne,
the area contained just three species of plant that
could sustain a flying fox. Starting in the 1970s,
garden tastes began to change: people in Australian
cities started to plant eucalypts and Morton Bay figs
as street trees; they introduced hundreds of native
Australian trees and plants to gardens and parks.
This meant a year-round bonanza for the bats, a
total remodelling of the local environment as a by-
product of urbanisation. People also tend to water
plants, abolishing droughts. As Melbourne's urban
forest grew and diversified, it became supremely
attractive not just to megabats but to lorikeets and
possums. The grey-headed flying fox has become urbanised, discovering Melbourne – and subsequently
another forty-two Australian cities – to be a forest-
like refuge from extinction.[22]

Australia is one of only seventeen megadiverse
countries. Yet thousands of its species are facing extinction. The flying fox is not alone: 46 per cent of
animals listed as threatened now live in the urban
environment. In fact, Australian cities contain
substantially more endangered species per square
kilometre than non-urban areas. The story is similar elsewhere. Driven out of their native range by
deforestation and farming, the tiny, endangered
Brazilian golden lion tamarin has found a refuge

among the generous suburbanites of Rio. During a drought in Rajasthan, India, between 1999 and 2001 the Hanuman langur population crashed in rural areas but remained unscathed in Jodhpur, where there were adequate food sources to ride out the troubles. When resources are scarce, black bears move into Aspen, Colorado, returning to their natural habitats in good food years.[23]

The experience of Australian megabats, Indian monkeys and American bears may well offer a forerunner for the climate emergency. The city could become an ark for certain species, a sanctuary from extreme conditions.

During the global lockdowns of 2020, as we sat bored and isolated in our homes, news services around the world tantalised us with stories about what was happening to our cities in our absence. Deer roamed freely into cities around the world; puma stalked Santiago, Chile; boar and wild pigs brazenly wandered the deserted streets of Barcelona and Paris; an elephant strolled through Dehradun in northern India; wild turkeys took over a school in San Francisco; otters hung out at a mall in Singapore and scampered through the lobby of a hospital. Less traffic and reduced noise and movement were all it took for curious animals to move into town. We don't need to do much to make the urban environment attractive to wildlife. Small interventions can reap big benefits in some cases.

Lit up bright at night, a city is a confusing place for animals, just as it interrupts our own circadian rhythms. Light pollution is one of the most significant dangers in the urban ecosystem, ranking alongside habitat loss and chemical pollution. The United States is estimated to waste $3.3 billion a year and release 21 million tons of carbon dioxide through unnecessary outdoor lighting. Millions of sea turtle hatchlings, fatally distracted by the bright lights of Florida, die unnecessarily, missing the subtle reflections of starlight and moonlight on the surface of the sea. Artificial light disrupts the migratory patterns of millions of birds. Illuminated buildings lure them to death-by-collision. Street lighting drastically reduces insect populations by increasing nocturnal predation and disrupting procreation. Plants suffer too, with artificial lighting tricking them into growing larger leaves and more stomatal pores, which makes them susceptible to pollution and drought. Back in 2001, Flagstaff, Arizona, became the world's first International Dark Sky City. Since then, it has been followed by dozens of other cities, including Tucson and Pittsburgh. Indeed, Pittsburgh went even further than other cities in 2022, switching away from bulbs that emit disruptive blue light in favour of cooler-temperature bulbs, saving itself $1 million a year in the process. It is also adding shielded fixtures to streetlamps, preventing illumination pouring upwards into the night sky. Small, but targeted, interventions can reap a lot of benefits, including for humans, who can once again reclaim their right to see the stars.

Howler monkeys take the overpass to avoid murderous traffic and dogs at street level. Travelling from one remnant patch of forest to another in Porto Alegre, Brazil, the threatened monkeys climb along powerlines, a risky way to move about the city. The introduction of inexpensive rope bridges high above the street has saved many brown howlers from electrocution, along with fellow urban climbers such as white-eared opossums and porcupines. In Costa Rica, sloths – hardly, one would think, a natural city slicker – are benefiting from such rope bridges. In relatively unkempt Berlin, it was recently discovered – to the surprise of researchers – that hedgehogs have a high level of gene flow. The findings suggested that there was enough interconnected greenery for creatures to travel across Berlin to find mates. Indeed, genetic analysis found that Berlin hedgehogs ranged further than their rural cousins. Hedgehogs do not travel far in just any circumstances; if they can traverse the green grid of the city – scuttling from one green stepping-stone to another by night via parks, gardens, cemeteries and areas of wild vegetation – so can other mammals and insects.[24]

As we know, cities contain within them ecological treasure houses. But they are often fragmented islands. What animals need is a citywide green metro system – a matrix of habitat highways cutting across the concrete and asphalt desert – connecting patches of dense vegetation. We are all familiar with the metro, bus and tram maps of our cities. Why not make the green map just as iconic and recognisable? An entire new city would take shape in our minds.

Pedestrianised streets, cycle lanes, railway tracks, riverbanks, tree-lined avenues, unmown verges, roof gardens, green walls and wetlands can all become links in the natural metro system. The city of Utrecht found extra foraging spots for bees when it planted sedum on the roofs of over 300 bus stops. When narrow ledge walkways were added to drainage culverts cut under roads in Brisbane it only took a few weeks for koalas, wallabies, possums, echidnas and goannas to learn how to navigate these dark underground passageways. Koalas were long assumed to be poor candidates for living in cities. But like so many other species, their capacity for adaptation to novel anthropic environments is stunning. Koalas are being given a helping hand in Moreton Bay, just north of Brisbane, with the widespread planting of the fast-growing Mount Beerwah mallee tree, a species of eucalypt which is itself listed as vulnerable. These trees will help ease the koala's way into the city, as it seeks a place of safety away from bushfires and droughts, providing food and habitat connectivity.[25]

Canopy rope bridges, ledges in tunnels and holes cut in suburban garden fences for hedgehogs are cheap ways of constructing a green grid. But some species require costly innovations. In Los Angeles, an enormous grassy bridge is being built at Liberty Canyon at a cost of $87 million so that wide-ranging mountain lions – along with skunks, deer and other animals – can cross the 101 Freeway, avoiding the 300,000 vehicles that speed along it every day. Only by opening up the city like this can cougars and bobcats be saved from genetic isolation and in-breeding. The ability of animals to traverse landscapes is essential to their long-term survival: we can, if we want, remove or modify the barriers we have thrown in the path of gene flow. It means redesigning cities so that they are hospitable not just to humans but to animals. The alternative is large-scale local extinctions in biodiverse hotspots around the globe, the places where urban expansion is most intense.

That brings us back to Melbourne's grey-headed flying foxes and Brisbane's koala bears. As we have seen, relatively modest modifications to the urban environment over the last four decades have trans-formed Australian cities into havens for some en-dangered creatures. Streets, parks, roadsides and gardens planted with diverse native and alien flora make cities highly attractive to numerous species. Cities all over the world – particularly those fast-growing ones in rainforests, savannahs, grasslands and deltas – need to emulate the best of Australia's innovation and avoid the worst of its sins. For the first time in history, cities in these hotspots have the opportunity to make conservation a central goal of urban planning, preserving large tracts of native habitats, interconnected by wildlife corridors, amid the expanding and sprawling cityscape. Animals are just at the beginning of their great migration to the city. It should be an urgent conservation priority to ease their passage so that threatened species can follow the path of flying foxes and koalas. We focus on upholding the habitability of unspoilt wildernesses, but cities should be seen in the same light. That means thinking bigger, reconsidering them as places packed with life and ecological benefits. Humans have affected every corner of the planet; perhaps the least we could do would be to support nature within one of the most destructive agents on the planet, the city.[26]

The success of wildlife in urban landscapes is surely a sign of a healthy city. Flying foxes have thronged to Melbourne precisely because it has blossomed with native plants in recent decades. What makes the metropolis good for megabats makes it good for people too. But when we are talking about mass extinction, there is a new urgency to greening modern cities. It goes beyond aesthetic preferences or even climate change adaptation. If we want to conserve species from oblivion, we need to make cities wilder, seeing nature not as a nice add-on but as critical to our survival.

We may very well find that our fate is bound up with those animals that are coming into the city. We may discover that making urban environments more hospitable for animals makes them healthier and happier for us too.

Epilogue
The End

Exhausted, half-starved and lost in the tropical forests, Andres de Avendano y Loyola and his men climbed hill after hill, their clothes and faces torn by thorns. At last, from one of the ridges, they saw something incredible. An enormous stone tower, covered with trees and vines, poked out above the thick canopy.

The Franciscan friar Avendano and his men were fleeing from their failed mission in 1695 to convert the king of the remote island city of Nojpetén to Christianity and convince him to accept the sovereignty of the Spanish crown. Nojpetén was the last holdout of the Mayans in the impenetrable rainforests of the Guatemalan lowlands; they had defied the Spanish for more than 150 years and were not prepared to accept Avendano's overtures. On the run, maddened with thirst, Avendano believed he must be in, or near, a settlement when he climbed the vegetated pyramid. But there was no city, nor even a village: the great pyramids were abandoned in the jungle. He did not realise it at the time, but Avendano was the first European to glimpse the lonely ruins of the great Mayan metropolis of Tikal, abandoned 500 years before in the face of climate change.[1]

Many years later, the American explorer John Lloyd Stephens heard rumours of this lost city in the rainforest, where white stone buildings jutted above the treeline. Stephens visited Tikal and other Mayan cities in 1839/40, and his descriptions and the engravings drawn by his fellow explorer Frederick Catherwood brought them to global prominence. 'In the romance of the world's history,' he declared, 'nothing impressed me more forcibly than the spectacle of this once great and lovely city, overturned, desolate, and lost; discovered by accident, overgrown with trees for miles around, and without even a name to distinguish it.'[2]

The contrast between an enigmatic, ruined civilisation and wild, entangling nature made the places he visited so intriguing. Stephens brought to life his exploration of the pyramids, ascending regular stone steps that were, in some places 'forced apart by bushes and saplings' and in others 'thrown down by the growth of large trees'. At the summit, he found large terraces thick with trees, including two gigantic ceibas, 'above twenty-feet in circumference, extending their half-naked roots fifty or a hundred feet around, binding down the ruins, and shading them with their wide-spreading branches'. The ceiba tree, with its long, straight trunk, umbrella-like canopy and huge, coiling buttress roots, was sacred to the Mayan people because it connected Xibalba, the underworld, with the sky via the terrestrial world. The triumph of the sacred ceiba, high above the forest floor with the great Mayan edifices in its tight embrace, seems particularly apt.

Descending the steps, Stephen and his party cleared an overgrown area with their machetes and ascertained it to be 'a square, and with steps on all the sides almost as perfect as those of a Roman amphitheatre'. Who had built this great city in the middle of a jungle? Stephens asked himself. 'All was mystery, dark impenetrable mystery', the immense forest shrouding the ruins 'heightening the impression . . . and giving an intensity and almost wildness to the interest'. The intense fascination with the lost cities of the rainforest has never gone away.[3]

Over the last decade, aircraft equipped with LiDAR scanners have circled 2,000 feet above the canopy, using laser pulses linked to GPS to make distance measurements and produce minutely detailed, three-dimensional, digital maps. LiDAR lays bare the ancient landscape, identifying features buried deep beneath the tangled rainforest, including a massive pyramid so covered with vegetation that it had always been thought to be a hill, the outlines of cities and networks of infrastructure such as roads, quarries, terraced fields, canals, reservoirs and irrigation systems. Human activity – particularly urbanisation – carves permanent records into the land that are never erased. The vegetation that returned to stressed soils caused by city building in the rainforest remains to this day different from the plants growing on untouched or lightly used ground. The digital topography showed that the size and sophistication of Mayan urbanism had been grossly underestimated, not least in the way it completely modified the vast tropical terrain in which it existed.

Where once there were region-sized megalopolises, there is today mile after mile of dense rainforest. We are, it appears, gripped by the idea of vegetation speedily consuming our greatest creations, whether it is Tikal in Guatemala, Angkor in Cambodia or the scenes of wildlife lording it over the toxic Chernobyl Exclusion Zone; as John Lloyd Stephen said, it is romantic. George Lucas used Tikal's ethereal qualities as the location for the rebel base on the fictional moon Yavin 4 in the first **Star Wars** film, its visual impact suggestive of forgotten ancient civilisations, decay and the remorseless cycle of history.

Our relish for the apocalyptic draws us to these sites: they are eerie premonitions of the fate of all that is humanmade, as roots, creepers and vines split stone and smother our mightiest buildings. They tell of the ultimate power of nature and its ability to reclaim and erase civilisation with astonishing speed. Above all, they serve as warnings to us.

There are few rivers in the Yucatán Peninsula, because rainfall drains quickly into gigantic sinkholes

100–150 metres beneath the spongy karstic lime-stone. The soil is thin and easily washed away; the climate is humid; there are no beasts of burden; and droughts are a frequent occurrence. Not a promising place for a city, let alone a network of cities, farms and villages comprising well over 10 million people. But the Mayans transformed the rainforest landscape.

Their urban civilisation flourished against the considerable constraints imposed by nature between CE 250 and 900 during the era known as the Classic period in Mayan history. Their prowess in architecture mirrored their strides in mathematics, astronomy and the arts. The Mayans were able to manipulate the hydrology of their region, turning underground sinkholes into reservoirs that fed an extensive irrigation system for their terraced farms. The rainforest was hacked back through intensive slash-and-burn agriculture. The ability to control the environment allowed the Mayan population to grow quickly during the Classical period. Monument construction – a sign of wealth and confidence – peaked towards the end of the period. Tikal's iconic tall buildings date to this time of frenetic boom. But then, at the moment this activity was accelerating, it all collapsed.

Just as LiDAR has revealed the sheer extent of the Mayan megalopolis, so modern technology has partly explained its descent into darkness. Stephen might have imagined the Mayans to have existed in cities shaded by the jungle canopy, but recent analysis of pollen samples shows that by the end of the eighth century CE, the Yucatán Peninsula had been deforested. Cities and fields sprawled over denuded plains. The great trees were felled and burnt to make plaster in industrial quantities; twenty trees had to be burnt to make one square metre of lime plaster. The denuded land was used for agriculture. With more and more mouths to feed, the ecosystem was pushed to its limits. The Mayans were adaptable, mitigating frequent droughts with sophisticated management techniques, but they could not adapt to the crisis that began around 760. Glacial samples taken from Greenland reveal that around this time, solar radiation suddenly declined. As temperatures plummeted in the northern hemisphere, global weather systems moved northwards. The Atlantic rain that watered the Yucatán did not arrive. Sediment samples taken from lakes in the region confirm that a long and exceptionally severe drought hit the Maya. This was a region, moreover, already suffering decreased precipitation as a result of the loss of rainforest.

Cities began to be abandoned one by one to nature in the face of this part-human and part-natural disaster. Soils throughout the peninsula were exhausted by deforestation, erosion and overexploitation. Climatic change made the land dry, but the Mayans had made it drier still through deforestation. In the face of scarcity, Mayan society slid into chaos. City fought city for dwindling resources. The trade routes that had crossed the lowlands and made it wealthy became seaborne traffic. By 900, Tikal was more or less empty, one of dozens of ghost towns. The rainforest swiftly returned. The ecosystem might have been fully restored by the time Andres de Avendano stumbled through the forests almost a millennium later, but cities never returned.

In Cambodia, a seemingly supernatural, giant banyan tree's roots clasp the magnificent edifices of Angkor, the largest city in the world between the eleventh and thirteenth centuries CE. Like Tikal, Angkor was a massive, dispersed, urban agglomeration, occupying territory the size of modern Paris and containing nearly a million people. In common with the Maya, it was reliant on an advanced hydraulic network. And like Mayan cities, this megalopolis put enormous strain on its ecosystem. The supersized urban area had been converted into a highly sophisticated infrastructure network of water catchment, retention and redistribution, made up of canals, irrigation ditches and reservoirs that coped with months of drought and intense monsoon rainfall. Urbanism on the lavish scale seen in Cambodia was possible because water was redistributed over a thousand square kilometres, making year-round farming possible. The urban machine was kept in operation by a large and highly controlled workforce. Urban land overlapped with rural land; in reality, there was no distinction between the two because Angkor was like an overgrown, continuous village in a wet landscape, with low-density housing clustered on mounds amid rice paddies. Hundreds of square miles of forest were stripped to create an open and highly engineered cityscape. The ability to manipulate the environment so completely was the source of Angkor's strength and its ability to feed a million residents. But it was also its greatest weakness.

The study of tree rings tells us that mainland south-east Asia was hit by climatic instability, caused by the shift from the Medieval Warm Period to the Little Ice Age. The canals became silted up with deposits swept down from the hills after unusually heavy rainfall and devastated the megalopolis with floods. But the deluges, tree rings tell us, came between extensive periods of drought in the fourteenth and fifteenth centuries: this time period was the wettest and driest in a millennium. The monsoon had become dangerously unpredictable, making a mockery of the elaborate engineering system, which had been designed for a relatively predictable (if challenging) climate and could not cope with the erosion and sedimentation caused in large part by centuries of deforestation. The population began to decline; jungle returned to gobble up the ever-shrinking edges of the dying city. As the vast workforce ebbed away, the intricate waterworks could no longer be maintained, making what remained of Angkor even more vulnerable to floods. The great city of the Middle Ages was eventually abandoned;

a small group of dutiful monks remained to observe religious rites. The tentacle roots of the city-shredding banyan tree crushed its stone buildings to death.

Modern system analysts have looked at what happened at Angkor and found a process of 'cascading failure of critical infrastructure as a result of climate extremes'. Angkor's water management was made of many interacting, interdependent components. Minor failures in this complex system, sparked by climate change, triggered a wave of escalating failures that reached a tipping point from which recovery was impossible. This was not a sudden, apocalyptic catastrophe; rather, it was a degeneration of the urban environment over a number of decades until abandonment became the only option. Medieval Angkor, the researchers argued, shares a number of functional characteristics with modern complex networks. We should take what happened as a warning.[4]

The fall of the Mayan cities and Angkor in the face of climatic instability are not isolated incidents. The Akkadian Empire of Mesopotamia experienced de-urbanisation as a result of the 4.2-kiloyear event, which saw the substantial cooling of the sub-polar Atlantic surface temperature from around 2200 BCE. The knock-on effect was global climate change, including aridification in south-west Asia. It also weakened the Asian monsoon, resulting in the abandonment of the dozens of enormous cities that made up the Indus Valley Civilisation from around

1800 BCE. The great cities of Mesopotamia, the cradle of urban civilisation, were eventually swallowed by the desert when sea levels receded, rivers changed course and irrigation systems fell into disuse. Much later, extreme weather events in CE 535/6 – perhaps caused by volcanic activity – had global consequences, not least the decline of Teotihuacan in the Valley of Mexico, the sixth-largest city in the world at the time. Cahokia, the biggest pre-Columbian Native American city (which existed between from CE 1050 near modern St Louis, Missouri) suffered a combination of drought and flooding from the Mississippi that led to its abandonment in the fourteenth century.

For a long time, the demise of Cahokia was put down to humanmade changes to the environment, particularly deforestation and over-farming. But modern scholarly consensus denies this accusation of ecocide. It is our modern anxieties about human-induced climate change that make us look back to the past in this way, projecting our present fears onto past societies. Natural climate change, it is true, has wrecked once-great urban civilisations. But the history of these past calamities can offer us hope, too.

The history of our species has been characterised by our ability to rebound after catastrophic events. What looks to us in retrospect like apocalypse were in reality slow-burning events, examples of gradual abandonment rather than sudden disaster. Angkor was deserted because of a changed climate, to be sure; but it had already been weakened by incessant war and the relocation of the royal family to Phnom Penh, along with large amounts of the population. The great public works were neglected after Angkor lost its primacy as the principal metropolis of Cambodia. Similarly, the Maya were gripped by endemic warfare and rivalries between city states. The fall of cities has happened for many reasons. Where climate has been involved, it has often been one factor among many. When disaster and abandonment have occurred, it has been not all at once but over generations. Populations dispersed to other regions, settling in other cities or taking up different ways of life. More often than not, societies have been able to regenerate after a cataclysmic event. Although individual cities disappear, urbanism does not. The Mayans are a rare example of a people that gave up on cities. When cities have been ceded to the jungle or the desert it has been because societies have been unable to foresee and adapt to changing environmental conditions.

We are in the position of being able to foresee and adapt. Cities are resilient, and so too are their inhabitants, capable of survival even in the face of devastating disasters, even nuclear attacks. In the history of cities you see a continual process of evolution and renewal. That ability to metamorphose is what has made our urbanised history over the last 6,000 years so durable and successful. Dense,

populous cities – many of them lying on coastlines –
are particularly vulnerable to climate breakdown.
Yet, living under the shadow of catastrophe, they
are showing signs of adapting.

Visitors to the tropical city state of Singapore are
immediately struck by the sheer amount of greenery draped over one of the most densely populated
and hypermodern places on the planet. Singapore
exemplifies to a strong degree the modern trend
whereby the distinction between the built environment and nature has become extremely blurry.
Few cities on earth have done more to adapt to
anticipated climate changes. In the BBC's **Planet
Earth II** (2016), David Attenborough described
Singapore as the supreme example of a city living
'in harmony with nature'.

On the face of it, that claim seems astonishing:
almost all of Singapore and its shoreline have undergone complete and irreversible anthropogenic transformation. After the British turned Singapore into
a trading post in 1819, the local environment came
under violent assault. By 1889, 90 per cent of the
old-growth forest on the island had been turned
into plantations, first for gambier and pepper and
then for rubber and agriculture. Lastly, it was urbanised. By the twenty-first century, Singapore's
primary vegetation had been beaten back to a miniscule 0.16 per cent of the island. Coral reefs once
covered one hundred square kilometres; now just

40 per cent remain. Less than a tenth of the seventy-five square kilometres of mangrove forests that were present at the time of the arrival of the British survive, and few of the pre-1819 sandy beaches. The aquatic ecosystem was murdered by development and by greedy land reclamation projects: since the 1960s, Singapore has expanded its territory by 25 per cent, from 581.5 square kilometres to 732. Much of its skyscrapered central business district, as well as its iconic Gardens by the Bay, occupies what was, in the 1960s, part of the sea separating Singapore from Indonesia. In wresting this land from the waves, Singapore has imported vast quantities of sand from Malaysia, Indonesia, Myanmar and the Philippines at severe ecological cost. For every 0.6 square miles of reclaimed land, 37.5 million cubic metres of sand – one of the world's most desirable commodities in the age of urbanisation, making up one quarter of standard concrete mix – is required, involving 1.4 million dump truck deliveries. Following ecological carnage on this scale and intensity, it is not surprising that as much as 73 per cent of the island's native flora and fauna has been driven to extinction.[5]

Singapore's history over the last 200 years has been defined by the engineering of nature to suit human needs. There is something a little familiar here: cities like Singapore, in their rush to remodel nature, act in ways not dissimilar to Tikal and Angor. After independence from the British in 1963 and its breakaway from the Federation of Malaya in 1965, Singapore's Promethean re-engineering of nature, however, has taken a decidedly different turn.

Prime Minister Lee Kuan Yew mobilised the authority and resources of the state to transform Singapore once again. Singapore was, in the 1960s, blighted with the ecological legacy of colonialism: plantations, pollution, sodden slums and rivers that had become open sewers. For Lee, turning Singapore into a supersized Garden City would not only symbolise its recovery from colonial degradation but attract wealth as the impoverished city state came to resemble the jungly cities of south-east Asia first encountered by Europeans. Lee dubbed himself the 'chief gardener'. Today, the legacy is readily apparent. Singapore's claim to be hypermodern is expressed not so much in its gleaming skyscrapers as in the lushness of the foliage that cascades over them and the vivid bougainvillea that overflows from bridges and other roadside structures. That striking juxtaposition of semi-wild nature and state-of-the-art architecture is what makes it look, in the age of climate emergency, futuristic.

Lee's Garden City was rebranded the 'City in a Garden'. For such a densely populated city, it is extraordinary to think that 56 per cent of Singapore's surface is covered in vegetation. The city leads the world in rooftop gardens and living walls, urban agriculture and reforestation, green buildings and wastewater recycling. Greening the city began as a means of making it more liveable for its citizens and appealing to investors. But low-lying Singapore – mortally threatened by rising sea levels, higher temperatures and flash floods – was one of the first cities, beginning in the 1990s, to begin future-proofing itself against climate change. By the 2020s, the reality of the Anthropocene was all too apparent on the island, with hotter temperatures and fiercer downpours.

Almost everything about Singapore looks and feels artificial. And, given the ferocity of anthropogenic alteration, the same is true of the island's nature. Singapore's famous Gardens by the Bay illustrates what has been called the metropolis's 'sci-fi botany' and 'technonature'. The nature park, opened in 2012 on reclaimed land, is dominated by its grove of eighteen colossal Supertrees, human-made arboreal structures with 160,000 tropical flowers, creepers and ferns clinging onto their steel frame. They are designed to act, as well as look, like real trees. Photovoltaic cells harness solar energy, mimicking photosynthesis; rainwater is harvested for irrigation; and their artificial canopies moderate temperatures by absorbing and dispersing heat. They act as air vents cooling the park's Flower Dome and Cloud Forest, two of the largest greenhouses in the world, which contain thousands of species of flora. The scene in **Planet Earth** praising Singapore for its harmonious relationship with nature was accompanied by a close-up shot of a hummingbird taking nectar from a vertical garden growing on one of the Supertrees. At the foot of these giants, a real tropical forest of living trees is maturing amid the skyscrapers and shipping terminals.[6]

Gardens by the Bay is Singapore's most popular tourist destination, receiving its 50 millionth visitor in 2018, six years after it opened. It is an apt symbol for the city's ecological aspirations – and perhaps for all cities. Brutally denuded of its native vegetation, Singapore has had to pioneer ways of coaxing biodiversity back, actively inserting greenspace in, on and around high-density buildings. It is a reminder that cities are novel ecosystems: only by sustained human interventions can a semblance of nature return to these supremely disturbed sites. Tropical Singapore has a stunning level of biodiversity, to be sure. But it is a fraction – as low as 27 per cent – of that which existed before urbanisation. This is a shocking revelation of ecocide. More worryingly, it shows what mass urbanisation has in store for the biodiversity hotspots of Asia and Africa – extirpation on a murderous scale.

Having destroyed so much in its path to prosperity, Singapore has self-consciously become a showcase of future city-building; rejuvenating its denuded environment is fundamental to national identity. In threading acres of greenery into what had formerly been grey, it is asking us to envisage a future where we have rethought urban space to maximise biodiversity, even in the densest of built environments.

Singapore has mandated that 80 per cent of all buildings, new and old, have to be greened by 2030. The city has actively promoted many of the themes explored throughout **Urban Jungle:** extensive re-forestation, the re-naturalisation of river systems, the creation of wetlands and floodplains, ecological recreation parks and sustainable architecture. It has found room for biodiversity by discouraging car-ownership, releasing land that would otherwise be given over to roads and parking spaces, and maintaining a high level of housing density. Very obviously in Singapore, nature is entwined with technology, biodiversity with futuristic architecture: such visual contrasts reinforce the idea that we will have to seek natural solutions to our self-created problems. Singapore's famous Supertrees symbolise that future in which biomimicry takes centre stage in technology.

Singapore is one of the wealthiest places on earth. It also has a strong, centralised government, leading to what has been called 'eco-authoritarianism', a no-nonsense, no-compromise, top-down imposition of environmental policies. Little wonder, then, that it has been able to deploy green infrastructure on a vast scale and at daunting cost. In Singapore, nature has always been a resource. More often than not, it was exploited to complete exhaustion. Today, the attitude towards nature is as utilitarian: it is being engineered to protect the city in the uncertain twenty-first century.

But other cities, less authoritarian and often not so prosperous, are also adapting, and relatively fast. Cities as diverse as Copenhagen, Wuhan and Philadelphia are switching from hard to soft engineering, using natural hydrology to manage floods. Rivers and coastlines are being rehabilitated in formerly blighted industrial areas. New parks such as Berlin's Südgelände and New York's Freshkills are examples of the trend towards wilder urban landscapes. Elsewhere, people are beginning to accept that spontaneous vegetation possesses an ecological value far higher than manicured nature. In almost all cities, there is an awareness that substantially re-naturalising the environment is the only way to safeguard their long-term survival: only large green areas, urban forests, wetlands and clean watercourses can lower temperatures and deal with excess water. This amounts to a tacit admission that, by defying the laws of nature, there was something fundamentally at fault with the way we urbanised over the last two centuries – or that, at the very least, modern cities, like Tikal or Angkor, were not designed for the climate extremes that are about to hit them.

Sometimes nature can be brought back into the city cheaply. It can certainly happen quickly; plants and animals recolonise urban areas with astonishing speed when we drive less and back off from our compulsion for tidying, mowing, weeding and spraying weedkiller about. Oftentimes, however, ecological restoration is an eyewateringly expensive business. The willingness of wealthy cities to invest in these schemes tell us how necessary they now are as mitigation strategies. It also tells us that it is more economical to plan cities around their environments as they expand, rather than forking out vast sums later to retrofit them with forests, floodplains, living shorelines and other safeguards.

Will we learn that lesson? Over the last four or five decades, rapid urbanisation has become the route for countries, and individuals, to better themselves. The rush to the city has been unplanned in many parts of the world, especially those parts of the world that are both abrim with biodiversity and vulnerable to heatwaves, floods, droughts and rising sea levels. Urbanisation of this magnitude and velocity often pays little regard to the environment: in that way, it is no different from urbanisation during the Promethean phase of history in the global north. Lessons may only be learnt too late, after grievous damage is done, when megacities begin to become uninhabitable.

Already, Jakarta is going the way of Tikal and Angkor. It may well be abandoned before it is reclaimed by the sea: the Indonesian government is spending billions relocating the capital to the rainforests of East Kalimantan on Borneo Island. In cities devoid of green space, such as Buenos Aires and Muscat, temperatures are rising much faster than the regional average, making them unbearable.

As we have seen, built-up areas that don't have generous canopy cover and open water can be 10°C
hotter than their surroundings. The water level in
Manila Bay is rising four times faster than the global
average, the result of obliterating the area's protecting forests of mangroves. Tianjin – one of China's
largest cities with a population of 14 million – may
be uninhabitable by the end of the century as a result
of extreme humidity and heat that will push average
temperatures between 2°C and 5°C above current
levels. Besides, by that time, most of the metropolitan area will likely be underwater unless it puts
in place mitigation strategies. So too will low-lying
cities in parts of the world that can't afford costly
adaptations; large swathes of Lagos, Alexandria,
Abidjan, Banjul and Dhaka will be underwater if
sea levels rise by between fifty centimetres and one
metre. The need for cities all over the world to emulate Singapore could not be clearer.

If only it was so simple.

Those cities that have the resources and political will to adapt and mitigate will most likely find
ways to do so. They will become the fortresses of
the Anthropocene, using hard and soft engineering
to maintain a reasonable quality of life. This will
inevitably widen the disparities between rich and
poor: as ever, living with greenery is a privilege of
the wealthy. Around a billion people reside in slums
and informal settlements. Half the urban population of Asia and Africa, and a quarter of that of

Latin America and the Caribbean, lack adequate basic infrastructure – electricity, clean water and sanitation – let alone open space, trees or drainage, the kind of green infrastructure now regarded as essential for microclimate regulation. Such places often occupy, by necessity rather than choice, flood-plains, drained wetlands, low-lying coasts, garbage dumps and hillsides; they are already vulnerable to natural disasters and are markedly deprived of the kind of ecosystem services described throughout **Urban Jungle.** They are inhabited by people who contributed very little to climate change but will bear its brunt. Cities such as Lagos, Dar-es-Salaam and Nairobi offer millions a route out of poverty; they could well be underwater or intolerably hot before they reach their potential.

Many megacities – particularly those lacking stable government – are becoming hazardous places. Even so, extreme weather conditions are already forcing rural people into cities for safety; they are bastions when things get dangerous, and we should expect to see many more millions of climate refugees swelling the global urban population. One important theme of **Urban Jungle** has been the clash between the kind of city people wanted and the actual cities that have developed. Protestors who marched out to defend the ancient heaths of London, the forests of Berlin, the peepal trees of Bangalore and the ancient forests of Delhi are examples of this. So too are the people in cities all over the world who asserted, time and again, their rights to farm the unforgiving urban terrain for pleasure and for sustenance. Cities once contained numerous common lands – often marginal and edgeland space – where city folk had access to rugged forms of nature for leisure and to glean resources.

That is because urban nature offers us generous returns in the form of ecological services. Trees shade us and beautify the concrete jungle. Biodiversity, wherever it is found, improves our mood and makes life bearable. And it has also provided people with foods and medicines. Slum-dwellers are most deprived of nature but most in need of it. Harini Nagendra, in her study of the ecology of informal settlements in Bangalore, found that what nature existed provided a range of public goods. Although these settlements had many fewer trees than more prosperous neighbourhoods, half of those that existed provided medicines – such as the drumstick, the neem, the peepal and the honge – and one-third were fruit trees, most commonly coconut, cherry, mango and jamun. Tall and slender, the drumstick tree can squeeze itself into cramped slums, providing shade for outdoor activities, seeds for cooking and leaves for eating, rich in iron and vitamins. Herbs are also frequently grown on windowsills and roofs and in discarded paint tins, old cooking pots, plastic bags and battery cans.

There is a serious nature deficiency in settlements like these around the globe. Nagendra's interviewees expressed a strong desire for more trees and plants: if they could design their own neighbourhoods, they would be thick with honges and neems, prized for their medicinal qualities and shady canopies alike. Urban planning puts green infrastructure way down the list of priorities when it comes to informal settlements; ecological sustainability rarely gets a mention. Many of the world's poorest and most challenging cities would become as lush as wealthier metropolises simply by the actions of local residents if they had more agency, if only because urban ecologies possess a higher value for the poorest who can't afford air conditioning, vitamin-rich food and medicines. Bangalore's assault on its nature over the last few decades, as it has grown at speed, has impacted heavily on its slum-dwellers and migrants. A city that once boasted a wide range of edible and medicinal plants has simplified its environment, prioritising ornamental plants and lawns over species that were foraged. Nature was once multi-use; now it is just for looking at. Urban commons have succumbed to development. The ecosystem favoured by the most disadvantaged, it seems, corresponds with one that is abundant and diverse in species, in contrast to the more pared back preferences of the wealthy. We have an instinct to beautify our environment and use nature as a source of sustenance and health; oftentimes, that instinct is restrained against our will, just as nature has long been restrained in cities.[7]

But no number of trees, clean rivers and ecological parks will reverse the looming catastrophe; they will only stave off the effects for a while. The concept of nature in the city has become increasingly important. But even more important is the question of the city in nature.

An ecosystem consists of complex interactions between its biotic and abiotic – living and non-living – components. The web of life is bound together by nutrient cycles and energy flows. Energy and carbon enter through photosynthesis and are transferred to organisms via the living tissue of plants. Nutrients are exchanged between plants, animals, microbes and the soil through feeding and the decomposition of dead organic matter and waste products. All ecosystems are subject to disturbances, sometimes violent; but they have the capacity to absorb and adapt to such shocks and return to equilibrium. This is known as 'ecological resilience'.

Like any ecosystem, a city in the twenty-first century needs to be able to react to serious and unpredictable environmental shocks. But even though cities are ecosystems, they do not behave like them. They suck in vast amounts of energy and nutrients, only to expel them as pollutants, sewage, heat and solid waste, or they lock them up in groundwater and landfills. In a wild ecosystem, flows are circular, with most inputs recycled back; in urban ecosystems, it is a linear process, a one-way street.

The environmental impact of organising cities as greedy input-output machines is grave. Today, just over 50 per cent of people are urbanised, but cities produce 75 per cent of carbon emissions. They extract 40 billion tons of the planet's material resources every year; by the midpoint of the century, it will be 90 billion. As we have seen, cities imbibe vast amounts of nutrients, which are never returned to fertilise the land from which they came. When cities ceased to be self-sufficient in terms of energy, fuel, food, water and other raw materials, they started to place heavier and heavier burdens on the planet; that appetite is becoming riskier as the urban population ramps up, and with it comes greater prosperity. Much of the ecological damage caused by cities was obscured, because energy, nutrients and consumer goods were imported through pipes, wires and long-distance supply chains and exported via sewers and landfills. Now, thanks to the use of big data, we can measure the footprints of cities and minutely analyse the flows of energy and resources from origin to expulsion. Some 63 per cent of CO_2 emissions from a city in the developed world derive from products and materials that were consumed in the city but produced elsewhere. Much environmental damage is unseen.

Cities are not sustainable. They stand in the frontline of environmental disaster; they will bear the brunt of its effects, along with the vast majority of the human race that lives in them. Climate change is an urban problem; as such, it calls for urban solutions.

A fully circular city: that's what Amsterdam is working to become by 2050. The Dutch capital was the birthplace of modern financial capitalism at the outset of the seventeenth century; today, it has a breathtakingly ambitious plan to reimagine capitalism in the twenty-first century. Pioneers in trade and finance, the people of the highly urbanised, low-lying Netherlands have always had to strike a balance with nature, learning to live with water and flooding. Dutch cities are highly vulnerable to climate change, hence Amsterdam's bold decision in April 2020, as Covid-19 was engulfing the world, to use science-based measures to achieve, by 2050, the 'ambition of performing at least as well as a healthy local ecosystem'.[8]

For a city to function like a natural ecosystem, it has to take account of all the multivarious material flows that enter and leave. Amsterdam held up a mirror to itself in the late 2010s. It did not like what it saw reflected back. The metropolis, like all cities in the developed world, consumes resources in a way that directly harms the planetary life-support system. It consumes voraciously without returning to the planet. At the heart of that problem is power.

Amsterdam is taking direct responsibility for its own energy needs. By 2030, it will produce 80 per cent of its energy by using nearby solar arrays, wind-farms and biomass generators. Half of this energy production will come from solar panels installed by neighbourhood co-operatives and businesses. This desire to become self-sufficient in energy production once again is not confined to Amsterdam. Cadiz owns its own power company, which supplies 80 per cent of households from renewable sources. Los Angeles is also fortunate in having a publicly owned energy utility. In 2021, Los Angeles City Council voted to mandate 100 per cent renewable energy by 2035. That is one advantage cities have: the density and scale of urban settlements mean much better resource efficiency. Cities possess greater power to control their flows of resources and implement large-scale changes tailored to their individual needs than central governments. Aware of their vulnerability, cities are prepared to act faster and deeper than nation states.

Amsterdam is going further than mere self-sufficiency in clean energy: it is attempting to close the energy loop. As long ago as 1851, Henry Mayhew said about ecology in cities: '[I]n Nature everything moves in a circle – perpetually changing, and yet ever returning to the point whence it started. . . . Up to the present time we have only thought of removing our refuse – the idea of using it never enters our minds. It was not until science taught us the dependence of one order of creation upon another, that we began to see what appeared worse than worthless to us was Nature's capital – wealth set aside for future production.'

'Waste does not exist –' declares the website of the Port of Amsterdam in the same vein – 'only value waiting to be discovered.' Establishing the kind of circularity envisaged by Mayhew – by emulating natural processes – is central to Amsterdam's ambitions in becoming a zero-waste city. Nutrients and chemicals are reclaimed from industrial and domestic organic waste in biorefineries. Discarded foods are converted into compost, green energy and heat; fat used for deep frying into biodiesel. Phosphates, calcite, cellulose and humic acid are extracted from sewage sludge and wastewater. The other side of that coin – food production – is being brought closer to the city, so that Amsterdam consumes from within its hinterland rather than importing from thousands of miles away. Self-sufficiency represents a step towards sustainability.

Better not to produce waste in the first place. Amsterdam wants to halve its consumption of primary raw materials by 2030 and become a fully circular, self-sufficient economy twenty years after that as a way of drastically limiting its impact on the environment. Making such radical reductions without sacrificing quality of life requires recycling,

reusing, repairing and repurposing on a titanic scale
so that the life cycles of most products are extended
indefinitely. The textile industry, for example, is one
of the world's most polluting industries, with an
enormous ecological footprint. Discarded clothing
creates mountains of waste – 36,500 metric tons
a year in the Amsterdam metropolitan area – and
that which is reclaimed is recycled into low-grade
materials. Amsterdam is prioritising the recycling of
textile fibres into high-quality clothing as a central
part of its emerging circular economy. The same
goes for electronics and furniture. To set an example
to consumers, the municipal government is using
its purchasing power to procure only used or re-
furbished electronics and office furniture. It is making the same habit easier for Amsterdammers by
sponsoring sharing platforms, second-hand shops
and repair services.

Buildings and their construction account for
39 per cent of all global carbon emissions, the majority coming from lighting, heating and cooling.
With the world's building stock expected to double
by 2060 as we urbanise even more, there is a hell
of a lot more carbon waiting to be released. If it
wants to reduce its carbon emissions by 95 per cent
and become a fully circular economy by the middle
of this century, Amsterdam will have to undergo a
spectacular series of interventions to renovate its existing building stock. Individual buildings have to
become self-sufficient in terms of energy generation

and water collection and re-use. New construction will have to recycle concrete and use biobased raw materials such as wood so that the very fabric of the city obeys the principles of circularity.

Amsterdam wants to live 'in harmony with nature' in a more profound way even than Singapore, where the imbrication of humans and wildlife is readily apparent. A liberal, cohesive and affluent city, Amsterdam is a promising place for an experiment of this magnitude, complexity and disruptiveness. It will rely on the city government inspiring individuals, neighbourhoods and businesses coming along with it. The outcome is far from certain, to put it mildly; it will not be achieved without a large degree of pain. At the very least, its striving for circularity in every aspect of life reveals starkly just how unnatural cities are in their metabolic processes. At the same time, fostering a circular economy is only possible within individual cities because the close proximity of businesses, consumers and producers provides a greater economic opportunity for the re-use and recycling of materials and energy, not to say greater efficiency and reduced transport costs. Cities can be agents of change when it comes to achieving more sustainable lifestyles; they are where innovation has happened throughout history. We have a sliver of a reason to be optimistic.

Amsterdam is striving to become a laboratory for a new way of doing things, just as it did in the Dutch Golden Age four centuries ago. Already, cities including Copenhagen, Philadelphia, Barcelona, Portland, Austin and Brussels are taking tentative steps towards policies of zero-waste, circular economies. As Amsterdam sees it, for a city to become a healthy ecosystem, it is not enough to plant thousands of trees, establish roof gardens, clean up rivers and wild green spaces; all this is futile if it merely conceals a ruthless assault on nature elsewhere.[9]

A stately hollyhock clad with bright pink flowers spears out of the pavement. Once, there were cars parked here and vehicles ceaselessly passing up and down the street. Now, they are gone, and in their place are the hollyhocks, purple loosestrife, salvias and climbing roses, growing alongside luxurious bushy shrubs, densely massed flowers, grasses and trees. This is now a social place, somewhere to meet, talk, play and dine, somewhere to spend time, not hurry through.

Here, in the streets of the Frans Halsbuurt district of Amsterdam, you discover complete tranquillity and striking greenness; the roar of traffic has given way to birdsong and the sound of children playing; greyness has been conquered by lushness. In the Netherlands, they call it the **knip** – the 'cut': barriers close off portions of long streets, allowing vehicle access only for deliveries and pick-ups. Amsterdam is on its way to being car-free. As space-hungry vehicles disappear, foliage and animals move in. As they do so, people get their streets back. They become, once again, places for mingling under the spreading canopy – a living area, not a dead one. Cars can take up to 40 per cent of public space in a city. Remove them, and you suddenly have a lot more room for hollyhocks and trees, not to say for people. Part of Amsterdam's vision for a circular economy is to create 'a city for people, plants and animals'. Perhaps we will realise one day that a city that benefits all three more or less equally is a good one in which to live. The Frans Halsbuurt district is a showcase for this new kind of metropolis.

These streets exemplify the best of the urban biome. The city is now our habitat, after all. Car-dependence has wrought havoc on cities, making streets less fun to be in, breaking up communities and introducing a lot of pollution into the air. Weaning ourselves off our private vehicles will not be easy; we are fearsomely addicted to them. But it is clear that the benefits of drastically reducing motor vehicles in cities, painful as it will be, will transform them for the better. They will become even greener, as trees and pocket parks reclaim parking spaces and wide roads. And, as in the quiet lockdowns of the 2020s, more wild animals will come to live among us.

Aside from the environmental benefits of making streets greener, living within a healthy ecosystem improves our lives immeasurably, reducing stress levels and depression and improving our physical fitness. The quest for biodiversity and sustainability should, as its ultimate goal, make the environment in which we reside the best it possibly can be for **us.**

Throughout history, density has made cities productive, profitable and sociable. Density is pretty good for the environment, too: when we stop spreading out, we leave more land for nature. We also burn less petrol; we walk, cycle and take public transport more. One of the reasons we sprawl ever further outwards is to get our nature fix, surrounded by gardens, big skies and open space, but we kill the things we love: unchecked urban expansion is fatal for nature. Things are changing, however, and they are changing fast. High human density no longer means you have to live without nature; across the planet, we are weaving wildlife into the urban fabric in a way unknown before. And perhaps more importantly, we are discovering that urban ecosystems have a vital role to play for planetary health.

In 2019, London became the world's first National Park City. And why not? Nearly half of it is green and 60 per cent is **not** built upon. There are 14,000 different species of plants, animals and fungi in the English capital; around 20 per cent of the metropolis's surface area consists of Sites of Importance for Nature Conservation. The designation is a clear acknowledgement of the prolific and unique biodiversity that is found in all cities. It signals a move

away from seeing nature as belonging only in designated urban spaces such as parks: nature in London
and, indeed, every city is ubiquitous, doing what it
does best or learning new tricks. As Daniel Raven-
Ellison, 'guerrilla geographer' and brain behind the
campaign to make London a National Park City,
said, the project was a way of making people see and
treat cities differently. By applying the national park
concept to London, it asked the question: 'what is
nature, and the boundaries between it and people?'[10]

Wander amid the emergent grasslands at Freshkills
Park in New York or the maturing forest in the
Südgelände in Berlin; step into a micro-jungle in
Bangalore or a wildflower meadow in Frankfurt;
meander along a re-naturalised river or through a
restored urban wetland; get lost in Dallas's Trinity
Forest or Delhi's Mangar Bani: wildness is becoming a pronounced feature of modern cities. The
public spaces of the future are being built around
such concepts of natural regeneration and wildness. But you don't even need to go to these places;
every street, wall, vacant space, building site, garden and crack in the concrete is home to an array
of life. If we learn to reread the city, an ecosystem
forms in front of our eyes. A stroll can become an
urban safari.

As we learn more about the natural processes
and animal life within cities, we will surely begin
to see our urban world very differently – as a thing

existing in nature, not apart from it. Our need for nature, and our need for sociability and culture, can be served all together if we let them. Cities should be the conservation sites of the twenty-first century. They are ecosystems deserving of our protection and nurture. Miracles happen on our doorsteps.

Notes

Introduction

1 C. Y. Jim, 'Old Stone Walls as an Ecological Habitat for Urban Trees in Hong Kong', **Landscape and Urban Planning,** 42/1 (July 1998); Christopher Dewolf, 'A Tree Worthy of Worship: Hong Kong's Banyans', **Zolima City Mag,** 1/6/2016; Chi Yung Jim, 'Impacts of Intensive Urbanization on Trees in Hong Kong', **Environmental Conservation,** 25/2 (June 1998), 115; Bureau of Forestry and Landscaping of Guangzhou Municipality, 'Description on the Improvement of Road Greening Quality in Guangzhou', 31/5/2021, http://lyylj.gz.gov.cn/zmhd/rdhy/content/post_7308343.html.
2 Anthony Reid, 'The Structure of Cities in Southeast Asia, Fifteenth to Seventeenth Centuries', **Journal of Southeast Asian Studies,** 11/2 (Sept. 1980), 241.
3 Richard A. Fuller **et al,** 'Psychological Benefits of Greenspace Increase with Biodiversity', **Biology Letters,** 3/4 (Aug. 2007).

1. On the Edge

1 T. McGee, 'Urbanisasi or Kotadesasi? Evolving patterns of urbanization in Asia', in F. J. Costa **et al**

(eds.), **Urbanisation in Asia** (Honolulu, 1989); T. McGee, 'The Emergence of Desakota Regions in Asia: expanding a hypothesis', in N. Ginbsberg **et al** (eds.), **The Extended Metropolis: settlement transition in Asia** (Honolulu, 1991); Stephen Cairns, 'Troubling Real-estate: Reflecting on Urban Form in Southeast Asia', in T. Bunnell, L. Drummond and K. C. Ho (eds.), **Critical Reflections on Cities in Southeast Asia** (Singapore, 2002).

2 Ross Barrett, 'Speculations in Paint: Ernest Lawson and the urbanization of New York', **Winterhur Portfolio,** 42/1 (Spring 2008); James Reuel Smith, **Springs and Wells of Manhattan and the Bronx, New York City, at the End of the Nineteenth Century** (New York, 1938), pp. 48–50, 97–8.

3 Ted Steinberg, **Gotham Unbound: the ecological history of Greater New York** (New York, 2014), pp. 90ff, 207, 217, 269.

4 **Ibid.,** pp. 269, 283, 293.

5 **Ibid.,** p. 281; Samuel J. Kearing, 'The Politics of Garbage', **New York,** April 1970, p. 32.

6 Steinberg, p. 269.

7 K. Gardner, **Global Migrants, Local Lives** (Oxford, 1995), p. 23.

8 Ben Wilson, **Metropolis: a history of humankind's greatest invention** (London, 2020), pp. 354f; Karen C. Seto, Burak Güneralp and Lucy R. Hutyra, 'Global Forecasts of Urban Expansion to 2030 and Direct Impacts on Biodiversity and Carbon Pools', **PNAS,** 109/40 (Oct. 2012); 'Hotspot Cities', Atlas for the End of the World, http://atlas-for-the-end

-of-the-world.com/hotspot_cities_main.html; B Güneralp and K. C. Seto, 'Futures of Global Urban Expansion: uncertainties and implications for biodiversity conservation', **Environmental Research Letters,** 8 (2013).

9 Kristin Poling, **Germany's Urban Frontiers: nature and history on the edge of the nineteenth-century city** (Pittsburgh, 2020), pp. 19ff.

10 C. D. Preston, 'Engulfed by Suburbia or Destroyed by the Plough: the ecology of extinction in Middlesex and Cambridgeshire', **Watsonia,** 23 (2000), 73; Sir Richard Phillips, **A Morning's Walk from London to Kew** (London, 1817), p. 156; Walter George Bell, **Where London Sleeps: historical journeyings into the suburbs** (London, 1926), p. 43.

11 Walter Besant, **South London** (London, 1912), p. 308; William Bardwell, **Healthy Homes, and How to Make Them** (London, 1854), pp. 45–50.

12 John Stow, **A Survey of London, written in the year 1598** (London, 1842), p. 38; Steinberg, pp. 214–15, 250; Poling, ch. 4.

13 Leigh Hunt, 'On the Suburbs of Genoa and the Country about London', **Literary Examiner,** 16/8/ 1823, p. 98; Thomas de Quincey, **Confessions of an English Opium-eater** (Edinburgh, 1856), pp. 189–90.

14 Ben Wilson, **The Laughter of Triumph: William Hone and the fight for the free press** (London, 2005), p. 360.

15 Michael Rawson, 'The March of Bricks and Mortar', **Environmental History,** 17/4 (Oct. 2012), 844.

16 Phillips, p. 171; Élie Halévy, **A History of the English People in the Nineteenth Century: England in 1815** (London, 1924), p. 202.

17 Neil P. Thornton, 'The Taming of London's Commons' [unpublished PhD thesis] (University of Adelaide, 1988), pp. 41ff.

18 Rawson, p. 848ff.

19 H. J. Dyos, **Victorian Suburb: a study of the growth of Camberwell** (Leicester, 1973), pp. 19–20, 56ff.

20 J. C. Loudon, 'Hints for Breathing Places for the Metropolis', **Gardener's Magazine,** 5, (1829), 686–90.

21 Alona Martinez Perez, 'Garden Cities, Suburbs and Fringes: the Green Belt in a global setting', in P. Bishop **et al** (eds.), **Repurposing the Green Belt in the 21ˢᵗ Century** (London, 2020), pp. 60ff.

22 Frank Lloyd Wright, 'Experimenting with Human Lives' (1923), in **Collected Writings,** i, p. 172.

23 Jens Lachmund, **Greening Berlin: the co-production of science, politics, and urban nature** (Cambridge, Mass., 2013), p. 29.

24 Barry A. Jackisch, 'The Nature of Berlin: green space and visions of a new German capital', 1900–45', **Central European History,** 47/2 (June 2014), 216ff; P. Abercrombie and J. Forshaw, **County of London Plan Prepared for the LCC, 1943** (London, 1943), p. 39.

25 Mark A. Goddard **et al,** 'Scaling up from Gardens: biodiversity conservation in urban environments', **Trends in Ecology and Evolution,** 25/2 (Feb. 2010), 90.

26 Sarah Bilson, ' "They Congregate in Towns and Suburbs": the shape of middle-class life in John Claudius Loudon's **The Suburban Gardener**', **Victorian Review** 37/1 (Spring 2011); Howard Leathlean, 'Loudon's **Gardener's Magazine** and the morality of landscape', **Ecumene,** 4/1 (Jan. 1997).

27 John Claudius Loudon, **The Suburban Gardener, and Villa Companion** (London, 1838), pp. 330ff.

28 Gillen D'Arcy Wood, 'Leigh Hunt's New Suburbia: an eco-historical study in climate poetics and public health', **Interdisciplinary Studies in Literature and Environment** 18/3 (Summer 2011), 530.

29 Susan M. Neild, 'Colonial Urbanism: the development of Madras City in the Eighteenth and Nineteenth Centuries', **Modern Asian Studies,** 13/2 (1979), 241ff; John Archer, 'Colonial Suburbs in South Asia, 1700–1850, and the Spaces of Modernity', in Roger Silverstone (ed.), **Visions of Suburbia** (London, 1997), pp. 1–25; Mark Girouard, **Cities and People: a social and architectural history** (New Haven, 1985), pp. 242, 277–80; Todd Kuchta, **Semi-Detached Empire: suburbia and the colonization of Britain, 1880 to the present** (Charlottesville, 2010), pp. 18ff; Eugenia W. Herbert, **Flora's Empire: British gardens in India** (Philadelphia, 2011), ch. 1.

30 Margaret Willes, **The Gardens of the British Working Class** (New Haven, 2014), pp. 251f, 271f, 338.

31 **Ibid.,** p. 318.

32 **Ibid.,** p. 319–20.

364   **Notes**

33 Charles S. Elton, **The Pattern of Animal Communities** (London, 1966) p. 78.

34 Jennifer Owen, **The Ecology of a Garden: a thirty-year study** (London, 2010).

35 For further studies in garden ecology see the list at http://www.bugs.group.shef.ac.uk/BUGS1/updates.html and comparative studies in Kevin J. Gaston and Sian Gaston, 'Urban Gardens and Biodiversity', in Ian Douglas **et al** (eds.), **The Routledge Handbook of Urban Ecology** (London, 2011), pp. 451ff.

36 K. Thompson **et al,** 'Urban Domestic Gardens (III): composition and diversity of lawn floras', **Journal of Vegetation Science,** 15 (2004); Herbert Sukopp, 'Berlin', in John G. Kelcey **et al** (eds.), **Plants and Habitats of European Cities** (New York, 2011), p. 65.

37 D. Macaulay **et al** (eds.), **Royal Horticultural Society Plant Finder 2002 – 2003** (London, 2002).

38 William H. Whyte, 'Urban Sprawl', **Fortune,** Jan. 1958, 103.

39 Christopher C. Sellers, **Crabgrass Crucible: suburban nature and the rise of environmentalism in twentieth-century America** (Chapel Hill, 2012), pp. 156, 164; Meghan Avolio **et al,** 'Urban Plant Diversity in Los Angeles, California: species and functional type turnover in cultivated landscapes', **Plants, People, Planet,** 2/2 (March, 2020), 144–156.

40 Sellers, pp. 157–9.

41 Norbert Müller **et al,** 'Patterns and Trends in Urban Biodiversity and Landscape Design', in Thomas

Elmqvist **et al** (eds.), **Urbanization, Biodiversity and Ecosystem Services: challenges and opportunities** (Dordrecht, 2013), p. 128; P. P. Garcilán **et al,** 'Analysis of the non-native flora of Ensenada, a fast-growing city in northwestern Baja California', **Urban Ecosystems,** 12/4 (Dec. 2009), 449–463; A. Pauchard **et al,** 'Multiple Effects of Urbanization on the Biodiversity of Developing Countries: the case of a fast-growing metropolitan area (Concepción, Chile)', **Biological Conservation,** 127 (Jan. 2006), 272–281.

42 R. Decandido, 'Recent Changes in Plant Species Diversity in Urban Pelham Bay Park, 1947–1998', **Biological Conservation,** 120/1 (Nov. 2004), 129–136; Decandido **et al,** 'The Naturally Occurring Historical and Extant Flora of Central Park', New York City, New York (1857–2007), **Journal of the Torrey Botanical Society,** 134/4 (2007), 552–569.

43 Greater London Authority, **Crazy Paving: the environmental importance of London's front gardens** (London, 2005).

44 **Ibid.;** Conor Dougherty, 'Where the Suburbs End', **New York Times,** 8/10/2021; Diederik Baazil, 'One Way to Green a City: knock out the tiles', Bloomberg City Lab, 5/1/2021, https://www.bloomberg.com/news/features/2021-01-05/how-dutch-cities-are-creating-more-green-space.

45 Preston Lerner, 'Whither the Lawn', **Los Angeles Times,** 4/5/2003.

46 **Ibid.**

47 John Vidal, 'A Bleak Corner of Essex is being hailed as England's Rainforest', **Guardian,** 3/5/2003.
48 Steinberg, p. 154.
49 Jodi A. Hilty **et al, Corridor Ecology: linking landscapes for biodiversity conservation and climate adaptation** (Washington D.C., 2019); Aysel Uslu and Nasim Shakouri, 'Urban Landscape Design and Biodiversity', in Murat Ozyavuz (ed.), **Advances in Landscape Architecture** (Rijeka, 2013); Briony Norton **et al,** 'Urban Biodiversity and Landscape Ecology: patterns, processes and planning', **Current Landscape Ecology Reports,** 1 (2016); Ellen Damschen **et al,** 'Corridors Increase Plant Species Richness at Large Scales', **Science,** 313 (Sept. 2006); Holly Kirk **et al,** 'Building Biodiversity into the Urban Fabric: a case study in applying Biodiversity Sensitive Urban Design (BSUD)', **Urban Forestry and Urban Greening,** 62 (July 2021).

2. Parks & Rec

1 Field Operations, 'Fresh Kills Park: draft master plan' (New York, 2006) https://freshkillspark.org/wp-content/uploads/2013/07/Fresh-Kills-Park-Draft-Master-Plan.pdf; Madeline Gressel, 'Reinventing Staten Island: the ecological philosophy of turning a garbage dump into a park', **Nautilus,** 12/7/2017, https://nautil.us/issue/62/systems/reinventing-staten-island-rp.
2 M. F. Quigley, 'Potemkin Gardens: biodiversity in small designed landscapes', in J. Niemelä **et al**

(eds.), **Urban Ecology: patterns, processes and applications** (New York, 2011).

3 Rabun Taylor **et al**, '**Rus in Urbe:** a garden city', in Rabun Taylor **et al** (eds.), **Rome: an urban history from antiquity to the present** (Cambridge, 2016).

4 María Elena Bernal-García, 'Dance of Time: the procession of space at Mexico-Tenochtitlan's desert garden', in Michael Conan, **Sacred Gardens and Landscapes: ritual and agency** (Washington D.C., 2007).

5 Ali Mohammad Khan, **Mirat-i-Ahamadi,** trans. Syed Nawab Ali, 2 vols. (Baroda, 1927–30), Supplement, p. 22.

6 The Marchioness of Dufferin and Ava, **Our Viceregal Life in India: selections from my journal, 1884–1888,** 2 vols. (London, 1890), i, p. 138.

7 F. L. Olmsted, 'Public Parks and the Enlargement of Towns', **Journal of Social Sciences: containing the transactions of the American Association,** 3 (1871), 27.

8 'Particulars of Construction and Estimate for a Plan of the Central Park', **Documents of the Assembly of the State of New York,** 64, 9/2/1860, appendix A, p. 14; Carol. J. Nicholson, 'Elegance and Grass Roots: the neglected philosophy of Frederick Law Olmsted', **Transactions of the Charles S. Peirce Society,** 40/2 (Spring 2004).

9 Tim Richardson, **The Arcadian Friends: inventing the English landscape Garden** (London, 2007), ch. 8 **passim.**

10 John Claudius Loudon, **The Suburban Gardener, and Villa Companion** (London, 1838), p. 137.

11 J. C. Loudon and Joseph Strutt, **The Derby Arboretum** (London, 1840), p. 83.

12 Morrison H. Heckscher, **Creating Central Park** (New York, 2008), p. 12.

13 Frederick Law Olmsted, **Walks and Talks of an American Farmer in England** (Columbus, Ohio, 1859), p. 62.

14 Charles E. Beveridge and Paul Rocheleau, **Frederick Law Olmsted: designing the American landscape** (New York, 1998), p. 48; Olmsted, 'Public Parks, 34; George L. Scheper, 'The Reformist Vision of Frederick Law Olmsted and the Poetics of Park Design', **The New England Quarterly,** 62/3 (Sept. 1989).

15 **The Times,** 7/9/1847.

16 Oliver Gilbert, **The Ecology of Urban Habitats** (London, 1989).

17 Maria Ignatieva and Glenn Stewart, 'Homogeneity of Urban Biotopes and Similarity of Landscape Design Language in Former Colonial Cities', in Mark McDonnell **et al** (eds.), **Ecology of Cities and Towns: a comparative approach** (Cambridge, 2009); Fengping Yang **et al,** 'Historical Development and Practices of Lawns in China', **Environment and History,** 25/1 (Feb. 2019).

18 C. M. Villiers-Stuart, **Gardens of the Great Mughals** (London, 1913), p. 336; cf. pp. 48, 53–5, 90, 208, 213, 240, 264–6.

19 **Ibid.,** p. 16; George Curzon, 1st Marquess Curzon of Kedleston, 'The Queen Victoria Memorial Hall in India', **The Nineteenth Century and After, a Monthly Review,** 39 (Jan.–June 1901), 949–959.

20 Maria Ignatieva and Karin Ahrné, 'Biodiverse Green Infrastructure for the 21st Century: from "green desert" of lawns to biophilic cities', **Journal of Architecture and Urbanism** 37/1 (March 2013) 3; Maria Ignatieva **et al,** 'Lawns in Cities: from a globalised urban green space phenomenon to sustainable nature-based solutions', **Land,** 9 (March 2020).

21 Nigel Reeve, 'Managing for Biodiversity in London's Royal Parks', lecture, Gresham College, 9/10/2006.

22 Fengping Yang **et al;** Ignatieva and Ahrné (2013); Ignatieva **et al** (2020); 'Blades of Glory: America's love affair with lawns', **The Week,** 8/1/2015.

23 Norbert Müller **et al,** pp. 136ff; C. Meurk, 'Beyond the Forest: restoring the "herbs"', in I. Spellerberg and D. Given (eds.), **Going Native** (Christchurch, 2004); G. H. Stewart **et al,** 'URban Biotopes of Aotearoa New Zealand (URBANZ) (I): composition and diversity of temperate urban lawns in Christchurch', **Urban Ecosystems,** 12 (2009).

24 Saraswathy Nagarajan, 'Woke Gardeners Replace Green Deserts with Urban Jungle', **Hindu,** 6/10/2021; Raghvendra Vanjari **et al,** 'The Other Side of Development IV: green carpet or green desert?', Small Farm Dynamics in India blog, https://smallfarmdynamics.blog/2018/09/04/green-carpet-or-green-desert/#_ftn1.

25 Harini Nagendra, 'Protecting Urban Nature: lessons from ecological history', **Hindu,** 10/10/2016.

26 'Encroachments on Epping Forest: demonstration on Wanstead Flats', **Illustrated Times,** 15/7/1871;

'The Epping Forest Agitation: meeting at Wanstead Flats', **Morning Advertiser,** 10/7/1871; 'The Epping Forest Agitation – Meeting on Wanstead Flats – Destruction of Fences', **Standard,** 10/7/1871.

27 'Wanstead Flats', **The Graphic,** 15/7/1871; Parliamentary Papers, **Special Report from the Select Committee on Metropolitan Commons Act (1866) Amendment Bill,** pp. 1868–69 (333), X, 507, q. 257.

28 Parl. Debs. (series 3) vol. 176, col. 434 (28/6/1864).

29 W. Ivor Jennings, **Royal Commission on Common Land 1955–1958** (London, 1958), p. 455.

30 Reeve.

31 Steen Eiler Rasmussen, **London: the unique city** (London, 1937), pp. 333–8.

32 Stefan Bechtel, **Mr Hornaday's War: how a peculiar Victorian zookeeper waged a lonely crusade for wildlife that changed the world** (Boston, 2012).

33 Ignatieva and Ahrné (2013).

34 Alec Brownlow, 'Inherited Fragmentations and Narratives of Environmental Control in Entrepreneurial Philadelphia', in Nik Heynen **et al** (eds.), **In the Nature of Cities: urban political ecology and the politics of urban metabolism** (Abingdon, 2006).

35 Tom Burr, 'Circa 1977, Platzspitz Park Installation', in Joel Sanders (ed.), **Stud: architectures of masculinity** (Abingdon, 1996).

3. The Crack in the Concrete

1 Jens Lachmund, 'Exploring the City of Rubble: botanical fieldwork in bombed cities in Germany after World War II', **Osiris**[2], 18 (2003), 242.

2 **Ibid.,** 239; **Washington Post,** 13/10/1946.

3 R. S. R. Fitter, **London's Natural History** (London, 1945), pp. 73, 132, 231; Job Edward Lousley, 'The Pioneer Flora of Bombed Sites in Central London', **Botanical Society and Exchange Club of the British Isles,** 12/5 (1941–2) 528.

4 Lousley, 529; 'Flowers on Bombed Sites', **Times,** 3/5/1945; Edward James Salisbury, 'The Flora of Bombed Areas', **Nature,** 151 (April, 1943); Fitter, appendix.

5 Philip Lawton **et al,** 'Natura Urbana: the brachen of Berlin', **The AAG Review of Books,** 7/3 (2019), 220.

6 Herbert Sukopp, 'Flora and Vegetation Reflecting the Urban History of Berlin', **Die Erde,** 134 (2003) 308.

7 Fitter, pp. 123ff; Lachmund (2013), p. 55; Sukopp, 'Flora and Vegetation' (2003), 310.

8 John Kieran, **Natural History of New York City** (NY, 1959), p. 18.

9 Lachmund (2003), 241; Lachmund (2013), pp. 52ff.

10 Lachmund (2013), pp. 54–9.

11 Herbert Sukopp and Angelica Wurzel, 'The Effects of Climate Change on the Vegetation of Central European Cities', **Urban Habitats,** 24 (Dec. 2003),

https://www.urbanhabitats.org/v01n01/climate change_full.html. On the international influence of Sukopp see Ingo Kowarik, 'Herbert Sukopp – an inspiring pioneer in the field of urban ecology', **Urban Ecosystems,** 23 (March 2020).

12 Sukopp, 'Flora and Vegetation' (2003), 310.

13 Lachmund (2013), p. 74; Sukopp, 'Flora and Vege-tation' (2003), 308.

14 Lachmund (2013), pp. 77ff, 84.

15 **Ibid.,** pp. 97f.

16 Herbert Sukopp **et al,** 'The Soil, Flora, and Vegetation of Berlin's Waste Lands', in Ian C. Laurie (ed.), **Nature in Cities: the natural environment in the design and development of urban green space** (Chichester, 1979), pp. 121–2, 123, 127, 130.

17 Neil Clayton, 'Weeds, People and Contested Places', **Environment and History,** 9/3 (Aug. 2003).

18 Herbert Sukopp, 'On the Early History of Urban Ecology in Europe', in John M. Marzluff **et al** (eds.), **Urban Ecology: an international perspective on the interaction between humans and nature** (NY, 2008), p. 84.

19 Fitter, p. 192.

20 Sukopp (2008), p. 81.

21 Zachary J. S. Falck, **Weeds: an environmental history of metropolitan America** (Pittsburgh, 2016), p. 27.

22 **Ibid.,** pp. 3–4.

23 **Ibid.,** pp. 36, 61–2.

24 Joseph Vallot, **Essai sur la Flore du Pavé de Paris Limité aux Boulevards Extérieurs . . .** (Paris, 1884), p. 2.

25 Falck, pp. 25ff.

26 **Ibid.,** p. 44.

27 'Urban Wildflowers', **New York Times,** 20/5/1985, col. 5.

28 **New York Times,** 1/9/1983.

29 Lachmund (2013), ch. 3 **passim.**

30 **Ibid.,** pp. 148ff.

31 Lachmund (2013), pp. 66–7, 165ff, 180ff.

32 **Ibid.,** pp. 172ff.

33 Falck, p. 95; Timon McPhearson and Katinka Wijsman, 'Transitioning Complex Urban Systems: the importance of urban ecology for sustainability in New York City', in Niki Frantzeskaki **et al** (eds.), **Urban Sustainability Transitions** (New York, 2017), pp. 71–2.

34 Richard Mabey, **Weeds: in defense of nature's most unloved plants** (New York, 2010), p. 20.

35 Peleg Kremer **et al,** 'A Social-ecological Assessment of Vacant Lots in New York City', **Landscape and Urban Planning,** 120 (Dec. 2013), 218–33.

36 Sébastien Bonthoux, 'More Than Weeds: spontaneous vegetation in streets as a neglected element of urban biodiversity', **Landscape and Urban Planning,** 185 (May 2019); Sukopp, 'Berlin' (2011), p. 71.

37 Adrian J. Marshall **et al,** 'From Little Things: more than a third of public green space is road verge', **Urban Forestry and Urban Greening,** 44 (Aug. 2019); Megan Backhouse, 'Nature Strips Gardening Enthusiasm Grows, But New Guidelines Dampen Cheer', **The Age,** 24/12/2021, https://www.tijdelijkenatuur.nl/.

4. The Canopy

1 Sohail Hashmi, 'Last Forest Standing', **Hindu,** 11/8/2012; Shilpy Arora, 'The Doughty Dhau, and why it's important to the Aravali ecosystem', **Times of India,** 7/1/2019; Pradip Krishen, **Trees of Delhi: a field guide** (Delhi, 2006), pp. 90ff.

2 Rama Lakshmi, 'Villagers Just Protected a Sacred Forest Outside India's Polluted Capital', **Washington Post** 1/5/2016.

3 **Ibid.**

4 Shily Arora, 'Saving Mangar Bani', **Times of India,** 4/10/2018.

5 Syed Shaz, 'Knock on Woods', **Hindu Businessline** 28/4/2021.

6 Tetsuya Matsui, 'Meiji Shrine: an early old-growth forest creation in Tokyo', **Ecological Restoration,** 14/1 (Jan. 1996); Shinji Isoya, 'Creating Serenity: the construction of the Meiji Shrine Forest', **Nippon.com,** 8/7/2020, https://www.nippon .com/en/japan-topics/g00866/.

7 Henry W. Lawrence, 'Origins of the Tree-lined Boulevard', **Geographical Review,** 78/4 (Oct. 1988); Henry W. Lawrence, **City Trees: a historical geography from the Renaissance through the nineteenth century** (Charlottesville, 2006), pp. 38f, 54ff.

8 Lawrence (2006), pp. 32ff.

9 **Ibid.,** pp. 34ff, 39ff.

10 **Ibid.,** pp. 42ff.

11 Peter Kalm, **Travels into North America,** 2 vols. (London, 1772), i, pp. 193–4.

12 David Gobel, 'Interweaving Country and City in the Urban Design of Savannah, Georgia', **Global Environment,** 9/1 (2016).

13 Franco Panzini, 'Pines, Palms and Holm Oaks: historicist modes in modern Italian cityscapes', **Studies in the History of Art,** 78 (2015), Symposium Papers LV.

14 Dinya Patel and Mushirul Hasan (eds.), **From Ghalib's Dilli to Lutyen's New Delhi** (Delhi, 2014), p. 61.

15 Kai Wang **et al,** 'Urban Heat Island Modelling of a Tropical City: case of Kuala Lumpur', **Geoscience Letters,** 6 (2019).

16 Food and Agriculture Organization of the United Nations, **Forests and Sustainable Cities: inspiring stories from around the world** (Rome, 2018), pp. 61ff.

17 James Fallows, ' "Gingko Fever in Chongqing": the billion-dollar trees of Central China', **The Atlantic,** 13/5/2011; https://www.theatlantic .com/international/archive/2011/05/gingko-fever -in-chongqing-the-billion-dollar-trees-of-central -china/238885/.

18 See introduction, note 1; Yuan Ye and Zhu Ruiying, 'Guangzhou Officials Punished for Axing City's Beloved Banyan Trees', **Sixth Tone,** 13/12/21, https://www.sixthtone.com/news/1009194/ guangzhou-officials-punished-for-axing-citys -beloved-banyan-trees.

19 T. V. Ramachandra **et al,** 'Frequent Floods in

Bangalore: causes and remedial measures', **ENVIS Technical Report,** 123 (Aug. 2017); Y. Maheswara Reddy, 'How Bengaluru Lost Over 70 lakh Trees', **Bangalore Mirror,** 2/3/2020; Harini Nagendra, **Nature in the City: Bengaluru in the past, present and future** (New Delhi, 2019), ch. 6 **passim;** Prashant Rupera, 'Banyan City Lost 50 per cent of its Canopy: MSU study', **Times of India,** 16/11/2020; Renu Singhal, 'Where Have All the Peepal Trees Gone?', **Hindu,** 11/5/2017.

20 Harini Nagendra, 'Citizens Save the Day', **Bangalore Mirror,** 19/6/2017; 'How the People of Delhi Saved 16,000 Trees from the Axe', BBC News, 9/7/2018, https://www.bbc.co.uk/news/world-asia-india-44678680.

21 Divya Gopal, 'Sacred Sites, Biodiversity and Urbanization in an Indian Megacity', **Urban Ecosystems,** 22 (Feb. 2019); Aike P. Rots, 'Sacred Forests, Sacred Nation: the Shinto environmentalist paradigm and the rediscovery of **Chinju no Mori**', **Japanese Journal of Religious Studies,** 42/2 (2015); Elizabeth Hewitt, 'Why "Tiny Forests" are Popping up in Big Cities', **National Geographic,** 22/6/2021; Akira Miyawaki, 'A Call to Plant Trees', Blue Planet Prize essay (2006), https://www.af-info.or.jp/blueplanet/assets/pdf/list/2006essay-miyawaki.pdf; 'Plant Native Trees, Recreate Forests to Protect the Future', **JFS Newsletter,** 103 (March 2011).

22 Lela Nargi, 'The Miyawaki Method: a better way to build forests?', JSTOR Daily, 24/7/2019, https://daily.jstor.org/the-miyawaki-method-a-better-way

-to-build-forests/; S. Lalitha, 'Miyawaki Miracle in Bengaluru', **New Indian Express,** 26/5/2019; 'Could Miniature Forests Help Air-condition Cities?', **The Economist,** 3/7/2021; Himanshu Nitnaware, 'Bengaluru Man Grows Urban Jungle of 1700 Trees on Terrace, Doesn't Need Fans in Summers', The Better India, 30/3/2021 https://www.thebetterindia.com/251997/bengaluru-engineer-terrace-gardening-urban-jungle-organic-food-compost-green-hero-him16/; 'How did this Man Create a Forest in the Middle of Bangalore City?', YouTube, https://www.youtube.com/watch?v=dUaOftgup6U; Nagarajan.

23 See http://senseable.mit.edu/treepedia.

24 Robert Wilonsky, 'Dallas Vows, Again, to Protect the Great Trinity Forest, but what does that even mean?', **Dallas Morning News,** 24/5/2019.

25 Andreas W. Daum and Christof Mauch (eds.), **Berlin–Washington 1800–2000: capital cities, cultural representation, and national identities** (Washington, D.C., 2005), p. 205.

26 Wilonsky, 'Dallas Vows'.

27 Herbert Eiden and Franz Irsigler, 'Environs and Hinterland: Cologne and Nuremberg in the later middle ages', in James A. Galloway, **Trade, Urban Hinterlands and Market Integration c1300–1600** (London, 2000).

28 James A. Galloway, Derek Keene and Margaret Murphy, 'Fuelling the City: production and distribution of firewood and fuel in London's region, 1290–1400', **Economic History Review,** NS, 49/3 (Aug. 1996); John. T. Wing, 'Keeping Spain

Afloat: state forestry and imperial defense in the sixteenth century', **Environmental History,** 17/1 (Jan. 2012); Paul Warde, 'Fear of Wood Shortage and the Reality of the Woodland in Europe, c.1450–1850, **History Workshop Journal,** 62 (Autumn 2006).

29 Jeffrey K. Wilson, **The German Forest: nature, identity, and the contestation of a national symbol, 1871–1914** (Toronto, 2012), pp. 41f, 66; Poling, pp. 67f, 104ff.

30 Wilson, **The German Forest,** ch. 3 **passim.**

31 NYC Environmental Protection, 'DEP Launches First Ever Watershed Forest Management Plan to Protect Water Quality', Press Release, 22/12/2011, https://www1.nyc.gov/html/dep/html/press _releases/11-109pr.shtml#.YelkqP7P3cs.

32 Yiyuan Qin and Todd Gartner, 'Watersheds Lost Up to 22 per cent of their Forests in 14 years. Here's how it affects your water supply', World Resources Institute, 30/8/2016, https://www.wri .org/insights/watersheds-lost-22-their-forests-14 -years-heres-how-it-affects-your-water-supply; Suzanne Ozment and Rafael Feltran-Barbieri, 'Restoring Rio de Janeiro's Forests Could Save $70 Million in Water Treatment Costs', World Resources Institute, 18/12/2018, https://www .wri.org/insights/restoring-rio-de-janeiros-forests -could-save-79-million-water-treatment-costs; Robert I. McDonald **et al,** 'Estimating Watershed Degradation Over the Last Century and its Impact on Water-Treatment Costs for the World's Largest Cities', **Proceedings of the National Academy of**

Sciences of the United States of America, 113 (Aug. 2016).

33 Fred Pearce, 'Rivers in the Sky: how deforestation is affecting global water cycles', Yale Environment, 360 24/7/2018, https://e360.yale.edu/features/how-deforestation-affecting-global-water-cycles -climate-change; Nigel Dudley and Sue Stolton (eds.), **Running Pure: the importance of forest protected areas to drinking water** (2003); Patrick W. Keys **et al,** 'Megacity Precipitationsheds Reveal Tele-connected Water Security Challenges, **PLoS One,** 13/3 (March 2018).

5. Life Force

1 Blake Gumprecht, **The Los Angeles River: its life, death and possible rebirth** (Baltimore, 2001), ch. 1 **passim.**

2 Barbara E. Munday, **The Death of Aztec Tenochtitlan, the Life of Mexico City** (Austin, 2015), ch. 2 **passim;** Beth Tellman **et al,** 'Adaptive Pathways and Coupled Infrastructure: seven centuries of adaptation to water risk and the production of vulnerability in Mexico City', **Ecology and Society,** 23/1 (March 2018).

3 New York District U.S. Army Corps of Engineers (USACE), **Hudson-Raritan Estuary Ecosystem Restoration Feasibility Study** (New York, 2020), ch. 5, p. 29.

4 **Ibid.,** ch. 1, p. 12.

5 Steinberg, pp. 138ff.

6 **Ibid.,** pp. 206ff.
7 **Ibid.,** pp. 198ff.
8 'Wetlands Disappearing Three Times Faster than Forests', United Nations Climate Change, 1/10/2018, https://unfccc.int/news/wetlands -disappearing-three-times-faster-than-forests.
9 'Staten Island's Wildlife Periled by Reclamation and New Homes', **New York Times,** 9/5/1960, 31.
10 USACE, **South Shore of Staten Island Coastal Storm Risk Management. Draft environmental impact statement** (June 2015); Georgetown Climate Center, **Managing the Retreat from Rising Seas. Staten Island, New York: Oakwood Beach buyout committee and program** (Georgetown, 2020); Regina F. Graham, 'How Three Staten Island Neighbourhoods are being Demolished and Returned Back to Nature in New York's First "Managed Retreat" from Rising Sea Levels', **Daily Mail,** 21/8/2018.
11 'Surveying the Destruction Caused by Hurricane Sandy', **New York Times,** 20/11/12, news graphic, https://www.nytimes.com/newsgraphics/2012/ 1120-sandy/survey-of-the-flooding-in-new-york -after-the-hurricane.html.
12 USACE, **Hudson-Raritan Estuary Ecosystem,** ch. 1, pp. 5–6.
13 **Ibid.**
14 Rachel K. Gittman **et al,** 'Marshes With and Without Sills Protect Estuarine Shorelines from Erosion Better than Bulkheads During a Category 1 Hurricane', **Ocean & Coastal Management,**

102/A (Dec. 2014); Gittman **et al,** 'Ecological Consequences of Shoreline Hardening: a meta-analysis', **BioScience,** 66/9 (Sept. 2016); Ariana E. Sutton-Grier **et al,** 'Investing in Natural and Nature-Based Infrastructure: building better along our coasts', **Sustainability,** 12/2 (Feb. 2018); Zhenchang Zhu **et al,** 'Historic Storms and the Hidden Value of Coastal Wetlands for Nature-based Flood Defence', **Nature Sustainability,** 3 (June 2020); Iris Möller **et al,** 'Wave Attenuation Over Coastal Salt Marshes Under Storm Surge Conditions', **Nature Geoscience,** 7 (Sept. 2014).

15 Brian McGrath, 'Bangkok: the architecture of three ecologies', **Perspecta,** 39 (2007)

16 Copenhagen Cloudburst Plans, https://acwi.gov/climate_wkg/minutes/Copenhagen_Cloudburst _Ramboll_April_20_2016 per cent20(4).pdf; 'Copenhagen Unveils First City-wide Masterplan for Cloudburst', **Source,** 1/3/2016, https://www.thesourcemagazine.org/copenhagen-unveils-first-city-wide-masterplan-for-cloudburst/.

17 Bruce Stutz, 'With a Green Makeover, Philadelphia is Tackling its Stormwater Problem', **Yale Environment 360,** 29/3/2018, https://e360.yale.edu/features/with-a-green-makeover-philadelphia-tackles-its-stormwater-problem.

18 Chris Courtney, **The Nature of Disaster in China: the 1931 Yangzi River flood** (Cambridge, 2018), ch. 1 **passim.**

19 'Wuhan Yangtze Riverfront Park', Sasaki, https://www.sasaki.com/projects/wuhan-yangtze-riverfront-park/.

6. The Harvest

1 E. C. Spary, **Feeding France: new sciences of food,.
  1760–1815** (Cambridge, 2014), ch. 5.
2 Francesco Orsini **et al,** 'Exploring the Production
  Capacity of Rooftop Gardens in Urban Agriculture:
  the potential impact on food and nutrition security,
  biodiversity and other ecosystem services in the city
  of Bologna', **Food Security,** 6 (Dec. 2014).
3 John Weathers, **French Market-Gardening:
  including practical details of 'intensive
  cultivation' for English growers** (London, 1909);
  William Robinson, **The Parks, Promenades and
  Gardens of Paris** (London, 1869), pp. 462ff; Eliot
  Coleman, **The Winter Harvest Handbook** (White
  River Junction, 2009), pp. 13ff.
4 Henry Hopper, 'French Gardening in England',
  Estate Magazine, Sept. 1908, p. 404
5 Andrew Morris, ' "Fight for Fertilizer!" Excrement, public health, and mobilization in New
  China', **Journal of Unconventional History,** 6/3
  (Spring, 1995); Joshua Goldstein, **Remains of
  the Everyday: a century of recycling in Beijing**
  (Oakland, 2021), pp. 82ff.
6 Kayo Tajima, 'The Marketing of Urban Human Waste
  in the Early Modern Edo/Tokyo Metropolitan Area',
  Environnement Urbain/Urban Environment, 1
  (2007).
7 Dean T. Ferguson, 'Nightsoil and the "Great
  Divergence": human waste, the urban economy,
  and economic productivity, 1500–1900', **Journal**

of Global History, 9/3 (2014); Susan B. Hanley, 'Urban Sanitation in Preindustrial Japan', **Journal of Interdisciplinary History,** 18/1 (Summer 1987); Marta E. Szczygiel, 'Cultural Origins of Japan's Premodern Night Soil Collection System', **Worldwide Waste: Journal of Interdisciplinary Studies,** 3/1 (2020).

8 Catherine McNeur, **Taming Manhattan: environmental battles and the antebellum city** (Cambridge, Mass., 2014), ch. 3ff; Marc Linder and Lawrence S. Zacharias, **Of Cabbages and Kings County: agriculture and the formation of modern Brooklyn** (Iowa City, 1999), p. 3.

9 Sellers, p. 148.

10 M. Crippa **et al,** 'Food Systems are Responsible for a Third of Global Anthropogenic GHG Emissions', **Nature Food,** 2 (March 2021); United Nations Environment Programme, **Global Environment Outlook 2000** (London, 2000).

11 Alan Macfarlane, 'The non-use of night soil in England' (2002), http://www.alanmacfarlane.com/savage/A-NIGHT.PDF; F. H. King, **Farmers of Forty Centuries: permanent agriculture in China, Korea and Japan** (1911), ch. 9.

12 Christopher W. Smith, 'Sustainable Land Application of Sewer Sludge as a Biosolid', **Nature Resources and Environment,** 28/3 (Winter 2014); Steve Spicer, 'Fertilizers, Manure, or Biosolids?', **Water, Environment and Technology,** 14/7 (July 2002); Maria Cristina Collivignarelli **et al,** 'Legislation for the Reuse of Biosolids on Agricultural Land in Europe: overview, **Sustainability,** 11

(2019); John C. Radcliffe and Declan Page, 'Water Reuse and Recycling in Australia – history, current situation and future perspectives', **Water Cycle,** 1 (2020).

13 Tracey E. Watts, 'Martial's Farm in the Window', **Hermathena,** 198 (Summer 2015).

14 'Shantytown', **Century Magazine,** 20 (May–Oct. 1880).

15 Poling, ch. 4.

16 **Ibid.,** p. 124.

17 Elizabeth Anne Scott, 'Cockney Plots: working class politics and garden allotments in London's East End, 1890–1918', MA Thesis (University of Saskatchewan, 2005), pp. 48–9.

18 **Ibid.,** p. 92.

19 **Ibid.,** p. 81; Willes, p. 298.

20 Barry A. Jackisch, 'The Nature of Berlin: green space and visions of a new German capital, 1900–45', **Central European History,** 47/2 (June 2014), 315.

21 Patrick Mayoyo, 'How to Grow Food in a Slum: lessons from the sack farmers of Kibera', **Guardian,** 18/5/2015; Sam Ikua, 'Urban Agriculture Thrives in Nairobi During COVID-19 Crisis', RUAF blogs, 11/6/2020, https://ruaf.org/news/urban -agriculture-thrives-in-nairobi-during-covid-19 -crisis/; United Nations Environment Programme, **Building Urban Resilience: assessing urban and peri-urban agriculture in Kampala, Uganda** (Nairobi, 2014), p. 17; Richard Wetaya, 'Urban Agriculture Thriving in East Africa During COVID-19', Alliance for Science, 3/8/2020, https://allianceforscience.cornell.edu/blog/2020/

08/urban-agriculture-thriving-in-east-africa-during
-covid-19/; 'Urban Farming in Kampala', BBC
News, 5/4/2019, https://www.bbc.co.uk/news/av/
business-47834804.

22 United Nations Environment Programme, **Urban
Resilience: assessing urban and peri-urban
agriculture in Dar-es-Salaam, Tanzania** (Nairobi,
2014); Emily Brownell, 'Growing Hungry: the poli-
tics of food distribution and the shifting boundaries
between urban and rural in Dar es Salaam', **Global
Environment,** 9/1 (Spring 2016); L. McLees,
'Access to Land for Urban Farming in Dar es
Salaam, Tanzania: histories, benefits and insecure
tenure', **Journal of Modern African Studies,** 49/4
(Winter 2011); H. S. Mkwela, 'Urban Agriculture
in Dar es Salaam: a dream or a reality?', in C. A.
Brebbia (ed.), **Sustainable Development and
Planning VI** (Longhurst, 2013).

7. Zootropolis

1 'Cheeky Boar Leaves Nudist Grunting in Laptop
Chase', BBC News, 7/8/2020, https://www.bbc.co
.uk/news/world-europe-53692475.

2 McNeur, pp. 25ff.

3 Hannah Velten, **Beastly London: a history of
animals in the city** (London, 2013), pp. 28, 72;
Alec Forshaw and Theo Bergström, **Smithfield:
past and present** (London, 1980), p. 36.

4 Mark Ravinet **et al,** 'Signatures of Human-
commensalism in the House Sparrow Genome',

Proceedings of the Royal Society B, 285/1884 (Aug. 2018).

5 Nishant Kumar **et al,** 'Offspring Defense by an Urban Raptor Responds to Human Subsidies and Ritual Animal-feeding Practices', **PLOS ONE,** 13/10 (Oct. 2018); Kumar **et al,** 'The Population of an Urban Raptor is Inextricably Tied to Human Cultural Practices', **Proceedings of the Royal Society B,** 286/1900 (April 2019); Kumar **et al,** 'Density, Laying Date, Breeding Success and Diet of Black Kites **Milvus migrans govinda** in the City of Delhi (India)', **Bird Study,** 61/1 (2014); Kumar **et al,** 'GPS-telemetry Unveils the Regular High-Elevation Crossing of the Himalayas by a Migratory Raptor: implications for definition of a "Central Asian Flyway"', **Scientific Reports,** 10 (2020).

6 Virna L. Saenz **et al,** 'Genetic Analysis of Bed Bug Populations', **Journal of Medical Entomology,** 49/4 (July 2012).

7 Velten, pp. 71ff; McNeur, pp. 17ff.

8 McNeur, pp. 135ff.

9 Sean Kheraj, 'The Great Epizootic of 1872–3: networks of animal disease in North American urban environments', **Environmental History,** 23/3 (July 2018); McNeur, **passim.**

10 Michael McCarthy, 'Are Starlings Going the Way of Sparrows?', **Independent,** 13/11/2000.

11 Fitter, pp. 128–9.

12 Sellers, p. 89.

13 Bob Shaw, 'Deer are Everywhere in the Metro Area – and cities are fighting back, **Twin Cities Pioneer Press,** 8/1/2011.

14 Christine Dell'Amore, 'City Slickers', **Smithsonian Magazine** (March 2006).

15 K. J. Parsons **et al,** 'Skull Morphology Diverges Between Urban and Rural Populations of Red Foxes Mirroring Patterns of Domestication and Macroevolution', **Proceedings of the Royal Society B,** 287/1928 (June 2020); Anthony Adducci **et al,** 'Urban Coyotes are Genetically Distinct from Coyotes in Natural Habitats', **Journal of Urban Ecology,** 6/1 (May 2020).

16 Pamela J. Yeh, 'Rapid Evolution of a Sexually Selected Trait Following Population Establishment in a Novel Habitat, **Evolution,** 58 (Jan. 2004); Trevor D. Price **et al,** 'Phenotypic Plasticity and the Evolution of a Socially Selected Trait Following Colonization of a Novel Environment', **American Naturalist,** 172/1 (July 2008).

17 Jonathan W. Atwell **et al,** 'Boldness Behaviour and Stress Physiology in a Novel Urban Environment Suggest Rapid Correlated Evolutionary Adaptation', **Behavioural Ecology,** 23/5 (Sept.–Oct. 2012); Killu Timm **et al, 'SERT** Gene Polymorphisms are Associated with Risk-taking Behaviour and Breeding Parameters in Wild Great Tits', **Journal of Experimental Biology,** 221/4 (Jan. 2018); Anders Pape Møller **et al,** 'Urbanized Birds Have Superior Establishment Success in Novel Environments', **Oecologia,** 178/3 (July 2015).

18 Atwell **et al,;** Stewart W. Breck **et al,** 'The Intrepid Urban Coyote: a comparison of bold and exploratory behaviour in coyotes from urban and rural environments', **Scientific Reports,** vol. 9

(Feb. 2019); Emilie C. Snell-Rood and Naomi Wick, 'Anthropogenic Environments Exert Variable Selection on Cranial Capacity in Mammals', **Proceedings of the Royal Society B,** 280/1769 (Oct. 2013).

19 Kristin M. Winchell, 'Phenotype Shifts in Urban Areas in the Tropical Lizard **Anolis cristatellus**', **Evolution,** 70/5 (May 2016); Charles R. Brown, 'Where has all the Road Kill Gone', **Current Biology,** 23/6 (March 2013); Stephen E. Harris **et al,** 'Urbanization Shapes the Demographic History of a Native Rodent (the white-footed mouse, **Peromyscus leucopus**) in New York City', **Biology Letters,** 12/4 (April 2016); Stephen E. Harris and Jason Munshi-South, 'Signatures of Positive Selection and Local Adaptation to Urbanization in White-footed Mice (**Peromyscus leucopus**)', **Molecular Ecology,** 26/22 (Oct. 2017).

20 Marc T. J. Johnson and Jason Munshi-South, 'Evolution of Life in Urban Environments', **Science,** 358/6383 (Nov. 2017); Lindsay S. Miles **et al,** 'Gene Flow and Genetic Drift in Urban Environments', **Molecular Ecology,** 28/18 (Sept. 2019); Jason Munshi-South **et al,** 'Population Genomics of the Anthropocene: urbanization is negatively associated with genome-wide variation in white-footed mouse populations', **Evolutionary Applications,** 9/4 (April 2016).

21 Pablo Salmón **et al,** 'Continent-wide Genomic Signatures of Adaptation to Urbanisation in a Songbird Across Europe', **Nature Communications,** 12 (May 2021).

22 E. McDonald-Madden **et al,** 'Factors Affecting Grey-headed Flying-fox (**Pteropus poliocephalus:** Pteropodidae) foraging in the Melbourne Metropolitan Area, Australia', **Austral Ecology,** 30 (Aug. 2005).

23 Christopher D. Ives **et al,** 'Cities are Hotspots for Threatened Species', **Global Ecology and Biogeography,** 25/1 (Jan. 2016); Australian Conservation Foundation, **The Extinction Crisis in Australia's Cities and Towns** (Carlton, 2020); Kylie Soanes and Pia E. Lentini, 'When Cities are the Last Chance for Saving Species', **Frontiers in Ecology and the Environment,** 17/4 (May 2019); Tom A. Waite **et al,** 'Sanctuary in the City: urban monkeys buffered against catastrophic die-off during ENSO-related drought', **EcoHealth,** 4 (2007); Sharon Baruch-Mordo **et al,** 'Stochasticity in Natural Forage Production Affects Use of Urban Areas by Black Bears: implications to management of human-bear conflicts', **PLOS ONE,** 9/1 (Jan. 2014).

24 Fernanaa Zimmermann Teixeira **et al,** 'Canopy Bridges as Road Overpasses for Wildlife in Urban Fragmented Landscapes', **Biota Neotropica,** 13/1 (March 2013); Sarah Holder, 'How to Design a City for Sloths', Bloomberg CityLab, 30/11/2021, https://www.bloomberg.com/news/articles/2021 -11-30/fast-paced-urban-living-can-be-stressful -for-sloths; Leon M. F. Barthel **et al,** 'Unexpected Gene-flow in Urban Environments: the example of the European hedgehog', **Animals,** 10/12 (Dec. 2020).

25 Darryl Jones, 'Safe Passage: we can help save koalas through urban design', **The Conversation,** 4/8/2016, https://theconversation.com/safe-passage-we-can-help-save-koalas-through-urban-design-63123; Stephen J. Trueman **et al,** 'Designing Food and Habitat Trees for Urban Koalas: tree height, foliage palatability and clonal propagation of **Eucalyptus kabiana**', **Urban Forestry and Urban Greening,** 27 (Oct. 2017); Moreton Bay Regional Council, 'Urban Koala Project', https://www.moretonbay.qld.gov.au/Services/Environment/Research-Partnerships/Urban-Koala-Project.
26 Erica N. Spotswood **et al,** 'The Biological Desert Fallacy: cities in their landscapes contribute more than we think to regional biodiversity', **BioScience,** 71/2 (Feb. 2021).

Epilogue

1 Philip Ainsworth Means (ed.), **History of the Spanish Conquest of Yucatan and of the Itzas** (Cambridge, Mass., 1917), ch. 9.
2 John Lloyd Stephens, **Incidents of Travel in Central America, Chiapas and Yucatan,** ed. Frederick Catherwood (London, 1854), p. 530.
3 **Ibid.,** pp. 61–2.
4 Dan Penny **et al,** 'The Demise of Angkor: systemic vulnerability of urban infrastructure to climatic variations', **Science Advances,** 4/10 (Oct. 2018).
5 Emma Young, 'Biodiversity Wipeout Facing South East Asia', **New Scientist,** 23/7/2003.

6 Matthew Schneider-Mayerson, 'Some Islands Will Rise: Singapore in the Anthropocene', **Resilience: A Journal of the Environmental Humanities,** 4/2–3 (Spring-Fall 2017).

7 Nagendra, **Nature in the City,** ch. 5.

8 Doughnut Economics Action Lab, **The Amsterdam City Doughnut** (Amsterdam, March 2020), p. 8.

9 City of Amsterdam, **Amsterdam Circular 2020-2050 Strategy** (Amsterdam, 2020).

10 Simon Usborne, '47 per cent of London is Green Space: is it time for our capital to become a national park?', **Independent** 26/9/2014.

Acknowledgements

For all their help, hard work and advice, I would like to thank Clare Conville, Bea Hemming, Alex Russell, Alison Davies, Lucy Beresford-Knox, Clara Irvine, Kristine Puopolo, Ana Espinoza, Anne Jaconette, Salvatore Ruggiero, Elena Hershey, Birgitta Rabe, Nicholas Rose and Roisin Robothan-Jones. And sincere thanks to Benjamin Voight, author of two vital books in the fight for greener cities: **A New Garden Ethic** and **Prairie Up: An Introduction to Natural Garden Design.**

Index

About the Author

BEN WILSON has an undergraduate and master's degree in history from Cambridge. He is the author of six previous books, including **Metropolis, What Price Liberty?,** for which he received the Somerset Maugham Award, and the **Sunday Times** bestseller **Empire of the Deep: The Rise and Fall of the British Navy.**

Printed in the United States
by Baker & Taylor Publisher Services